DISCARDED

The Templar Treasure

An Investigation

Tobias Daniel Wabbel

Published by:
Trine Day LLC
PO Box 577
Walterville, OR 97489
1-800-556-2012
www.TrineDay.com
publisher@TrineDay.net

Library of Congress Control Number: 2013937959

Wabbel, Tobias Daniel
The Templar Treasure: An Investigation—1st ed.
p. cm.
Includes references and index.
Epud (ISBN-13) 978-1-937584-35-1
Mobi (ISBN-13) 978-1-937584-36-8
Print (ISBN-13) 978-1-937584-34-4
1. Templars--History. I. Wabbel, Tobias Daniel. II. Title

Translated by Sarah Downing of Aardwolf Text Services (www.aardwolf.de)

FIRST EDITION
10 9 8 7 6 5 4 3 2 1

Printed in the USA
Distribution to the Trade by:
Independent Publishers Group (IPG)
814 North Franklin Street
Chicago, Illinois 60610
312.337.0747
www.ipgbook.com

Dedicated to my wife Anja and Douglas J. Preston

Table of Contents

Jaques de Molay, the last Grand Master of the Knights Templar. © Public Domain

Prologue

The Virgin and the Dragon

We do not follow maps to buried treasures and X never, ever marks the spot.

—Dr. Henry Jones Jr.

Friday October 13, 1307

At dawn, the troops of King Philip IV stormed the headquarters of the Templar Order. The surprise attack on the little fortress inside of Paris, which was dubbed the *Temple*, was frighteningly easy. The resistance of the Knights Templar was soon broken. At the same time, arrests were taking place throughout the whole of France.

At first, Jacques de Molay, Grand Master of the Knights Templar, seemed unaware of the hopeless situation. According to the papal bull *Omne Datum Optimum* issued by Pope Innocent II in 1139, the only person to whom the Templars were answerable was the Pope himself, which had lulled him and his brothers into a false sense of security. Jacques de Molay was the godfather of one of the King's children and the King had granted the Templar Grand Master his protection in 1303 because the Templars had always managed his assets. How could the King be so unscrupulous? A furious letter from the Pope to Philip IV, who was also known as *Phillip the Fair*, was simply ignored.

When King Philip IV's militia forced their way into the *Temple* to plunder the vaults in which the Templar gold was stored, they were disappointed. Only a tiny amount of the immeasurable riches remained. The Templars had already removed the gold, knowing full well that in his desperation the King would resort to violent measures to refill his empty state coffers with fresh gold.

Jacques de Molay realized that the King had his eye on their money, which since their founding in 1129 had been given to them as generous gifts, and there were also the funds they managed for European nobles and kings, and then there was the capital which had grown into exorbitant amounts as the result of credits and loans throughout Europe. The Templars were the inventors of cash-free payments.

In 1307, Philip IV was in dire financial straits. But the Templars were rich – at least that's what Philip the Fair thought. The King had no other choice but to take action against the Templars. Philip IV needed the Templars' money. In the past, he had even attempted to become a member of their Order, to access their riches. Jacques de Molay had seen through all of Philip's plans up to this point. But it appears he hadn't expected such a perfectly organized attack as the wave of arrests that took place on October 13, 1307. Before Jacques de Molay could protest, he and 546 other Templars throughout the whole of France were put in chains.

After the arrest of the Templars in France, Pope Clement V gave in to the pressure of the King and his crafty chancellor Guillaume de Nogaret. On November 22, 1307, the Pope issued his papal bull *Pastoralis praeeminentiae*. It decreed that nobody was above the Church, not even the Templars. He didn't utter a word about the innocence of the order of warrior monks. Instead, Clement V ordered the arrest of Templars throughout the whole of Europe and the seizure of their properties. A surprising change of mind. Soon after, Templars in England, Ireland, Wales, Italy, Germany and Spain were arrested and accused of heresy.

The wave of arrests was preceded by decisive political events. In 1306, Jacques de Molay had offered Philip IV shelter in the *Temple* when the starving population was hunting the King through the streets of Paris because he had devalued their currency. This may have been when Philip the Fair glanced in the Templar treasury.

On April 8, 1307, Jacques de Molay defiantly refused an offer of Pope Clement V to merge the Knights Templar with the Order of St. John. This proposal had been based on a crafty strategy of Philip the Fair to take advantage of the political weakness of Pope Clement V. The Knights of the Order of the Hospital of St. John of Jerusalem – Knights of St. John for short – were subject to the direct orders of the King, but the Templar Order was not.

De Molay knew that the merging of the Templars with the Knights of St. John would mean an end to all of their privileges. These included the exemption from all taxes, the right to build their own churches and the duty to display absolute obedience only to the Pope. Jacques de Molay knew that if he said yes, the Templars would lose their identity and become the King's pawns.[1] So he refused the offer of Pope Clement V. The King must have been fuming when he read De Molay's answer that a unified order would be so strong and powerful that it could defend its rights against anyone, even the King. A clever manipulation of the King.

When Philip's ruse failed, he was left with only one way to violently destroy the Templar Order: to accuse them of heresy. This happened a lot in the Middle Ages. Previously, Philip IV had used slander and denunciation to disempower Pope Boniface VIII who had decreed in 1302 that the Church held ultimate authority over all worldly, and thus regal, powers. With no further ado, Philip IV had Boniface arrested and he died a few weeks later, a shocked and broken man.

Philip's plans to destroy the Templars were already so far progressed that on August 24, 1307, Pope Clement V gave in to the pressure of the King and commissioned Grand Inquisitor Guillaume Imbert to investigate their crimes. On September 14, 1307, Philip IV, who was burdened with debts as a result of the wars he had been embroiled in, sent out a sealed order to the King's Seneschals and bailiffs throughout the whole of France to arrest all Templars in the land on October 13.[2]

The charges consist of seven main accusations and a total of 127 items. The most severe accusations were: denying Christ, the Virgin Mary and spitting or urinating on the cross; worshiping idols; denying the sacraments and, not least, homosexual acts as part of the initiation rites. The Templars were accused of the most severe heresies you could commit in the Middle Ages. Jacques de Molay was soon painfully aware that he had underestimated the King.

---

1   Demurger, Alain, Der letzte Templer, Munich: C.H. Beck, 2004, p. 207.
2   Barber, Malcolm, Der Templerprozess, Düsseldorf: Patmos Verlag, 2008, p. 232f.

The trial against the Knights Templar lasted until 1312. The interrogation methods were imaginative, to put it mildly: The accused's hands were bound behind his back, he was pulled off the ground with ropes and then suddenly dropped, breaking his bones and tearing his tendons. But the incredible torture repertoire also included hot irons, crushed fingers and feet, torn out teeth and hair and burning feet over hot coals and fires. Subjected to these torture methods, the Templars would confess anything.

Often, the mere threat of torture or simply witnessing the torture of another Templar was enough to make individual Templars talk or break their resistance. No matter what the Templars testified, one thing is clear: the accused were already convicted before they even had a chance to defend themselves.[3]

Pope Clement V and some of his cardinals also personally interviewed seventy-two Templars in Poitiers – including Grand Master Jacques de Molay. Following this investigation, Pope Clement V decided to dissolve the Order – possibly to prevent any embarrassing secrets being revealed about the Church. At a council in the Burgundian town of Vienne, he decreed the end of the Templar Order by issuing the papal bulls *Vox excelso* and *Vox clamatis* on March 22, 1312. On May 2, 1312, Pope Clement V issued the bull *Ad povidendam*, and thus handed over all Templar possessions to the Knights of St. John.

Almost two years later, on March 18, 1314, Jacques de Molay and Geoffroy de Charney, Preceptor of Normandy, were burned at the stake in Paris – after recanting the confessions they had made in Poitiers. Legend has it that through the murderous flames, Jacques de Molay foretold that King Philip IV and Pope Clement V would both die within the year.

And in fact, on April 20, 1314, Pope Clement died a horrible death that is subject to academic speculation to this day. On November 29, 1314, Philip IV died as the result of a hunting accident. Coincidence? We will never know. In 2001, Italian historian Barbara Frale rediscovered among the documents of the Vatican Secret Archives a missing document that was dubbed the *Chinon*

---

3   Finke, Heinrich, Papsttum und Templerorden, Vol. I, Münster i.W.: Verlag Aschendorff, 1907, p. 151.

Parchment, which has since been causing quite a stir. In it Pope Clement V states that he considers the *Templars to be innocent.*[4]

So was there ever a treasure? In a statement made before the papal investigation commission in 1308, Templar Jean de Châlon stated the following as the 46th witness: "The night before the wave of arrests, the treasure of the Grand Visitor of the Paris Temple, Hugues de Pairaud, was brought by Hugues de Châlon and Gerard de Villiers on three carts with fifty horses out of the *Temple* to the Templar port of La Rochelle. Subsequently, 18 ships set sail with an unknown destination. Moreover, he said that he knew of high-ranking Templar brothers who had been aware of the impending arrests before they occurred."[5]

However, it is very improbable that Hugues de Châlon and Gerard de Villiers would have been able to drive their horses and carts to the coast and avoid the streets that had been blocked off the night before by Philip IV's sentries. Any ships setting sail would have attracted attention and undoubtedly been boarded. The only thing we can be certain of is that Jean de Châlon was one of the thirty Templars who knew ahead about the wave of arrests and was able to escape it. Fifteen of the 30 escapees were arrested and brought before the Grand Inquisitor. Twelve escapees were listed, of whom two – Hugues de Châlon and Gerard de Villiers – were able to get away.[6] Therefore, it does seem certain that the treasure from the *Temple* was transported away by Hugues de Châlon and Gerard de Villiers to an unknown destination.

But where did the gold end up? It's apparent that Hugues de Pairaud was already aware of Philip IV's order to arrest the Templars before it took place. On October 1, 1307, Hugues de Pairaud appeared in the presence of the Pope, protested and announced that he planned to save his life as well as the lives of his brothers.[7] But if

4   Frale, Barbara, La storia dei Templari e l'apporto delle nuove scoperte, Il Papato e il processo ai Templari. L'inedita assoluzione di Chinon alla luce della diplomatica pontificia, Roma, 2003, p. 9-48.

5   Finke, Heinrich, Papsttum und Templerorden, Vol. II, Münster i.W.: Verlag Aschendorff, 1907, p. 339.

6   Ibid., p. 74.

7   Schottmüller, Konrad, Untergang des Templerordens, Vol. I, Berlin:

Hugues de Pairaud had informed his Grand Master of the planned arrest by Philip's militia before October 13, 1307, why did Jacques de Molay allow them to arrest him without putting up a fight? Jacques de Molay was never tortured.[8] So why did he confess to the accusations of denying Christ which were brought against the Order? Why did the Templar Pierre Brocart of the Paris *Temple* confess in the presence of the Pope in Poitiers, without being subjected to any kind of torture, that he had spat on the cross and denied Christ? We can find all these reports in the trial records. The Templars denied Christ and openly admitted to sacrilege. Out of 138 Templars questioned, only four insisted they were innocent.[9] Why?

The Templar trial records from the South of France mention statements about an idol worshiped by the Templars that some referred to as *Baphomet* or *Bahumet*.[10] According to the trial statement of the Grand Visitor of the Temple, Hugues de Pairaud, it was golden, had what looked like two heads and four feet.[11]

A few months before his death, Jacques de Molay was imprisoned in the Norman Château de Gisors. Shortly before his death, he carved graffiti into the walls: including drawings of a virgin and a dragon speared by the martyr St. George, the patron saint of the Knights Templar. Even today, these puzzling pictures can still be admired. What do they mean? Are they a clue to the hiding place of the actual Templar treasure: the *Bahumet*? What was this *Bahumet*? Where did the Templar treasure disappear to? And the most important question: is the treasure still waiting to be discovered today?

Ernst S. Mittler & Sohn, 1887, p. 128; cf. Michelet, Michel, Procès des templiers, Imprimerie Royale, Paris, 1841, Vol. II, p. 373.

8   Finke, Heinrich, Papsttum und Templerorden, Vol. II, Münster i.W.: Verlag Aschendorff, 1907, p. 143.

9   Finke, Heinrich, Papsttum und Templerorden, Vol. I, Münster i.W.: Verlag Aschendorff, 1907, p. 164.

10   Charpentier, John, Die Templer, Frankfurt am Main: Klett-Cotta, 1981, p. 159.

11   Krüger, Anke, Das Baphomet-Idol, in: Historisches Jahrbuch 119, 1999, p. 132.

Chapter One

God's Army

We cannot afford to take mythology at face value.

— Dr. Henry Jones Jr.

The Founding of the Templar Order

My search for the Templar treasure begins in the French region of Champagne. If you take Route Nationale 19 that runs from Troyes in north-east France in the direction of Provins you will pass the commune of Payns after about six miles. This is a sleepy little community located on the left bank of the Seine in the midst of seemingly endless chalk-white fields. As I pass the entrance to the commune, on the left side of the road I spy a light yellow water tower with an impressively oversized Templar painted on it.

Two minutes later, I turn into Voie Riot 10. The *Musée Hugues de Payns* is located in a modest town house next door to a gravel car parking lot. For a long time, the Museum was only open for a few Sundays each year. Now, following the hysteria about a missing Templar treasure, it's open almost every day and is run by two young women on a voluntary basis on behalf of Dr. Thierry LeRoy, the founder of *Fondation Hugues de Payns*. In addition to merchandising items such as T-shirts, mugs, pens and stickers with Templar red crosses, interested visitors can also purchase various reading materials on the subject. Display boards and cases with medieval coins, pottery fragments and broken off spear tips document the dramatic history of the Templar Order that began here with the Knight Hugues de Payns.

The life-sized model of an armed Templar defending himself with a shield stares at me with lackluster eyes. Unfortunately, this figure of Hugues de Payns cannot speak and reveal the secrets of how the Templar Order came to be.[1] But after in-depth research some aspects become increasingly clear ....

The commune of Payns is located about 15 kilometers to the north-west of Troyes, in the midst of seemingly endless chalk-white fields. © Tobias D. Wabbel

Hugues de Payns was born 1080 in Payns. He was the Lord of Montigny-Lagesse and owned expansive estates in the Burgundian commune of Tonnerre. He was knighted at an early age. He probably served during the First Crusade between 1095 and 1099 in the army of the Count of Blois and Champagne and returned to France in 1100. Hugues de Payns had two brothers, Baldwin and Eustace of Boulogne. His cousin, Baldwin of Bourg, was Count of Edessa and under the name Baldwin II was crowned King of Jerusalem.[2] Hugues' wife gave him a son Thibaud, who was made the Abbot of Saint Colombe at Sens Abbey[3] – and became unpopular with the Abbey's monks because he pawned the Abbey's treasure to finance his participation in the Second Crusade.[4] Through his wife,

---

1 The leading (but not error-free) experts on the topic of the Knights Templar are Alain Demurger from Paris-Sorbonne University and Malcolm Barber from the University of Reading in England..

2 Charpentier, Louis, Macht und Geheimnis der Templer, Herrsching: Pawlak Verlagsgesellschaft, 1986, p. 23.

3 Demurger, Alain, Die Templer, Munich: C.H. Beck, 2000, p. 22.

4 Demurger is wrong here: The Abbey of Saint Colombe lies on the outskirts of the town of Sens and not in Troyes, an error that is frequently repeated by other authors.

Hugues de Payns was related to the Montbard line, and the family of the Abbot Bernard of Clairvaux on his mother's side.[5]

Hugues had excellent contacts to the Cistercian order and Count Hugues I of Champagne, whose estates were larger than those of the French King. He became an officer of the Count. Most historians assume he was close friends with or even closely related to the noble family of Champagne, because in 1100 Hugues de Payns was mentioned several times in official documents with them, including in connection with the Counts of Bar and Ramerupt.[6] So he was a well-known nobleman who moved in the highest circles and enjoyed considerable political influence.

Little is known about the years between 1100 and 1103 in the life of Hugues de Payns. In the year of our Lord 1104, it is documented that he embarked on a pilgrimage to Jerusalem together with his brother Stephen and the Count of Champagne. Whose initiative this was is unknown. But it is probable that this was at the instigation of the highly devout Count Hugues I of Champagne, a well-known sponsor of the Cistercian Order and friend of Abbot Bernard of Clairvaux.

And then things get a little mysterious. Directly after their return to France in 1108, Count Hugues I of Champagne sought out the Cistercian abbot Stephen Harding. Following in the footsteps of the founder Robert of Molesme and the second Abbot Alberic, Harding was the third Abbot of the Cistercian monastery Cîteaux from 1109 to 1134. A scriptorium was built there from 1109 to 1134, and Harding was often found there. Harding is famous for his revision of the incorrectly translated Latin Bible (Vulgate), which had been in use since Late Antiquity. He corrected this, and in particular many texts of the Old Testament, based on true-to-the-original translations from the Hebrew.[7] Harding himself noted that he debated in French with the rabbis of Burgundy about problem-

Cf. Wilcke, Ferdinand, Die Geschichte des Ordens der Tempelherren, Wiesbaden: Marix Verlag, 2005, p. 51. Cf. Charpentier, Louis, Macht und Geheimnis der Templer, Herrsching: Pawlak Verlagsgesellschaft, 1986, p. 23.

5   Demurger, Alain, Die Templer, Munich: C.H. Beck, 2000, p. 22.
6   Ibid., p. 22.
7   Dinzelbacher, Peter, Bernhard von Clairvaux, Darmstadt: Wissenschaftliche Buchgesellschaft, 1998, p. 22; cf. Auberger, Jean-Baptiste, L'Unanimité Cistercienne Primitive – Mythe Ou Réalité, Achel, Belgium, 1986, p. 327; Zaluska, Yolanta, L'Enluminure et le Scriptorium De Cîteaux au XIIe Siècle, Cîteaux, 1989, p. 274f.

atic passages of the Old Testament and then corrected these in the Latin. He described the process as follows:

> Astonished therefore at the discrepancies in our books, which all come from one translator, we approached certain Jews who were learned in their Scriptures, and inquired most carefully of them in French about all those places that contained the particular passages and lines we found in the book we transcribed, and had since inserted in our own volume, but did not find in the many other Latin copies. The Jews, unrolling a number of their scrolls in front of us, and explaining to us in French what was written in Hebrew and Aramaic in the places we questioned them about, found no trace of the passages and lines that were causing us so much trouble. Placing our trust therefore in the veracity of the Hebrew and Aramaic versions and in the many Latin books, which, omitting these passages, are in full agreement with the former, we completely erased all these unnecessary additions [...][8]

The leading biographer of St. Bernard of Clairvaux, Elphège Vacandard, wrote the following about Stephen Harding: "For the Old Testament, which was lacking the original and instead contained a Hebrew or Chaldaic text that had been passed down by word of mouth, he did not hesitate to consult with the neighboring Jewish rabbis."[9]

The result was the famous Harding Bible, and a contact between Harding and the Jewish rabbis who explained unknown, non-canonical Bible passages and the Talmud to him. Thus, Talmudic secrets were revealed to Harding that had been unknown to any other Christian cleric before him. As we can see, Cistercians and Jewish Bible and Talmud experts in the region worked together.[10] At a time in which Jews were often victims of attacks and discrimination, this was remarkable.

---

8   Stephen Harding, The Admonition of Stephen Harding, in: The Cistercian World: Monastic Writings of the Twelfth Century, translated and published by Pauline Matarasso, London: Penguin Books, 1993, p. 11f.
9   Vacandard, Elphège, Das Leben des Heiligen Bernard von Clairvaux, Mainz: Verlag Franz Kirchheim, 1897-1898, Volume 1, p. 110-112.
10   David Kaufman, Les Juifs et la bible de l'abbé Etienne Harding de Citeaux, Revue des etudes juives XVIII, 1889, p. 131-133; cf. Smalley, Beryl, The Study of the Bible in the Middle Ages, University of Notre Dame, New York, 1964, p. 79; cf. Auberger, Jean-Baptiste, L'Unanimité Cistercienne Primitive – Mythe Ou Réalité, Achel, Belgium, 1986, p. 21-22.

After Count Hugues I of Champagne sought out his friend Abbot Harding, he ordered more precise Bible studies of the Old Testament.[11] It is possible that the greatest Bible and Talmud scholar of his time, Rabbi Solomon Bar Isaac, known as Rashi, participated in these studies in Troyes. Rashi was the leading Jewish expert in the field of the Torah, the Five Books of Moses.[12] In addition, Rashi lived in the direct neighborhood of the Cîteaux Monastery and had very good relations to Christians and in particular to the Count of Champagne, partly because of his wine-growing that he used to finance his Bible studies.[13]

The Synagogue of Troyes in Champagne. This was founded by Rabbi Solomon Bar Isaac, known as Rashi, who ran the Talmudic school. His sons were consulted by the Cistercian abbot Stephen Harding to provide the correct translation into Latin of Bible passages from the Old Testament. The poet Chrétien de Troyes also came in contact with the city's Talmud scholars. The Jewish influences in his Grail epic Le Conte del Graal are proof of this. © Tobias D. Wabbel

11   Charpentier, Louis, Macht und Geheimnis der Templer, Herrsching: Pawlak Verlagsgesellschaft, 1986, p. 26.
12   Clayton-Emmerson, Sandra, Key Figures in Medieval Europe, CRC Press, 2006, p. 557-558. The suspicion of some authors that Rashi and Harding cooperated is pure speculation, as historian Gilbert Dahan asks us to consider. Dahan deems it very probable that his sons, who were also Bible scholars, cooperated with Abbot Stephen Harding, as Rashi died in 1105. Personal correspondence of the author with Gilbert Dahan from October 26, 2008. Even today, the Rashi Institute still exists at Rue Brunneval 2, opposite the Synagogue of Troyes.
13   Oliel-Grausz, Évelyne, Raschi von Troyes, in: Raschi 1105-2005, Worms: Worms-Verlag, 2005, p. 13.

Why Hugues de Payns and Count Hugues I of Champagne worked with Stephen Harding and Jewish rabbis to study Hebrew texts of the Five Books of Moses and the Talmud (the Jewish commentary on the Old Testament) is initially unclear. However, the texts obviously seem to have been interesting enough to justify another journey to Jerusalem. This fact leads us to a compelling conclusion that we will discuss later.

But let's get back to Hugues de Payns. He was mentioned in documents from 1113 as a lord of the manor in Payns.[14] In 1114, he and Hugues I of Champagne set off for Jerusalem again. This time Hugues de Payns stayed there. On the other hand, his friend, the rich and powerful Count, returned to France. About six years later, something amazing happens.

In 1120, there was a secret meeting in Jerusalem. Its background is still a little vague today.[15] Hugues de Payns and his representative Godfrey de St. Omer, appeared at the court of King Baldwin II and Garimond, the Patriarch of Jerusalem. Later, they were joined by the knights André de Montbard, Payen de Montdidier, Archambaud de St. Amand, Geoffroy Bisol and three other contemporaries who were either knights or monks: Roral (sometimes referred to as Rosal), Gondemar and Godfrey.[16]

André de Montbard was the uncle of St Bernard of Clairvaux, the spiritual father of the Order whom we will talk about in more detail soon. André was related to the Count of Burgundy, his sister was the wife of Tescelin le Roux, the father of St. Bernard of Clairvaux. Godfrey de St. Omer, Payen de Montdidier and Archambaud de St. Amand were knights of medium-ranking nobility in Picardy, the "breadbasket" in north-east France, and the ground on which the most beautiful Gothic cathedrals were to be built. The only thing we know about

14   Barber, Malcom, Die Templer, Düsseldorf: Patmos Verlag, 2005, p. 18.
15   Hiestand, Rudolf, Kardinalbischof Matthäus von Albano, das Konzil von Troyes und die Entstehung des Templerordens, in: Zeitschrift für Kirchengeschichte 99, 1988, p. 295ff. Although Hiestand claims to have proven that according to historical accounts the Templar Order was founded in 1120, it is much more probable that it was already founded circa 1114 when Hugues de Payns and Count Hugues I of Champagne went to Jerusalem. A document mentions the "Militia Christi" as early as 1114.
16   Historians often write the names of the Templar founders in different ways. For instance, John Charpentier writes Archambaud de St. Amand's name as Archambaud de St. Agnan in his work "L'Ordre des Templiers" ("The Order of the Templars"). The publicist Manfred Barthel refers to Geoffroy Bisol in his work "Die Templer" ("The Templars") as Geoffroy Bisot. In the Rule of the Templars from 1128, however, the names Geoffroy Bisol and Archambaud de St. Amand are used. These are the conventions I use here.

Geoffroy Bisol, Roral and Godfrey is that they attended the Council of
Troyes in 1128. Chroniclers remain silent about Gondemar.

Together with the Patriarch of Jerusalem, King Baldwin II debated the proposal of Hugues de Payns to allow him and his friends
to settle in the royal palace. He subsequently granted them space
for a headquarters in a wing of the former Al-Aqsa Mosque.[17] This
was also very remarkable. Without further ado, a king made space in
his palace for what must have appeared to have been a disorganized
troop of knights. But the King gave the nine knights the Al-Aqsa
Mosque which was built on the grounds of the former Temple of Solomon – not just any old building in the Holy City. Without doubt, it
was Hugues de Payns and Godfrey de St. Omer who asked for these
quarters – and not the other way round. From then on, the nine pilgrims would go down in history as *The Poor Fellow-Soldiers of Christ
and of the Temple of Solomon,*[18] Knights Templar for short. The chronicle of William of Tyre also reported that Hugues and his men vowed
to henceforth be chaste, poor and obedient in accordance with the
rules of the Benedictine and Augustine Orders.

In 1120, the influential and very wealthy Count Fulk V of Anjou,
the future King of Jerusalem and Baldwin II's successor, joined the
Templars. He supported them financially. According to the official historical accounts the Templars were living off donations and alms. Up
until 1121, Fulk V remained an unofficial member of the Order and
gave them his continued support with thirty Angevin pieces of silver.[19]
It is highly unlikely that Hugues and his friends went hungry. It was
also unlikely that they lived in poverty because their noble origins
stood in opposition to their plans to deprive themselves like abstinent
monks. Even if they may have wanted to, they wouldn't have voluntarily subjected themselves to this ascetic fate. Hugues de Payns' familial
relationship to King Baldwin II leads us to conclude that he received
financial support from the King and the Barons.[20]

17   Bulst-Thiele, Marie-Louise, The Influence of St. Bernard of Clairvaux on the Formation of the Order of the Knights Templar, in: The Second Crusade and the Cistercians,
New York: St. Martin's Press, 1992, p. 57.
18   The Latin term is: Pauperes commilitones Christi templique Salomonici Hiero-
salemitanis.
19   Wilcke, Ferdinand, Die Geschichte des Ordens der Tempelherren, Wiesbaden:
Marix Verlag, 2005, p. 44.
20   Ibid., p. 43.

Hugues de Payns, Lord of Montigny-Lagesse in Champagne, first served under Count Hugues I of Champagne as his vasall. Later, Count Huges I of Champagne swore an oath of fealty to his subordinate after Hugues de Payns was appointed the first Grand Master. © Tobias D. Wabbel

In 1125, something else mysterious happens: Count Hugues I of Champagne joined the nine inhabitants of the Temple Mount.[21] But first he transfered his titles to his nephew Theobald II, separated from his wife and denied that he was the father of his child. The Count suddenly shocked his very pregnant wife Elizabeth of Varais with the news that he was impotent – and so she couldn't have born him a child. Instead "his" child was the result of an affair of Elizabeth.[22] A crass accusation.

All in all, the Count was a strange fellow. Born circa 1074 as the third son of Theobald I, he was the first to hold the title "Count of Champagne." He didn't take part in the First Crusade, settled down in Troyes and did an active business with Jewish merchants. He also had an excellent relationship with the Jews in the region. As Count of Champagne, he had connections to Rabbi Rashi and his Talmudic school. In 1104, Count Hugues was the victim of an assassination attempt, but he survived. The reasons are unclear. There is also proof that he gave the Templars a huge piece of property. Even today, there is a forest and lake named after the Templars: Forêt de Temple and Lac du Temple, to the south-east of Troyes. During his lifetime, Count Hugues I of Champagne was one of the most powerful men in France. So it was all the more astonishing and inexplainable when he decided to join an order of knights. A letter to Count Hugues I of Champagne from the year 1125 documents the thoughts of St. Bernard of Clairvaux about the Count joining the Templar Order:

> If it is for God's sake that you from being a count have become a simple soldier, from being a rich man have become poor, then it is right that I should congratulate you, and glorify God in you, seeing in this a change of the right hand of the Most High [...] But that your joyous presence which, were it possible, I would never be without, should be removed from me by the inscrutable judgement of God, this is something hard to bear with equanimity. How can I forget your long-standing affection and generosity to this house?[23]

21   Barber, Malcom, Die Templer, Düsseldorf: Patmos Verlag, 2005, p. 18.
22   Wilcke, Ferdinand, Die Geschichte des Ordens der Tempelherren, Wiesbaden: Marix Verlag, 2005, p. 44.
23   The letters of St. Bernard of Clairvaux, translated by Bruno Scott James, Cistercian Publications, Kalamazoo, Michigan, 1998, Letter 32, p. 65.

These words display Bernard's great admiration, but also his regret. The Cistercian Abbot Bernard of Clairvaux, who in the 12th century was more powerful than the Pope, expressed his disappointment over the fact that Count Hugues I of Champagne was not joining the Cistercian Order, but was instead rushing to Jerusalem to join the knights at the Temple Mount. We can tell from this that the Count previously had a close relationship to Bernard and the Cistercian Order – and very probably was a frequent visitor to the Cîteaux Monastery. In his letter, Bernard also refered to the generous gift of land in the forest of Bar-sur-Aube by the Count of Champagne on which he had erected his monastery, the world-famous Clairvaux Abbey, in 1115. Thanks to this gift and the close friendship of Count Hugues I of Champagne, Bernard was henceforth an avid supporter of the Templar Order.

But what were Hugues de Payns and his friends doing in Jerusalem? After Count Hugues I of Champagne joined the Templars, neither he nor Hugues de Payns and his seven followers took part in battles although there were plenty of opportunities to participate in armed disputes. In 1119, the armies of Seljuqs from present-day Syria and Fatimids from Egypt attacked the Kingdom of Jerusalem. Baldwin II successfully drove back both armies – but the Templars with Hugues de Payns did not fight. In 1123, Baldwin II was captured by Seljuqs and not liberated until 1124 – the Templars didn't rush to his aid this time either. The same year, Baldwin II had lain siege to the Syrian town of Aleppo – but once again without any Templar support. In 1125, he defeated the army of Seljuqs in the Battle of Azaz – without the involvement of the Templars. It really did not seem as if the Templars were the least bit interested in battles and were in fact pursuing other goals.

But the Kingdom of Jerusalem was not just threatened by armed disputes. In 1125, after its conquest by the Crusaders (1095 -1099), because of its Biblical sites Jerusalem became a popular destination for Christians from the whole of Europe. Particularly the Church of the Holy Sepulchre. But, due to the lack of militia, many pilgrims were regularly attacked, robbed, kidnapped or even killed. Thus, Crusades chronicler William of Tyre described the task of Hugues de Payns' Knights Templars as being that of guarding the pilgrimage routes. Since then, this explanation has been unquestioningly accepted by the majority of historians.[24]

Several facts clearly refute this explanation. First and foremost, William of Tyre wasn't born until 1130. Therefore, it was impossible for him to report directly on the founding of the Templar Order. William of Tyre didn't compose his chronicle of the crusader states until 1170. William based it on preserved and accessible documents and eyewitness accounts of chroniclers and survivors – decades after the Templar Order had been founded in Jerusalem.

Therefore, it is conceivable that Hugues de Payns and his followers were considering guarding the pilgrimage routes between Jaffa and Jerusalem as a *possible future task*. However, they were most certainly not capable – with nine and occasionally 10 men – of fighting against tens of thousands of bloodthirsty highway robbers who wouldn't shy away from murder. This concept is rather absurd.

In contrast, English historian Malcolm Barber from the University of Reading states that the Templars initially led a rather secluded life as lay brothers with secular clothing behind the walls of the Al-Aqsa Mosque. They did not fight. And yet it appears to be the case that the community of the Templars already existed before their official founding. The German biographer of Bernard of Clairvaux, August Neander, writes the following about the founding of the Templar Order in 1120: "For ten years the association subsisted without the observance of any fixed rule, and without any great extension of their fame, or any addition to their number."[25] So the connection between Hugues de Payns and his eight comrades-in-arms had existed for much longer – at least 10 years – not to mention Hugues' acquaintance with the Count of Champagne.

In 1137, a certain William, Castellan of St. Omer, reported in a document that the "Patriarch Garimond and the Barons" had advised the Templars to defend Jerusalem.[26] This shows us that King

---

24   Alone the fact that both the Rule of the Templars, which was approved at the Council of Troyes in 1129, and the eulogy De laude novae militiae by Bernard of Clairvaux from the same year don't mention a single word about guarding the pilgrimage routes suggest that this was not the case.

25   Neander, August, Der Heilige Bernhard und sein Zeitalter, Gotha: Verlag Friedrich Andreas von Perthes, 1865, p. 26.

26   Document CG, no. 141, p. 99, mentioned in Barber, Malcolm, Die Templer, Düsseldorf: Patmos Verlag, 2005.

Baldwin II, the Patriarch and the King's barons had asked the Templars to guard the pilgrimage routes – years after they had set up their headquarters at the Temple Mount. So it was clearly not originally an idea of Hugues de Payns and his men. This task appears to be only *assigned* to them once they were already living on the Temple Mount.

Another argument refuting the theory of guarding the pilgrimage routes is also the logistically and strategically senseless procedure of Hugues de Payns and Godfrey de St. Omer: They would have done well to gather the financial funds from counts and princes in France *before* founding an order of knights and not waiting until after they arrived in Jerusalem, living there for eight years on a few donations and watching the buildings on the Temple Mount to continue to fall into ruin due to the lack of funding. So Hugues de Payns' Templars must have had a different mission when they came to Jerusalem. They didn't originally intend to simply guard the pilgrimage routes – this explanation was one that was later posited. There's no longer any doubt about this.

What's rather strange is the fact that King Baldwin II unhesitatingly granted them a part of his palace in the former Al-Aqsa Mosque. Apparently, it came in handy that Hugues de Payns was related to King Baldwin II. What's even stranger is that Hugues de Payns and Godfrey de St. Omer didn't first discuss their plan with any noblemen to secure the necessary financing, providing further evidence that the idea of guarding the pilgrimage routes did not originate from Hugues de Payns and the nine Templars.

It's also strange that Count Hugues I of Champagne embarked on three pilgrimages to Jerusalem. His behavior suggests great haste and obsessiveness. He seemed to have a constant goal and an extremely important mission in sight because he was obviously not frightened off by the great perils that such a journey posed to life and limb. Whatever happened in Jerusalem was much more significant than guarding the pilgrimage routes. But if the Templars had a different mission, what were Hugues de Payns' Templars doing during the eight years they resided on the Temple Mount? What was so important that Count Hugues I of Champagne and Hugues de Payns immediately sought out Stephen Harding in 1108 to study the

Bible? And what was so important that in 1125 Count Hugues I of Champagne practically disowned his family and gave up his titles in France just to live a reclusive life on the Temple Mount and shy away from battles?

They were digging. The chronicler of the First Crusade, Fulcher of Chartres, reports that in the 1120s the Templars did construction work on a large section of the western Temple area and exposed *Solomon's Stables* beneath the Al-Aqsa Mosque, which – according to the German pilgrim Theoderich – could house about 10,000 horses with their stable boys. The dimensions of the vaults are so huge that a single shot with a longbow would scarcely reach from one end to the other of the construction, neither lengthwise nor widthwise. Furthermore, according to Theoderich, in and to the west of the Al-Aqsa Mosque, construction work was performed on the buildings.[27]

In the 1980s, the Israeli archaeologist Meir Ben-Dov explored a tunnel that dates back to the 12th century. This tunnel had been previously discovered by the archaeologists of the *Palestine Exploration Fund* in the 1860s under the direction of archaeologist Charles Warren. The tunnel is situated thirty meters from the Southern Wall of the Temple Mount beneath Solomon's Stables – and thus directly below the former Templar headquarters. The shaft was obviously constructed to enable people to access the Temple Mount's passageways and caves further below ground. A map from the 12th century, known as the *Cambrai manuscript*, shows a side door described as *Poterna*. Meir Ben-Dov dubs this shaft a secret tunnel because it is *beneath* Solomon's Stables. There is no doubt in his mind that this was created by the Templars.[28]

Circa 1120, King Baldwin II moved out of the Al-Aqsa Mosque into the new royal palace at the Jaffa Gate in the west of Jerusalem. The Templars then had free reign. Circa 1128, the Al-Aqsa Mosque and the entire grounds were converted to the Templar headquarters. Hugues de Payns and his men were hard at work. It is very

27   Fulcher von Chartres, Historia, 1. 26, p. 291.
28   Ben-Dov, Meir, In the Shadow of the Temple, New York: Harpercollins, 1985, p. 346f. Cf. Gibson, Shimon und Jacobsen, David M., Below the Temple Mount in Jerusalem, Oxford: Tempus Reparatum, 1996 (BAR International Series 637); Palestine Exploration Fund, London or Wilson, Charles, Ordnance Survey of Jerusalem, Authority of the Lord's Commissioners of her Majesties Treasurers, London, 1886.

probable that they had even more men helping them to convert the Temple Mount. However, this suspicion is not historically documented. But just as it would have been impossible for nine men to guard the pilgrimage routes, it would have been equally impossible for nine men to complete such construction activities without the help of additional workers.

So the question is: Why did nine men, many of whom were noblemen, gather at the foundation walls of the former Temple of Solomon to live a reclusive life as a newly founded order of knights and dig beneath the Temple Mount to explore the grounds? What were they looking for?

The Council of Troyes

This question becomes particularly controversial when we consider what Hugues de Payns was doing in Jerusalem from 1115 until the official founding of the Order in 1120. The chronicler of the First Crusade, Albert of Aachen, reported that, before founding the Order, Hugues de Payns and some of his fellow knights were supposedly under the protection of the Prior of the Church of the Holy Sepulchre in Jerusalem. Therefore, Hugues de Payns and Godfrey de St. Omer would have been able to undertake investigations without any interruptions. It wasn't until 1119 that several hundred pilgrims were attacked and murdered not far from Jerusalem by highway robbers and marauding bandits – an event that Albert of Aachen claims triggered the founding of the Templar Order for the protection of the pilgrimage routes.[29] This is merely a conjecture, as we have seen, Hugues and his men didn't participate in any battles between 1115 and 1128, and lived a secluded life as lay brothers who were diligently focusing on their excavation activities. A letter from St. Bernard of Clairvaux to the Patriarch of Jerusalem from 1130 illustrates that the Patriarch apparently didn't have much patience with the Templars because they were not fulfilling their task of guarding the pilgrimage routes, but instead undertaking excavations:

> Give a thought, I pray you, to the soldiers of the Temple, and
> of your great piety take care of these zealous defenders of the

---

29   Albert von Aachen, Book 12, Chapter 33, p. 712-713.

Church. If you cherish those who have devoted their lives for their brethren's sake you will do a thing acceptable to God and well-pleasing to man.[30]

Bernard practically beseeched the angry Patriarch because apparently the Templars have not done enough for their pilgrim brothers. When King Baldwin II noticed the endeavors of the Abbot of Clairvaux, he suggested to Hugues de Payns and his eight Templars to found a new order of knights that is granted a Rule at a Council and was endorsed by the Pope in Rome.

The Patriarch was outvoted. Hugues was forced to agree. King Baldwin II sent André de Montbard and Brother Gondemar with an encyclical to France to ask Bernard of Clairvaux to compose a document advocating the new knighthood of the Templars.[31]

But first King Baldwin II sent Hugues de Payns to France circa 1127 to embark on a recruitment journey through Europe. They stopped off in Rome to consult with Pope Honorius II, who granted them his blessing and refered Hugues de Payns and his companions to the papal legates Matthew of Albano and Bernard of Clairvaux.[32]

Hugues' recruitment journey served to garner the support of influential noblemen for the Templar Order to finance their stay in Jerusalem, and accelerated the process of new brothers joining the Order. Hugues' journey took him to France, England and Scotland. In Scotland, he met King David I who gave the Templar Order a gift of lands near Ballantrodoch, today known as Temple, not far from Edinburgh. Hugues returned with dozens of volunteers who were ready to join the Order.

On his return, a Council was convened for January 13, 1129, in Troyes to confirm a Rule for the Order, which Hugues de Payns had already composed with the help of his friend Bernard of Clairvaux. At this time, this was an extremely strange procedure for an order of knights. After all, in 1109 the Knights of the Order of the Hospital of St. John of Jerusalem – Knights of St. John – had formed in

30   Bernhard von Clairvaux, Sämtliche Werke, Volume 2, Innsbruck: Tyrolia-Verlag, 1995, Letter 175.
31   Wilcke, Ferdinand, Die Geschichte des Ordens der Tempelherren, Wiesbaden: Marix Verlag, p. 44.
32   Ibid., p. 23.

Jerusalem to take care of the sick and provide medical care for pilgrims. The Order's hospital had been recognized by Pope Paschal in 1113 as an independent and necessary institution, but without convening a council.

This shows the significance the clergy ascribed to the Knights Templar Order because Hugues de Payns and his eight acolytes could have simply joined the Knights of St. John. But evidently they realized that it would be much more advantageous to found an order of their own. The great attention that they were given by the French bishops, King Baldwin II, and also Pope Honorius II, confirms their excellent standing. Possibly this was also due to a discovery under the Temple Mount in Jerusalem. Many things suggest that they found what they were looking for under the Temple Mount, because the preamble of the French Templar Rule contains a strange formulation: "God works well with us and our saviour Jesus Christ; he has sent his friends from the Holy City of Jerusalem to the marches of France and Burgundy."[33]

This *work* – finding the Templar treasure – was undoubtedly part of the debate at the Council of Troyes. And, the list of attendees confirms the extraordinary significance of this mysterious gathering of bishops. It begins with Hugues de Payns and Godfrey de St. Omer, the knights Godfrey, Roral, Geoffroy Bisol, Payen de Montdidier and Archambaud de St. Amand. In fact, seven of the founding Templar members were present in Troyes. And as Bernard had frequently communicated with the Patriarch and the King of Jerusalem in the run-up to the Council, it's hardly surprising that he also attended the meeting, together, with Abbot Stephen Harding of Cîteaux.[34] In addition, other Cistercian abbots were invited to the Council which was presided over by the papal legate of France Cardinal Matthew of Albano.

The highest-ranking dignitaries in the land entered the city. The archbishops of Reims and Sens, the bishops of Chartres, Soissons, Paris, Troyes, Orléans, Auxerre, Meaux, Châlons, Laon, Beauvais. These were the bishops of the towns where just a few decades later France's famous Gothic cathedrals would be erected.

33   Charpentier, Louis, Macht und Geheimnis der Templer, Herrsching: Pawlak Verlagsgesellschaft, 1986, p. 48.
34   Originally, Bernard had cancelled the Council due to illness, but the papal legate persuaded him to change his mind.

The Seneschal of Champagne, André de Baudement, also attended the synod as did the Count of Nevers and Theobald II, the nephew of Count Hugues I of Champagne, who before the death of his uncle in 1126 inherited his fortune and titles.

So what did they debate at the Council? The founding of the Templar Order was only one item on the agenda. It is unknown which other topics were discussed. What is clear however is that the initially 72-paragraph long Latin Rule of the Templar Order was endorsed at the Council of Troyes by the attending bishops and, in particular, the papal legate Matthew of Albano.

Hugues de Payns personally presented the clauses that are based on the strict Rule of the Cistercian Order. These were regulations for daily life as a brotherhood. Here we can find the instructions about accepting potential new brothers. We find out that children are not allowed to join the Order, but secular knights who have been previously expelled from the Church were; only that the Knights of Christ may wear a white linen shirt in the Holy Land due to the scorching heat; too thick hair or long clothes are forbidden, a brother must be internally and externally pure before God.

Here we also find the instructions that the brothers had to dine together in the refectorium and listen to the words of the Bible during their noonday and evening meals; two brothers had to eat from one dish if there were insufficient dishes available; every brother had to always have an equal portion of wine in their cup. Apart from feast days such as Christmas or All Saints' Day, meat could only be eaten three times a week as it corrupted the body. The remaining weekdays Monday, Wednesday and Saturday were for the consumption of pulses and vegetable broth. Out of respect for Lord Jesus Christ, the Templars fasted on Fridays, apart from the brothers who were sick and weak. A refreshment was always to be taken before Compline – evening prayer. It was up to the Master to choose what this consisted of. Contact with women was forbidden because this could lead some brothers to stray from the path to Paradise – bearing children was even more reprehensible. Every brother was allowed to have three horses and a squire whom they were not allowed to hit if he performed his service voluntarily and without pay. Pompous reins and decorated lances, falconry, linen or wool nose bags, boasting about your foibles and sins or spreading nasty rumors and slandering your brothers were also forbidden. And so on and so forth. The code of behavior of the Templar Rule is long and strict and it is blatantly obvious that this was inspired by the advice of Bernard of Clairvaux and the Cistercian rules.[35]

But the clauses regarding the ownership of land and chattels, farmers and fields and the levying of interest were incredibly laid back. The individual Templar had to take a vow of poverty, but the Order was allowed to accept and own (charitable) gifts. This paragraph provided the stirring reason for the Order's immeasurable riches.

The scribe present at the Council, Jean Michel, noted that the bishops and abbots listened devoutly to Hugues' words. As a result of the Order's development, the French Templar Rule later grew to a total of 686 paragraphs.

The Templar constitution gave rise to the reputation of the warrior monk, but also to a military hierarchy. Hugues de Payns became the first Templar Grand Master who presided over all members of the Order – squires, chaplain brothers, warrior monks. His representative was the Seneschal who counseled the Grand Master on all military matters. It was the Preceptor's job to make sure that the Templar brothers were keeping to the Rule and to manage the finances. Lands owned by the Templars were divided into commanderies. If the Grand Master was indisposed or captured in battle, he was represented by the Grand Commander until his return. In battle, the Marshal was responsible for battle formations and tactics. He also appointed the Standard Bearer. During battle, the Templars were split into squadrons and each of them was led by a Constable.

The Council of Troyes also laid the foundations for the public appearance of the Order at that time. The Templars now had to exchange their laymen's clothing for white surcoats that they then wore over the top of their armor or chainmail. It would have been impossible for Hugues de Payns and Bernard of Clairvaux to have

35   Bauer, Martin, Die Tempelritter – Mythos und Wahrheit, Munich: Wilhelm Heyne Verlag, 2003, p. 37.

thought all this up in a single day off the top of their heads. Instead, it seems more probable that the Templar Rule and the military hierarchy were developed over the years. At the Council of Troyes, the Order was given structure and prepared for war in the Holy Land. There were regulations covering practically every minutia of behavior for the Templar brothers.

But a most important thing seems to be missing: *not a single word* was mentioned about guarding the pilgrimage routes as a possible mission statement for the Templar Order.

St. Bernard of Clairvaux

Without the influence of Bernard of Clairvaux, the Templar Order would never have been founded. Bernard was born circa 1090 as the third of seven children of the knight Tescelin le Roux and his wife Aleth of Montbard at the castle of Fontaine-lès-Dijon.[36] Bernard's father was a feudal lord and very loyal servant to the dukes of Burgundy. Like her brother, the Templar founder André de Montbard, his mother Aleth was related to none other than the counts of Burgundy. Aleth was devoutly religious and it was of her own volition to entrust a monastery with the care of her seven children. She would have liked to have entered a convent to become a nun and serve God had Tescelin le Roux not won her heart. She nursed little Bernard herself instead of putting him in the care of a wet nurse – this was certainly unusual for the time as it was a sign of poverty. But this family was anything but poor.

Aleth frequently confronted her children with her personal religious views and read to them from the Bible. As a result, Bernard came into contact with Latin from a very early age. It is not known why he was not sent to be raised in a Benedictine monastery as a child. It is probable that at this time his father had too great a secular influence.

From 1098, Bernard attended the monastery school Saint-Vorles in Châtillon-sur-Seine. It was here that he learned reading, writing, rhetoric, grammar and dialectics. The quickest way he found to learn Latin was by learning Bible psalms by heart, which he sang together with his fellow scholars. The future Abbot of Clairvaux was spared

---

36   Most biographers, such as Elphège Vacandard, assume that Bernard was born in 1090, but there is no precise information about this in any of the sources.

the horrors of higher math – some of today's schoolchildren would have loved to trade places with the shy, pale, slight little boy with strawberry blond hair. Despite his lack of education in the natural sciences, Bernard became a model pupil and once he mastered Latin he was obsessed with reading the Bible and became a devout Catholic. When his mother Aleth died, Bernard was about 17-years-old. He blossomed and found friends among noble youths of his age. This soon led to the formation of cliques of which Bernard – thanks to his charismatic charm and rhetoric skills – rapidly became the leader.

It was not until 1109 that Bernard of Clairvaux's life became really strange: a contemporary, Herman of Laon, reported that Bernard had joined the Church – years before his decision to become a monk. Bernard was seriously considering traveling to Cologne to study at its cathedral school. The fact that Herman of Laon described him as a cleric before his actual life as a monk suggests that Bernard was already studying Biblical, natural science and philosophical texts.[37]

On the other hand, Bernard's feelings towards the fair sex were completely mortal. In spite of a young woman's attempt to seduce him, he was not known to have had any close relationship with women. In contrast: Bernard did his utmost to ensure he did not fall into temptation because he considered fulfilling his sexual needs to be an infernal sin. Bernard mitigated the consequences of the constant threat from his carnal desires and the danger of the damnation of his soul by entering a monastery.

In 1112, together with 30 other laymen of the Burgundian nobility who were his friends and relations (including four of his brothers), he asked to be admitted to Cîteaux Monastery.

The Cîteaux Monastery, founded on March 21, 1098, by Benedictine monk Robert of Molesme (1028-1111) is situated in the middle of a damp valley overgrown with reeds and surrounded by a deep forest.[38] The name Cîteaux is probably derived from *Cistel*, the old French word for reed. Robert was accompanied by 20 monks and the Duke of Burgundy, Odo I. Here we notice how close the clergy were to the region's nobility because Bernard's father, Tescelin le Roux,

---

37   Manitius, Geschichte III, 531ff., quoted according to Dinzelbacher, Peter, Bernhard von Clairvaux, Darmstadt: Wissenschaftliche Buchgesellschaft, 1998.

38   Exordium, p. 63; quoted according to Vacandard, Elphége, Leben des Heiligen Bernhard von Clairvaux, Mainz: Verlag Franz Kirchheim, 1897, Volume 1, p. 91.

had also served Odo I. Robert of Molesme had been forced to watch how the Rule of St. Benedict of Nursia (480-547) was increasingly deteriorating due to the excessive lifestyle and negligence of the abbots and monks of the Benedictine Order. The Rule of St. Benedict consisted of a prologue, as well as 73 chapters and was particularly based on the principles of poverty, prayer, work, chastity, humility and obedience. Chastity became increasingly rare within the walls of the Benedictine abbeys and the vow of poverty was increasingly broken due to extravagant living in Cluny Abbey, which was relatively close to Cîteaux, and had a church that surpassed the huge dimensions of Old St. Peter's Basilica in Rome thanks to generous financial gifts from the nobility.[39]

So it's no surprise that Bernard joined Cîteaux Monastery and did not put his trust in the Benedictines in Cluny. When Bernard knocked on the door of Cîteaux, the abbey was being run by Stephen Harding. Harding originally joined the Benedictine Order under Robert of Molesme and also disapproved of breaking the Benedictine Rule. Following Robert of Molesme and Alberic (1050-1109), Harding (who was born in the English town of Merriott in Dorsetshire in 1059) was at the time the third Abbot of Cîteaux. Harding had spent his childhood in Scotland and studied theology in the Irish town of Lismore, in Paris and in Rome. Then, on a trip to Rome he stayed in Molesme Abbey to join Abbot Robert of Molesme and established the Cîteaux Monastery.

Harding intended to introduce reform to restore the old strict virtues of St. Benedict. For many applicants who knocked on the doors of Cîteaux Monastery, the strictness of the Cistercian Order was off-putting. The monks in their white habits worked more than they prayed and abstinence was part of their daily lives. Stephen Harding is described in a contemporary chronicle as a fervent advocate of the life of the Order, poverty and the disciplinarian Rule. He is said to have followed and preached the Rule of the Benedictines as strictly as the Israelites their Mosaic Law.[40] Their ascetic stringency was based on the Desert Fathers.[41] In 1113, Harding

39   Neander, August, Der Heilige Bernhard und sein Zeitalter, Gotha: Verlag Friedrich Andreas von Perthes, 1865, p. 30.
40   Ordericus Vitalis, Historia Ecclesiastica 8, 26, 61, ed. Cîteaux, documents 208.
41   Dinzelbacher, Peter, Bernhard von Clairvaux, Darmstadt: Wissenschaftliche

composed the *Charta Charitatis* and gave the Cistercian Order a constitution. Thus, he made a significant contribution to the Order's success. Harding is also credited with writing the *Exordium parvum*, a chronicle about the history of the Cistercians.

Abbot Stephen Harding proved to be the perfect master for the inquisitive and highly gifted Bernard of Clairvaux. It is probable that the young novice was also present at the visits of Count Hugues I of Champagne when the latter was doing Bible study together with Abbot Harding. So right from the outset Bernard was initiated into the secrets of the Templar Order thanks to Count Hugues I of Champagne, as well as his uncle André de Montbard.

Bernard's novitiate was filled with at least six hours of church services, working in the fields and in the monastery, as well as studying the Bible. His meals were strictly rationed and it was perfectly normal for him to abstain from wine and meat because he believed that wine led to lasciviousness. Life in Cîteaux Monastery was not for the weak at heart, but Bernard denied himself more than all other monks in Cîteaux by excessively following the Benedictine Rule. This resulted in lifelong stomach problems and nausea during meals. His body was greatly weakened so that Bernard was only capable of doing light work. On the other hand, Bernard's asceticism of hunger, thirst, lack of sleep and physical suffering led to a hyperactivity that gave him the physical strength to write pages and pages of letters, sermons and Bible commentaries until late at night.[42]

The novitiate ended in 1114 with Bernard's public profession – the vow to henceforth live in poverty, obedience and chastity. The gray cowl was bestowed upon him. His head was shaved in a tonsure as a sign of the consecration of his life to the Virgin Mary.

Over the years, monastic life seemed to have become increasingly attractive to the population, because around 1115 the Cîteaux Monastery was no longer able to cope with the flock of new applicants. This resulted in the founding of sister monasteries, known as filiations: In 1113, La Ferté Abbey was founded, followed by Pontigny in 1114 and Morimond and Clairvaux in 1115. These four abbeys were dubbed primary abbeys from which sister monasteries could

---

Buchgesellschaft, 1998, p. 21.
42   Ibid., p. 26.

Today, Clairvaux Abbey serves as a prison. Only a few buildings survived the destruction of the French Revolution. © Tobias D. Wabbel.

be founded. As early as 1118, Trois-Fontaine was founded, followed by Fontenay in 1119 and Foigny in 1121. The wooded region of Burgundy was filled with hectic Cistercian construction activity. From the founding of Cîteaux, all these monasteries are dedicated to the Virgin Mary.

Abbot Stephen Harding let Bernard found his own monastery that was erected on the former property of Count Hugues I of Champagne. In 1115, Count Hugues I of Champagne was on his second pilgrimage to Jerusalem where he planned to meet Hugues de Payns. Count Hugues I of Champagne had his Viscount Gosbert de La Ferté officially transfer his property to the Cistercians. This Gosbert was one of Bernard's cousins. Clairvaux Abbey was constructed in the wooded wilderness of the Valley of Wormwood, 72 miles from Cîteaux, in the northern Diocese of Langres. The monks included Bernard of Clairvaux's four brothers, their uncle and two of Bernard's cousins.[43] Clairvaux was a family -run institution.

43   Fossier, Robert, L'installation et les Premières Années de Clairvaux, p. 79; Bouchard, Constance Brittain, Sword, Miter, and Cloister: Nobility and the Church in Burgundy, 980-1198, Cornell University Press, Ithaca, New York, 1987, p. 237f., quoted in: Dinzelbacher, Peter, Bernhard von Clairvaux, Darmstadt: Wissenschaftliche Buchgesellschaft, 1998, p. 31

Bernard gave the valley in which the wormwood plant grew a new name: Clairvaux, or the valley of light. And because a lot of trees first had to be chopped down to create the right setting, Bernard gave the Abbey a financial gift in accordance with the Second Book of Moses (Exodus) 23:15 – God orders the Israelites after the Exodus from Egypt to make sacrifices on the three festivals. This happened directly before the covenant with God when Moses meets God on Mount Sinai and is given the two stone tablets with the Ten Commandments. Once again, we notice this particular affiliation of the Cistercians with Judaism.[44] Stephen Harding and Bernard of Clairvaux seemed to be particularly impressed by this.

Shortly afterwards, Bernard received the blessing of the Bishop of Châlons-sur-Marne, William of Champeaux, to found the Abbey. The meeting with Champeaux was to dramatically change Bernard's life because throughout his lifetime he came and went from the Bishop's house and was always assured of his paternal protection. He developed a deep friendship to the man who taught philosophy at the Notre Dame Cathedral School in Paris. What is remarkable here is that Bernard was only twenty-five although the minimum age for an abbot was usually 30. It speaks for Bernard's outstanding intellect that the Bishop of Châlons-sur-Marne spent time with the young man to hold philosophical and theological debates with him.

Following the blessing of the Bishop of Châlons-sur-Marne, there was an increase in the financial contributions to Clairvaux Abbey which enabled Bernard to remedy the original construction deficits. The bitter cold in autumn and winter gave way to milder weather, which proved to be more conducive to the monks' health. On his trips to Châlons-sur-Marne, Bernard repeatedly brought back other novices who were willing to face the hard and ascetic monastic life. The reputation of the Abbey under the leadership of the outstanding Bernard of Clairvaux spread throughout the valleys of Burgundy – and beyond.

Bernard worked like a man possessed. Today, 545 letters, 300 sermons and numerous treatises are a testament to how influential Bernard was during his lifetime. The slight, pale Abbot of Clair-

---

44   Regula 58,24, quoted in: Dinzelbacher, Peter, Bernhard von Clairvaux, Darmstadt: Wissenschaftliche Buchgesellschaft, 1998, p. 31.

vaux even put popes and kings in their place in his letters – and they were amazingly obedient to him. Bernard was the first person people consulted on clerical matters rather than the Pope in Rome.

In 1124, Bernard of Clairvaux composed a memorable text of epic length on the Virgin Mary: *De laudibus Virginis Matris*. On the Praises of the Virgin Mother. According to one legend, three drops of milk shot from the breast of the Virgin Mary into Bernard's mouth who was henceforth obsessed with love for her. The Praises of the Virgin Mother are made up of a series of four sermons – *homilies* – that show how Bernard was influenced by the Cistercian abbots Robert of Molesme, Alberic and Stephen Harding. Robert of Molesme dedicated his abbey and Cîteaux to the Virgin Mary. Whereas Robert of Molesme, Alberic and Harding merely worshiped the Virgin Mary, Bernard was practically obsessed with her. His rapturous work *De laudibus Virginis Matris* is the highlight of Mariolatry and also a testament to his influence on the Templar Order because each new member of the Order of warrior monks had to swear an oath of fealty to the Virgin Mary. The Templar Order served her in the figurative sense of the word.

On January 13, 1129, Bernard turned 38. His asceticism had made him ill and he attended the Council of Troyes together with the Abbot of Cîteaux, Stephen Harding and the Bishop of Châlons-sur-Marne, William of Champeaux. Bernard opened the Council and, together with other Cistercian abbots and bishops, listened attentively to the words of Hugues de Payns who was presenting the constitution of the Templar Order.

In Praise of the New Knighthood

After the Council of Troyes, Hugues de Payns asked his friend Bernard of Clairvaux to compose a propaganda letter for the Templar Order. After initial hesitation, Bernard agreed and wrote his famous treatise for the Templars *Liber ad milites templi – De laude novae militiae*. In this praise of the new knighthood, Bernard writes:

> If I am not mistaken, my dear Hugh, you have asked me not once or twice, but three times to write a few words of exhortation for you and your comrades. You say that if I am not

permitted to wield the lance, at least I might direct my pen against the tyrannical foe, and that this moral, rather than material support of mine will be of no small help to you [...][45]

This almost sounds as if Bernard regreted not being able to take up the sword because his monastic existence forbade it. Here we can also see that it was Hugues de Payns' intention to obtain a clerical legitimation for the Templar Order and his friend Bernard of Clairvaux was the first instance – even before the Pope. Whoever has the Church's blessing on their side was beyond all criticism. The wording of Bernard's treatise is characterized by clever wit and Biblical references.

Initially, Bernard took the worldly knights severely to task. He scolded them for being vain fools who cover their horses with silk blankets and decorated their armor with fabrics and cloths, who painted their spears, shields and saddles and dressed up their reins and spurs with gold, silver and precious stones. Bernard condemned the surplus fripperies that are part of knighthood because in his opinion these detracted from the true mission of a knight: to fight for God. His cynical conclusion was not without humor: "And then in all this glory you rush to your ruin with fearful wrath and fearless folly." Then Bernard wondered whether all this pomp on horseback was for the sake of military honor or rather effeminate vanity.[46]

Bernard wrote that the swords of the foes will not be turned back by the gold of the worldly knight. The foes would not spare the jewels or be unable to pierce the silks. The reader recognizes that Bernard was not sad for these men in pompous armor who compete in tournaments or fall to the ground dead in battle. After dealing with the arrogant "swashbuckling" of these *adventures*, which was later so gloriously described in the courtly novels of the High Middle Ages by writers such as Chrétien de Troyes and Wolfram von Eschenbach, Bernard focused on his own creation: the warrior monks.

Subsequently, he declared the new knighthood of the Templars to be noble warriors who are going into battle against the princes

---

45   St. Bernard of Clairvaux, Liber ad milites templi. De laude novae militiae, published in: The Works of Bernard of Clairvaux, Treatises III, In Praise of the New Knighthood, translated by Conrad Greenia, Cistercian Publications, Kalamazoo, Michigan, 1977, p. 127.
46   Ibid., p. 132.

of darkness "with the strength of God's mighty hand." Bernard was enthused on how the Templar's "soul was protected by the armor of faith just as his body was protected by armor of steel. He is thus doubly armed and need fear neither demons nor men." The Templar, the warrior of the new Knighthood of Christ, "gladly and faithfully (…) stands for Christ, but he would prefer to be dissolved and to be with Christ, by far better the thing." This meant that the Templar's death in battle was not only expected, but also required for the glory of the cause. This view barely differed from the fanatic Ismaelite murder sect, the Assassins, which formed in Persia and set off on suicide missions from the mountain stronghold Alamut on behalf of the "Old Man of the Mountain," Rashid ad-Din Sinan. In his treatise Bernard was asking nothing but unconditional self-sacrifice for God – to the death. You can tell that he didn't yet feel at ease with this because the blood flowing through his veins appears more clerical than knightly. It was not in vain that he worked on the Templar Rule together with Hugues de Payns and elegantly gave the Order Cistercian influences. Obedience was one of the greatest virtues of the Cistercians. It was Bernard's belief that "death in battle is more precious as it is the more glorious." That was easy for him to say as a Cistercian abbot of such repute, because he didn't have to fight. Now the Cistercian Order had its own army and it can be sure that its warrior monks would be indoctrinated with a healthy portion of fanaticism.

Bernard's declarations become ecstatic: The Templars "set their minds on fighting to win rather than on parading for show." They sought to induce formidable teeth-chattering from their foes rather than coming across as flamboyant. "At the same time, (the Templars) are not quarrelsome, rash, or unduly hasty, but soberly, prudently and providently drawn up into orderly ranks." After all this transfiguration, it is practically a miracle that Bernard openly described the actual mission of the Templars and then got to the point.

And things get mysterious again. Bernard writes: "Indeed, the true Israelite is a man of peace, even when he goes forth to battle." Bernard of Clairvaux whose Cistercian Order already identified with Judaism

– may I remind you of Stephen Harding's cooperation with the Jewish Talmud experts – compared the Templars to the Israelites who wandered through the Sinai desert and whose leader Moses received the Ten Commandments from God on Mount Horeb (also known as Mount Sinai).

But Bernard went even further. He said that the Templars were the *true Israelites*. The Templars were fighting for the Lord of armies Zebaoth, an Israelite term for Yahweh in the Old Testament, which told of an epoch in Jewish history where God was only allowed to be named with synonyms and not named by name. The actual mission of the Templars becomes even clearer when in his treatise Bernard gets worked up about the "pagan" Muslims in Jerusalem: "They busy themselves to carry away the incalculable riches placed in Jerusalem by the Christian peoples, to profane the holy things and to possess the sanctuary of God as their heritage."

The Temple of Solomon played a very important role for Bernard. Subsequently, Bernard listed all places in the Holy Land that he believed are of particular significance. But first and foremost he lists the Temple of Solomon – and not the Church of the Holy Sepulchre that stands on the foundations of Golgotha where Jesus Christ was once buried and which was in Bernard's era the most important pilgrimage destination. The Temple of Solomon was followed by Christ's birthplace, Bethlehem. Then Nazareth, the town of Jesus' parents. This was followed by the place where Jesus held his Sermon on the Mount, the Mount of Olives. Then Bernard named the River Jordan in which Jesus was baptised by John the Baptist. The crucifixion site Golgotha. The Church of the Holy Sepulchre. The village of Bethphage in which two of Jesus' disciples borrowed a donkey for the Savior to ride into Jerusalem. In addition, we find Bethany, the birthplace of sisters Mary (whom some Christian traditions believe to be Mary Magdalene) and Martha of Bethany and their brother Lazarus whom Jesus raised from the dead.

But in spite of all these places that are important in Bible stories, the most important site in the Holy Land for Bernard of Clairvaux and the Poor Fellow-Soldiers of Christ was still the Temple of Solomon. Bernard addressed the "Holy Sepulchre" with these incredibly

The fact that Bernard of Clairvaux regarded the Templars as the true Israelites and this message was incorporated in the medieval art of the time is illustrated by this sculpture of the west portal of Reims Cathedral. The Jewish
patriarch Abraham is receiving the blessing by the high priest Melchizedek.
Abraham is depicted as a Templar, which is recognizable by his pilgrim staff
and the monk's habit over his knight's armor. © Tobias D. Wabbel

unspectacular words: "Somehow the Holy Sepulcher seems to be the most attractive of the holy places. I do not know exactly why the devout are more drawn to the place where his dead body rested than to where he lived and worked [...]"[47] When Bernard wrote that the Holy Sepulchre is *somehow* – so *not really* – the first place among the holy sites in Israel, the Church of the Holy Sepulchre is only mentioned in 11th place in his treatise to the Templars. In other words: Bernard felt forced to write a few well-meaning words about the Church of the Holy Sepulchre, but his true love was still the Temple of Solomon, which he mentioned in first place. Bernard prefered the Old to the New Testament. A further proof of Bernard's affinity to the Israelites. He concluded: "Do you not see how frequently these ancient witnesses foreshadowed the new knighthood?"[48]

Rather presumptuously Bernard added that the presence of the Templars had now made the Temple of Solomon the greatest sanctuary of all. It was not the gold on the walls that made the Temple of Solomon valuable, but the manifold virtues and holy acts of the warrior monks. How can an act be holy if it doesn't in some way refer to the search for a holy relic? The fight against marauding highway robbers who were mugging and murdering pilgrims certainly can't be seen as a holy act because Hugues de Payns' Templars didn't dedicate any time to this at all. Instead, Bernard can only have meant the excavation activities beneath the Temple Mount and the successful completion of their search. Because he wrote in the preamble of the Primitive Rule of the Knights Templar he helped to compose that "God works well with us."

So the Templars' task was clearly described: to protect the treasures of the Holy City – and to search for them – before they are stolen by "pagans." After conquering Jerusalem in 1099, the army commander Godfrey of Bouillon succeeded in securing a piece of Christ's cross in Jerusalem for Christendom.[49] In his treatise, Bernard of Clairvaux didn't mention a single word about guarding the pilgrimage routes. Instead, the Templars' actual mission now becomes clear: Bernard asked the Templars to hunt for relics in the Holy Land and, in

47   Ibid., p. 154
48   Ibid., p. 137
49   Runciman, Steven, Die Geschichte der Kreuzzüge, Munich: DTV, 1995, p. 280

particular, in Jerusalem. But which holy relics were Hugues de Payns and his men looking for in Jerusalem to make Bernard of Clairvaux claim in his treatise that the Templars are the true Israelites?

Bernard's treatise paved the way for the unstoppable victory of the Templar Order. Nobles throughout Europe declared their willingness to give the Templars large sums of money and lands. Even the clergy seemed amenable to the forceful methods of the warrior monks.

On March 29, 1139, Pope Innocent II granted the Templars exemption from episcopal authority in the papal bull *Omne datum optimum*. The Templar Order was now only answerable to the Pope – and no one else. Henceforth, the Grand Master was only chosen by his brothers in the Order and at the same time his power over his brothers was strengthened. Innocent II permitted the Templars to appoint their own priests – an important step that ensured the secrecy of the Order's internal matters. Confessions were thus heard by a Templar priest and not by an outside cleric. Even more important was the fact that the Templars were exempted from paying any tithes. The Templars didn't have to pay any taxes. This was one of the basis of the incredible riches of the warrior monks that was their undoing on October 13, 1307. Further privileges followed bit by bit: On February 9, 1143, Pope Innocent II extended the privileges of the Templars with his papal bull *Milites templi*. Chaplains of the Templar Order were now allowed to perform mass once a year.

On April 7, 1145, Pope Eugenius III, a former Cistercian abbot and pupil of Bernard of Clairvaux, issued the papal bull *Militia dei*, which permitted the Templars to build their own churches and own their own cemeteries. We will go into more detail about this privilege and Pope Eugenius III. Pope Eugenius III also issued another order: Henceforth, the brothers of the Order should wear a red cross pattée on the left shoulder of their white surcoats – the charismatic symbol of the Order of warrior monks. White represents innocence; red represents the blood of Christ. Now, the Templars were an uncontrollable power who exerted considerable political influence over the Pope and Kings – throughout the whole of Europe.

In 1129, Hugues de Payns, accompanied by Count Fulk V of Anjou, returned to Jerusalem. They led a small army of normal knights

A gravestone in the church of the Cistercian Abbey of Fontenay, which was founded in 1119 and was an affiliate abbey of Clairvaux. This photograph shows a Templar, who is recognizable by his knight's armor under his monk's habit and his prayer position. © Tobias D. Wabbel

to take part in a battle, because there were not yet sufficient Templar brothers who have joined the Order. That same year, under the leadership of Hugues de Payns, the Templars battled the Seljuqs when they laid siege to Damascus. Hugues suffered bitter losses and the Syrians regained possession of the city. The battle was in vain and Hugues de Payns died on May 24, 1136, in a battle against the Saracens.

Back to the present and back to Troyes. One of the two ladies running the Musée Hugues de Payns willingly answers my questions that I stammer in my amateur schoolboy French.

A few newspaper articles in the exhibition have caught my attention. In September 1998, Dr. Thierry LeRoy flew over the fields around Troyes in a plane. During this, on photographs he discovered the outlines of remains of ruins in the earth. After archaeologists exposed the area, it became obvious that this was the first Templar commandery that Hugues de Payns had given to the Templar Order. Based on the reconstructions, the commandery must have comprised two hundred hectares of land. The building, a type of farm, was three hectares in size and it also included a rectangular, 20.6-meter long and 9-meter wide Cistercian chapel made of chalk limestone that was surrounded by a cemetery. The excavations of the chapel were performed very carefully, but only superficially. Remains of glass and lead have led us to believe that the chapel had lead glass windows. Fresco fragments adorned the walls of the ruins and colorfully glazed terracotta tiles gave the impression of a typical Cistercian chapel of that period. Archaeologists have found several hundred silver coins in the earth – a small and rather modest treasure.

I leave the museum and drive on to the N29 in the direction of Troyes to take a closer look at the excavation. After just over half a mile, I take a sharp right on to the D442 that leads to Pavillon-Sainte-Julie. After about two hundred meters, I stop. Dust fills the air and the sparse vegetation casts a harsh shadow in the midday sun. Far and wide, there is no car to be seen. I get out of my car and search the fields with the aid of my binoculars.

After a few minutes, my breath catches in my throat. I spy the light outlines of a building complex that seems to be behind a fence in the furrows of the fields. My heart sinks as I suddenly realize: the excavation area has been paved over. Apparently, there was no one willing to finance the excavations and the farmer whom the field belonged to didn't seem to have any patience with the archaeologists.

To sum up my previous findings:

- Count Hugues I of Champagne, one of the most powerful men in France, goes on a pilgrimage to Jerusalem in 1105. But it was probably more of a research trip. On his return, he contacts the Cistercian abbot Stephen Harding, who subsequently meets with the Jews of Champagne and Burgundy to study Hebrew Biblical texts of the Old Testament and the Talmud.

- Nine noble knights meet on the Temple Mount in Jerusalem in 1120, including Hugues de Payns, Hugues I of Champagne and André de Montbard, the uncle of Saint Bernard of Clairvaux. They are all related to the noble houses of Champagne, Picardy and Burgundy.

- The Templars don't participate in any battles.

- It is only the Patriarch of Jerusalem who suggests that Hugues de Payns and his followers should guard the pilgrimage routes. So it wasn't the Templars' mission when they came to Jerusalem.

- Archaeological research under the Temple Mount proves that Hugues de Payns and his men performed excavations and were obviously looking for something in particular.

- In 1125, Hugues I of Champagne joins the Templars – after three pilgrimages to the Holy Land. But first he disowns his wife and child and transfers his property to his nephew Theobald II to join the Templar Order and ironically swear an oath of fealty to his former vassal Hugues de Payns.

- Bernard of Clairvaux and Abbot Stephen Harding of Cîteaux identify with Judaism.

- In 1129, Bernard writes in the preamble of the Primitive Rule of the Knights Templar, which he co-authored with Hugues de Payns: "God works well with us and our saviour

Jesus Christ; he has sent his friends from the Holy City of Jerusalem to the marches of France and Burgundy (...)." Bernard thereby confirms that the mission of Hugues de Payns and his companions has been accomplished.[50]

• In his treatise of 1129, *De laude novae militiae*, Bernard of Clairvaux praises the Templar Order and calls for the protection of the treasures and sacred objects of the Holy Land before they fall into the hands of the "pagans."

• Thus, Bernard calls for the hunt for relics and dubs the Templars "the true Israelites" whose acts make the Temple of Solomon a sanctuary.

And I can't help wondering: What were Hugues de Payns and his followers looking for under the Temple Mount – and what did they ultimately find? I get back in my car and drive back to Troyes.

---

50   Upton-Ward, Judith M., The Rule of the Templars, The French text of the Rule of the Knights Templar, Boydell Press, Woodbridge, Suffolk, 1992, p. 19. The Primitive Rule of the Templars endorsed on January 13, 1129, at Troyes was later translated into French some years after the Council and expanded.

DeMolay's graffitti at Gisors © Gérard de Sède, "Die Templer sind unter uns" (original title: "Les templiers sont parmi nous ou l'énigme de Gisors"), Ullstein Verlag, Berlin, 1962

Chapter Two

God's Relics

You call this archaeology?

— Dr. Henry Jones Sr.

For decades, there have been some pretty wild speculations about what Hugues de Payns' men were searching for under the Temple Mount between the years of 1105 and 1128. As we have seen, this search appears to have been successful. The clues they left behind are clearly visible. To find out where the Templar treasure is located, it is important to ask which relic they were secretly searching for over the years. It is, however, also possible that *subsequent Grand Masters* of the Templar Order were guarding a treasure. Thus, it is necessary to investigate the plausibility of the current theories on the possible nature of the Templar treasure. And that is precisely what we are going to do now.

The Enigma of Gisors

The French journalist Gérard de Sède told an astonishing story in his book *The Templars are Amongst Us*, which was published in 1962. During World War II, Gérard de Sède worked in the French *Resistance*, was briefly imprisoned by the Germans and after the Liberation received two awards from Paris at the end of the War. He had many jobs, including selling newspapers and building tunnels, before working for ten years as a journalist for a large French news agency and then retiring as a farmer. A former guardian of the Gisors Castle in Normandy, Roger Lhomoy, confided in de Sède that he had made a strange discovery.

But let's not get ahead of ourselves. Roger Lhomoy, born April 17, 1904, in Gisors, originally intended to become a clergyman and live the modest life of a country pastor. Lhomoy even received his minor orders so apparently he was very serious about this. But then he renounced the Church at the age of twenty-five. A few years later, he married and soon became the father of two children. From 1929, Lhomoy became obsessed with the idea that the Templar treasure could be hidden in the Gisors Castle. Obviously his enthusiasm was fueled by the fact that the Gisors Castle had been owned by the Templars for some years. Lhomoy repeatedly sent letters of application to the Gisors town council, recommending himself as a guardian of the Castle.[1]

In 1929, Lhomoy's perseverance finally paid off when he was hired as a castellan and gardener. In 1941, Lhomoy began digging. It is not known how he knew where to dig to possibly find a treasure. He exposed a well, behind the defense tower that is standing on a man-made mound – a "motte" – and dug 30 meters underground. Lhomoy broke his leg when the earth above fell on him. As soon as the castle gates closed at night to the visitors, Lhomoy would begin his work. Three years passed.

In January 1944, things got serious. Lhomoy dug another well, 15 meters from the first one, and laboriously carved a funnel-shaped shaft into the depths of the earth, which had neither support beams nor a ventilation shaft to protect him from life-threatening gases. A crazy business because the weight of the earth above him could have caused the shaft to cave in at any moment. The darkness of his underground world was only illuminated by an electric lamp. But Lhomoy didn't care about safety. His initial idea had developed into a manic obsession to find the Templar treasure.

Lhomoy didn't care about the Allied Forces who stormed the beaches of Normandy on D-Day, June 6, 1944. Actually, in view of the German Occupation, he had good reason to celebrate. Lhomoy shoveled like a madman as he penetrated deeper and deeper into the soil of Gisors Castle. When he reached a depth of 16 meters, he discovered a four by four meter room. It was completely empty.

---

1   Sède, Gérard de, Die Templer sind unter uns, Berlin: Ullstein Verlag, 1963, p. 11ff.

The "motte" (mound) of the defense tower of Gisors in Normandy was excavated by the castellan of Gisors Castle, Roger Lhomoy, in his search for the Templar treasure. Finally, the French military had the Castle blocked off on the instruction of Charles de Gaulle. The official explanation was that this was to prevent the tower caving in due to the many underground galleries. In the dungeon of the defense tower there are depictions of a virgin and a dragon which the last Templar Grand Master, Jacques de Molay, left behind before his death. © Tobias D. Wabbel

His old friend Lesenne, who recommended Lhomoy as a castellan, helped him to dig. He said he witnessed Lhomoy's discovery of the little underground room. But Lhomoy filled in the hole.

At the foot of a new hole, he dug another nine meter long horizontal gallery of about 50 centimeters in height behind the well. Lhomoy obtained an excavation permit from the Secretary of State for Fine Arts in Paris. However, his project exceeded the registered size of the original excavation site – up to this point, Lhomoy had moved 50 tons of earth and it was getting difficult to hide the excavation site. Lhomoy was getting cold feet because he felt that someone might fall into his excavation side and grievously injure themselves. So he carefully asked the Mayor who surprisingly informed him that he would support him once he had found something of significance.

Lhomoy continued to dig. But the shaft led to a dead end. Inspired by his obsession, Lhomoy dug another lateral shaft, but this one went vertically down. It was so deep that he then no longer got any air and had to periodically return to daylight. He used his bare hands and a crowbar to push onwards because the gallery was too narrow for the use of a spade or a pickax. After four meters, Lhomoy came across a wall of hewn stone. In a real tour de force, he used his crowbar to push out one stone after the other. When the hole was big enough, he crawled through it. As soon as Lhomoy brought his electric lamp into the room, he spied what he estimated to be a 30 meter long, 9 meter wide and 4.5 meter high Roman chapel. On the left side, Lhomoy saw an altar and on the right statues of Jesus Christ and the 12 apostles. On the walls he recognized the outlines of 2 meter long and 60 centimeter wide stone sarcophagi, as well as 30 chests made of precious metal which Lhomoy estimated to be about 2.5 meters long, 1.80 meters high and 1.60 meters wide.

The underground vaults of Gisors Castle still hold their secrets. © Tobias D. Wabbel.

The next day, Lhomoy informed the town council in detail of his discovery. One volunteer, Lhomoy's brother and the Parisian town councilor Marcel Lhomoy, agreed to be let down into the well. However, he gave up after a few meters due to fear of it collapsing. A second volunteer went down into the hole. He was the local chief of the Gisor fire service, Emile Beyne, a former military officer and a man of integrity who was held in high regard in the community. When he reached the underground wall, he threw a stone through the hole to the chapel. He didn't see anything, but heard a loud echo that was caused by the impact of the stone. When he got short of breath, Beyne hurried back to the daylight because he too was over-come with fear that hundreds of tons of earth could fall on him and bury him alive.

Lhomoy asked the Mayor for another permit for further excava-tions, but this time he was disappointed. The Mayor forbade him to perform any further excavations – and fired Lhomoy. The authorities were afraid of visitors to the Castle falling into the shaft, the defense tower becoming instable and the foundations collapsing. It is in this *donjon* (keep) that the last Templar Grand Master Jacques de Molay was imprisoned and interrogated by the French King's chancellor Guil-laume de Nogaret. The main reason for the shut down was most proba-bly because Lhomoy failed to bring to the surface a single piece of proof for his outlandish claim.

It was March 1946, a few German prisoners of war were filling in the holes and the matter was initially forgotten. Roger Lhomoy was then without a job. And as if that weren't bad enough, his wife and her two children left him.

Years passed. Lhomoy was a broken man and disappointed about the lack of enthusiasm from the Mayor and the authorities who thought he was a madman and predicted that in the next few years he would end up in an insane asylum if he didn't come to his senses soon. But Gérard de Sède stressed in his book that Lhomoy always appeared to be thinking clearly.

Lhomoy refused to give up. In 1952, he tried again. Meanwhile, he had been able to convince a rich industrialist, a hotel owner and two businessmen from Versailles to search for the treasure under Gisors Castle. An architectural draftsman completed what was more or less an exact map of the underground chapel based on Lhomoy's descriptions. Together with other documents on the excavation activities, the consortium filed a new application for an excavation permit for Gisors to the Secretary of State for the Fine Arts in Paris. They received the permit without delay. But the town of Gisors demanded four-fifths of any possible treasure found – as compensation for any damage that may be incurred. This discour-aged Lhomoy's sponsors because they would not make any profit if they found a treasure, but would only have to spend even more money. Subsequently, they distanced themselves from the daring project. Lhomoy was as far from his goal as his first cut of the spade. He had nothing to lose – and continued to dig in Gisors at night. When he reached the underground chapel and glanced through the walls that he had opened with his own hands, to his utter horror he saw – nothing. The chapel had been emptied out.

Years after these events, Gérard de Sède and two witnesses – Pierre Branche and Daniel Lefebvre – checked Roger Lhomoy's information that showed the excavation gallery. Even though de Sède does not get to see the underground chapel with his own eyes, he and his colleagues swore that Lhomoy's information is correct and was even understated.

Finally, in 1961, de Sède published his book *The Templars are Amongst Us*, that studies the Enigma of Gisors. The book became a national bestseller. The media sensationalism also attracted numerous treasure hunters. In his desperation, Roger Lhomoy contacted the French President Charles de Gaulle, who had become curious about Gisors due to the reports and commissions the Minister for Cultural Affairs André Malraux to perform further excavations. At Malraux's instructions, the police force and the military of the 5th Engineer Regiment of Rouen blocked off the Castle in 1964, but after months of excavations threatened the foundations of the defense tower, the work was discontinued.

Whatever the military might have found – is pure speculation. To the present day, it is forbidden to perform any excavations in Gisors. In his book, Gérard de Sède reported that the chapel that was dedicated to St. Catherine of Alexandria could have been the possible storage place for documents of the Templar Order. The cupboard-like objects supposedly suggested this. To his death, Roger Lhomoy continued to assert that he had seen and found the Templar treasure. The fact that Roger Lhomoy performed excavations under the defense tower of Gisors Castle is as proven as the fact that the French police force blocked off the area around the Castle. If the underground chapel ever existed, the objects contained therein could have very probably already been removed. If Lhomoy's story is true, the chapel was probably explored in his absence by the French authorities. But this is not proven, merely an educated guess.

The idea that the Templar treasure, which was found by Hugues de Payns and his followers under the Temple Mount in Jerusalem, might be hidden under Gisors Castle is not as crazy as it might initially seem. Gisors plays a special role in the history of the Templars. Construction began on the Castle in 1090 by Theobald who was a nephew of the first Templar Grand Master Hugues de Payns. The purchase contract for the Castle was signed by Othon de St. Omer, the brother of the founding Templar Godfrey de St. Omer. From 1158 to 1161, King Louis VII of France left the castle in the care of three Templars. Richard of Hastings, Toestes de St. Omer and Robert de Pirou.[2] In 1184, Gisors Castle was completed and in the care of Henry II Plantagenet.

It is possible that documents or other relics of the Templars have been stored down there since that time or are even still stored there because they were left behind by the Templars. Without proof, however, Roger Lhomoy's discovery was no more than an exciting story because it would require further excavations to find out whether a chapel or similar underground rooms really do exist beneath the defense tower. The French military remains silent.

An official letter from the Norman Ministry of Culture in Caen from October 1971 disputed that an underground chapel ever existed in Gisors.[3] Whoever would like to search for this in Gisors can do so by ultrasound. However, Professor Michel de Boüard of the Ministry of Culture in Caen, the author of the letter, must be present at the measurements. The Ministry was expressly granting people permission to search for the treasure in Gisors. In 1961, the frescoes of Gisors were examined by the aforementioned Professor Michel de Boüard who had been commissioned by the Minister for Cultural Affairs André Malraux. But, it was very probable that this does not

2   Wilcke, Wilhelm Ferdinand, Die Geschichte des Tempelherrenordens, Leipzig: Verlag Hartmann, p. 49.

3   Official document of the Ministry of Culture, October 19, 1971, No. 651/71/ C.A.H., Circonscription des Antiquités Historiques, Ministére d'État Chargé des Affaires Culturelles, Centre des Recherches Archéologiques, Université de Caen, initialed by Michel de Boüard.

refer to any medieval wall paintings, but instead to the graffiti that the last Templar Grand Master Jacques de Molay left in the defense tower during his imprisonment in Gisors. If not, this would be rather strange because officially there are no known frescoes in Gisors. On the other hand, back in 1971, whoever asked the Mayor of Gisors, Marcel Larmanou, for permission to perform ultrasound measurements received a harsh refusal. To date the population of Gisors has mixed opinions on the existence of an underground chapel in Gisors.

Gisors, present day, the area is still in danger of collapse. Cédric makes an exception because I am stubborn and push him to let me visit it so that I might perhaps come closer to the secret of Gisors. It is cold and dark in the vaults. The air smells of moist sandstone. A damp gust of air brushes past my face like a centuries-old ghost. The sparse light is lost in the darkness of the vaults. I shudder.

Finally, Cédric says something. "Ici!" He points the beam of his flashlight at a hole in the wall on our right. Cédric, a matter-of-fact man in his late twenties, works as a guide in Gisors Castle when he is not studying medieval history and, in particular, the Crusades.

The hole he shows me is not far from the stairs that lead to the underground vaults of Gisors Castle – vaults that were once a storage place for food and wood and in which there were kitchens and other rooms. But this hole in the wall behind bars stands out in a strange way. Cédric nods briefly in the direction of the hole. "That's where they dug for the Templar treasure." He is unable to suppress a mocking grin. The hole was driven horizontally into the wall. The entrance to the gallery leads to the defense tower. No doubt these are traces of digging left behind by Roger Lhomoy. Debris has filled in the hole.

As I look around, I wonder whether the Templar treasure was hidden here. If Roger Lhomoy really did discover a chapel and it exists, what happened to the Templar treasure? What might the military have discovered?

"Did the military find a treasure?" I ask Cédric.

The beam of the flashlight flits eerily through the underground vaults. Cédric grins ambiguously. We go up the stairs to the daylight. "Look somewhere else. It was never here because a chapel never existed."

This gallery which Roger Lhomoy dug under the donjon (keep) of Gisors Castle was covered over and secured with bars. © Tobias D. Wabbel.

So why did the military block off the area for several months?

"Because of all the treasure hunters," says Cédric. "They made the site unsafe. It wasn't until they came along that Gisors Castle gained the reputation of being the Templar treasure castle. Every hobby treasure hunter suddenly started digging here."

If this is to be believed, the story of a Templar treasure in Gisors is more of a fairytale than actual history.

We are in the dungeon of the defense tower when Cédric suddenly points out some graffiti scratched into the stone which is obviously from the Templars who were imprisoned here in 1314 and were interrogated during their trial.

I recognise a virgin and a dragon.

Cédric says: "*This* is the true treasure of Gisors. Even today, nobody knows what it means."

Virgin and dragon? Why should Jacques de Molay have scratched these symbols into the wall while awaiting certain death by being burned at the stake? Is this a clue to the location and nature of the Templar treasure? I will encounter Jacques de Molay's symbols of the virgin and the dragon again under dramatic circumstances.

The Secret of Rosslyn Chapel

B ut Gisors is not the only place that people believe to be the hiding place of the Templar treasure. In his book *The Head of God*,
the British anthropologist and BBC documentary filmmaker Keith
Laidler claims Rosslyn Chapel in Scotland is the hiding place of a
more than 2000-year-old relic that the Templars found in Jerusalem
beneath the Temple Mount and brought to Scotland prior to the
wave of arrest of October 13, 1307. This relic matches the description of *Baphomet*, whom the Knights Templar supposedly worshiped
according to the trial records and whose existence they had admitted
to as they were subjected to multiple rounds of torture.

But – one thing at a time. The Collegiate Chapel of St. Matthew,
the proper name for Rosslyn Chapel, is about 12 miles south-east
of the Scottish capital of Edinburgh. Whoever takes bus number
15 in the direction of Penicuik from the St. Andrews Square stop
in Edinburgh will enjoy an approximately 20-minute drive through
the lovely landscape of Midlothian and subsequently arrive at the
little village of Roslin. The village only has two restaurants, two
telephone boxes and a corner shop, as well as the Roslin Institute
in which the famous sheep Dolly was cloned. But in spite of the international fame of the village of Roslin due to Dan Brown's novel
The Da Vinci Code and the subsequent film adaptation with Tom
Hanks, the village is characterized more by the hectic bustle of a tax
office during the lunch break. But terror lurks around the corner:

As I turn off the main street and then follow the sign through
an alley in the direction of Rosslyn Chapel, I pass car parks with
bus loads of tourists. I am rather shocked by the admission prices
at the cash desk. A few years ago, they were just £5 and now, since
The Da Vinci Code, they have been raised to £7. The Sinclair family
on whose property the Chapel is located tells me how the restau-
rant prices have also risen and how the Chapel recently received £7
million in funding from the *National Trust for Scotland*. I beat the
tourists to it, buy my ticket and squeeze through the souvenir shop
to get to the Chapel.

The small, late Gothic-style church that is 30 meters in length
lies in the valley of the River Esk in the Pentland Hills and was

Rosslyn Chapel is a unique architectural gem. It was planned circa 1440 by William St. Clair and is located in the Pentland Hills on the bank of the River Esk, about 20 kilometers south-east of Edinburgh in the Lothian region. © Tobias D. Wabbel

planned in 1440 by William St. Clair, First Earl of Caithness and Third Earl of Orkney.[4] The construction process began in 1456. His grandfather William St. Clair fought at the side of Robert the Bruce against the English in the Battle of Bannockburn. The St. Clair family is originally from Normandy – over time, the name St. Clair turned into Sinclair. From 1028 to 1514, all St. Clair barons were alternately named either William or Henry.[5]

William St. Clair was originally planning a much bigger church. He died in 1484, two years before the Chapel was completed. What is interesting is that William St. Clair himself oversaw the stone masonry and first designed most of it so that nothing was left up to chance. As a result, the visitor to the inside of the Chapel is overwhelmed by the wealth of intricate stone masonry: engrailed crosses; the death mask of the Scottish King

4   Slezer, J., Theatrum Scotiae, 1693, quoted in: Laidler, Keith, Das Haupt Gottes, Munich: Scherz Verlag, 1999, p. 347.
5   Hay, Richard Augustin, Genealogy of Rosslyn, Edinburgh: Thomas G. Stevenson, 1835, p. 2ff.

Robert the Bruce; an angel holding the heart of Robert the Bruce; a knight on horseback; bagpipe-playing angels; the Lamb of God; an angel holding the Holy Chalice; pentagrams; Moses; Lucifer; a carving showing William St. Clair himself, as well as many heathen symbols such as the Green Man from Celtic legend. The Chapel is full of mysterious iconography references which some enthusiasts interpret as clues to the Templar past of the St. Clair family. Suspicions that Rosslyn Chapel also contains Freemason symbols are also very popular. Supposedly some stones have enigmatic Masonic symbols carved into them and even the depiction of a Freemason rite of initiation.

Keith Laidler and other authors claim that the Chapel has the same dimensions as the Temple of Solomon in Jerusalem.[6] In any case, the Chapel allegedly has many Jewish attributes. For instance, you can supposedly find the hexagram here, which is the Seal of King Solomon, who ordered the construction of the first Jerusalem temple. A reference to this Temple of Solomon in Jerusalem is also made by the imaginative stone masonry of the Master Pillar, as well as the Apprentice Pillar, in the eastern part of Rosslyn Chapel.

Legend has it that a master sculptor completed the left pillar that is today known as the Master Pillar. William St. Clair instructed the Master to carve the right pillar according to his plans, but the Master admitted to his client that his skills weren't good enough. And so he travelled to Europe to improve his artistic sculpting abilities. In the absence of his Master, the apprentice asked William St. Clair if he could try out his skills. When the Master returned months later, he was overcome by the beauty of the Apprentice Pillar and, out of envy, killed the apprentice by hitting him in the head with a mallet. It is very probable that the two bronze pillars Boaz and Jachin in the Temple of Solomon in Jerusalem served as the prototypes for the Master and Apprentice Pillars. The legend of the Master murdering his apprentice also resembles the story of the Tyrian Grand Architect Hiram-Abiff who was asked by King Solomon to build the Temple. In the Book of Chronicles the Bible describes the legend of Hiram Abiff who was struck dead by

---

6   Laidler, Keith, *Das Haupt Gottes*, Munich: Scherz Verlag, 1999, p. 349ff.

three workmen because he was unwilling to divulge the secret of the Temple construction.[7]

Keith Laidler suspects that the head of God, the mummified head of Jesus Christ, is hidden under this Apprentice Pillar. He believes that Hugues de Payns' Templars found this under the Temple Mount during their stay in Jerusalem and worshiped it as *Baphomet*. Laidler derives his theory from the possibility that mummified heads have been worshiped as holy relics since the time of Moses and the Exodus from Egypt. Thus, Laidler draws a hypothetical dynastic line from the first monotheist pharaoh of Egypt, Akhenaten, and the Hebrew patriarchs Moses, Abraham, Isaac, Jacob, Joseph, to King David, right through to Jesus, the Merovingians and a mysterious secret society known as the Prieuré de Sion (Priory of Sion), which is supposedly an offshoot of the Templar Order, still exists today and claims to count the direct descendants of Christ among its members. This ominous Prieuré de Sion was also propagated by the authors Henry Lincoln, Michael Baigent and Richard Leigh in their book *Holy Blood, Holy Grail*. It was one of the basis for *The Da Vinci Code*. Dan Brown cleverly features the Prieuré de Sion in his novel to explain the secret of the Holy Grail – that Jesus Christ had children with Mary Magdalene and this blood line of *Sang Real* (holy blood) is still alive today. Laidler stubbornly holds fast to the concept of the Prieuré de Sion.

Laidler believes that before the wave of arrests of October 13, 1307, a few Templars escaped on board 18 ships from the port of La Rochelle with the treasure to Scotland, where thanks to the gift of King David I they acquired some lands and thus a refuge in Ballantrodoch. In 1314, the Scottish King Robert the Bruce was excommunicated by Pope Clement V because the former had his archrival for the royal throne, John Comyn, murdered in the Grey Friars Church of Dumfries by his companion Roger de Kirkpatrick.[8] The murder happened on sacred church ground and thus Robert the Bruce was actually anathematized by Pope Clement V, which is the same as an excommunication. Laidler argues that Robert the Bruce was not subject to Pope Clement V's dictate to arrest all Templars

---

7   1 Kings 7
8   Barbour, John, The Bruce, Edinburgh: Canongate Books, 1997, p. 78f.

Despite the fame that Rosslyn Chapel acquired by Dan Brown's novel *The Da Vinci Code*, this strange religious building has nothing to do with the Templars. Nevertheless, the ornaments are impressive and it pays homage to the best European stonemasons of the 15th century. © Tobias D. Wabbel

and hand them over to the Inquisition. In contrast, Bruce welcomed the escaped Templars with open arms and let them hide the treasure somewhere in Scotland. Laidler claims that the Templars thanked him by subsequently helping the inferior Scottish troops of Robert the Bruce to achieve a victory in the Battle of Bannockburn on June 13 and 14, 1314, against the English army of King Edward II – as we know, the consequence was two hundred years of independence from England's royal house.

As the Bruce clan was friends with the St. Clair family, Laidler speculates that Robert the Bruce gave them the treasure in the form of the mummified head of Jesus. If Laidler's suspicion is correct, the head of God would have been hidden under the famous Apprentice Pillar some time between the years of 1440 and 1482, where it is today waiting to be discovered.

So what should we make of Keith Laidler's theory? Without a doubt, Hugues de Payns and his men would not have looked for the skull of Christ under the Temple Mount which was once the location of the Temple of Solomon. Looking for the mortal remains of Jesus under the Temple Mount would have made about as much sense as traveling to Paris to see the Cologne Cathedral. If they were looking for possible relics or even the mummified head of Jesus Christ, it would have made more sense to look under the Church of the Holy Sepulchre, which is supposed to have been built on top of Christ's tomb. But there is no chronicle that talks of any excavation activities by the Templars inside the Church of the Holy Sepulchre. And Hugues de Payns and his companions wouldn't have known whether it was the skull of Jesus Christ even if they had found a strange mummified skull. As a result, traders in relics, who were traveling to Jerusalem in 1099, could have tried to deceive them into buying any shrunken head that was available at the time. But Hugues de Payns never mentions anything about a mummified head.

As we have seen in Bernard of Clairvaux's treatise *De laude novae militiae*, the Holy Sepulchre is at the bottom of his list of priorities after the Temple of Solomon. The discovery of the mortal remains of Jesus Christ would have been a sensation and at first glance it appears that after the First Crusade the Templars were interested in any kind of relic that would have increased their power. The trade with holy relics was flourishing. But exhibiting a relic such as the head of Jesus Christ would have been regarded as the most extreme blasphemy – after all, the Christians believe that a Crucifixion Jesus rose from the dead and ascended to heaven. Such a relic would have completely undermined the Biblical Salvation History and called into question the Vatican's right to exist. One result, at that time, was the Church condemned the worshiping of relics, mainly for fear of fake heads, fingers, foreskins, hair and other body parts.[9] So findings of Christ's physical body would have had catastrophic consequences. If the Templars had been interested in earning money from relics by having pilgrims from Europe pay them to see this head, this news would have spread within a very short time. But nothing of the kind has been recorded.

It would have been a very outlandish claim to say that the Templar Order secretly worshiped a mummified head as the Inquisition commissioned the King's chancellor *before the arrest* of October 13, 1307, to apply the most brutal torture methods to force the arrested Templars to confess to worshiping an idol. So the idea that the Templars owned a bearded head is from the Inquisition and does not have any foundation of truth within the Order itself. It was merely an excuse to press charges against the Templars. The statements of the tortured Templars contained extremely varying descriptions of *Baphomet* – proof that the Templar Order was not worshiping a head. The only thing we can definitely tell from the interrogation records is that this idol was called *Baphomet* or *Bahumet*. But we still don't know what it was. Keith Laidler is happy to overlook these facts.

It is proven that King David I of Scotland bequeathed some lands to Hugues de Payns and the newly founded Templar Order in 1128 in order to support the continuation of the order of knights. These were located at the site of the present-day village of Temple, which is 10 miles from Roslin. But there are no historical recordings that might prove that a fleet of Templar ships landed on

9   Shalem, Avinoam, Reliquien der Kreuzfahrerzeit – Verehrung, Raub und Handel, in: Die Kreuzzüge, kein Krieg ist heilig, Mainz: Verlag Philipp von Zabern, 2003, p. 216.

the Scottish west coast of Argyll in 1307. Clues only exist in the form of gravestones around the community of Kilmartin, between Oban and Lochgilphead, which show knights with Norman nasal helmets and long swords. Judging by the iconography, these refer to Norman knights and not Templars.

In the history of Scottish King Robert the Bruce, which was composed in verse form in 1355 (just a few decades after Robert the Bruce's death) by John Barbour, an ecclesiastic of Dunkeld Cathedral, there is not a single suggestion that knights in white surcoats with red crosses pattées rushed to the aid of the Scottish troops in the Battle of Bannockburn against the English.[10] Alone the sight of the charging Templars would likely have frozen the English to the spot in terror and led them to flee in panic. It is very improbable that the contemporary chronicles would have failed to mention such an important event as the involvement of the Templars. But even if it sounds strange that the Scottish troops, which were inferior in number, dealt a crushing defeat to the seemingly unconquerable army of King Edward II, there is a lack of any proof that Robert the Bruce was even in contact with the members of the Templar Order.

The much cited connection of the Templars to Rosslyn does not hold up first and foremost because the St. Clair family themselves commissioned a genealogy to be drawn up that does not remotely mention a connection to the Templars.[11] But is it possible that ancestors of William St. Clair cooperated with the Templars?

As I enter the Chapel through the north portal and inspect the building's stone iconography for unambiguous traces of the Templar Order, the silence is constantly interrupted by the loud chatter of American tourists who have obviously forgotten that they are on holy ground. Several times I hear the name Dan Brown. A tour guide with a Boston accent explains the story of the Apprentice Pillar to the tourists.

I approach the pillar from the south front as the guide, an attractive lady in her mid-forties with dark curls, explains: "There

---

10   Barbour, John, the Bruce, Edinburgh: Canongate Books, 1997, p. 440ff.
11   Hay, Richard Augustin, Genealogy of Rosslyn, Edinburgh: Thomas G. Stevenson, 1835f.

British anthropologist Keith Laidler claims that the "head of God," the mummified skull of Jesus Christ, was hidden under the Apprentice Pillar of Rosslyn Chapel after the Templars fled to Scotland following the arrests of October 13, 1307. However, there is no proof whatsoever to suggest that the Templars fled to Scotland. Moreover, there is no proof to suggest a connection between the St. Clair family and the Templars. © Tobias D. Wabbel

are cavities under this Chapel that are still unexplored because the National Trust for Scotland does not permit excavations or ground radar measurements to be carried out here. The cliff on which the Chapel stands is perforated by passageways, just like the Temple Mount of Jerusalem. People suspect that the Templar treasure is hidden down there." She whispers in a purposely conspiratorial tone something about the "Holy Grail" and the tourists respond by collectively nodding their heads, accompanied by astonished murmurs. "Incredible!" says an older man with a Boston Red Sox baseball cap in realization.

These ominous cavities are nothing but crypts that hold the remains of the St. Clair family that have been blocked off for many years. Supposedly there are scan displays of the foundation and the earth beneath the Chapel, but to date the St. Clair family has not agreed to publish these. Recently, thermal measurements showed that there are no cavities *in* the Chapel.

On a capital on the north-east façade, I discover a symbol that remotely resembles a cross with splayed ends. If I really use my imagination, I can make out the shape of a Templar cross pattée. In another place, I make out the Lamb of God with a flag, a symbol of the warrior monks, but also of Jesus Christ and Jesus' victory over death by his Resurrection. I can't find the Seal of Solomon or the Star of David anywhere.

As I turn around, I remotely catch sight of something above a window that remotely resembles corn. In another place, I discover the stone depiction of a plant that is similar to the Mexican aloe plant, but could also be some kind of imaginary plant. In view of the fact that America wasn't officially discovered until 1492, the existence of pre-Columbian depictions of Central American plants would be a sensation in Scotland. Some authors suspect that William St. Clair, together with members of the seafaring Clan Gunn, could have reached the East Coast of the USA and Massachusetts via Iceland and Newfoundland before Columbus. In the coastal town of Westford, Massachusetts, a cliff with an unclear carving of a Scottish knight with a shield and sword is supposedly proof of this. In their book *Die Ewigkeits-Maschine* (The Eternity Machine), authors Peter and Johannes Fiebag posit that the Templar treasure was a machine to produce Biblical manna that the Hebrews ate when they were wandering through the Sinai Desert for 40 years. They believe the machine to be proof of the existence of extraterrestrial intelligences who came into contact with humans millennia ago. They go on to explain that the God that Moses met on Mount Sinai was merely an extraterrestrial. They believe that a manna machine is what Hugues de Payns and his followers were searching for and found beneath the Temple Mount.

Before the destruction of the Templars by Philip the Fair on October 13, 1307, this Biblical popcorn machine was supposedly brought on board a ship to Scotland. William St. Clair and Clan Gunn then brought the machine to America where it today stubbornly refuses to be retrieved at the bottom of the Oak Island *Money Pit*, off the coast of Nova Scotia, Canada. But this theory isn't plausible either because the *Westford Knight*, according to many, is a schoolboy prank from the 19th century.

Now we know that a supposed connection between the Templars and the St. Clair family cannot be proven. Furthermore, the ominous Prieuré de Sion never existed, but is merely a product of the imagination of the antisemitic and criminal Frenchman Pierre Plantard, who called himself St. Clair, and through forged documents created a fictitious family tree from King David, Jesus Christ, the Merovingians through to himself. Plantard fabricated one of the greatest historical frauds of the 20th century and Keith Laidler, Dan Brown and the sensationalist authors Lincoln, Baigent and Leigh fell for it. So our search for traces of the Templars in Scotland is only limited to ambiguous stone carvings in Rosslyn Chapel. And that is precious little.[12]

When the American tourists move on to look at the death mask of Robert the Bruce, I can now freely examine the Apprentice Pillar. It is decorated with a spiral-shaped plant. At its base is the Nordic snake Nidhöggr. These are obviously spirals of leaves

---

12   The authors Peter and Johannes Fiebag also claimed that Hugues de Payns was married to Catherine St. Clair. But unfortunately this ominous Catherine St. Clair is only mentioned in the forged documents of Pierre Plantard's fictitious Prieuré de Sion. As we have already seen, Hugues de Payns was married to a relative of the Montbard family.

around the World Tree Yggdrasil. The Tree of Life is a symbol for Jesus Christ and the Resurrection – art historians are still uncertain whether the Nordic reference to Jesus here in Rosslyn Chapel is applicable. As I take a closer look at the Pillar, I see several notches that lead me to believe that the Pillar has been opened and a part replaced. Whatever lies behind it is definitely not the mummified head of Jesus Christ, but solid stone.

A Spanish group of tourists now enters the Chapel. I decide to leave. After five hours of intense study and several hundred photographs from every angle of the Chapel and the crypt, as I'm leaving I get one last look at the bearded, stocky figure of William St. Clair, who high above the west façade on a chapter hides from the view of inattentive tourists. And the gravestone of Sir William from the year 1482, on the right next to the exit, pronounces with a modern caption: Knight Templar. I sign the guestbook with a comment: "Wonderful building. But no Templar treasure."

Rosslyn is entrenched in many fantastic myths. But the Templar treasure has nothing in common with the chapel of the St. Clairs.

The Mystery of Lirey

But let's return to France and Troyes in the Champagne region. When you turn on to the ring road and then take the Route nationale N77 to the south-west in the direction of Auxerre you can stop off in the small village of Lirey via the D88 country road. It was here in Lirey that French knight Geoffroy de Charny was ordered by King John II the Good of France to erect a collegiate church to house a relic which – if it were real – would be one of the most amazing Biblical testimonials of all.

The inside of St. Mary's Church is shrouded in twilight. Outside, storm clouds are blacking out the sun. The scent of incense from the last service hangs like a ghost in the air. An older, fragile looking lady is sitting on one of the rear benches, engrossed in prayer. As I reach the altar, I notice dark strips of fabric that are hanging on the walls to the left and right. Curious, I examine the fabric. As I take a closer look, I give a start. I rub my eyes and look again. It's a kind of negative of the naked body of a man. I can clearly recognize a bearded face. And I can make out wounds on his forehead. These strips of fabric are obviously reproductions of the famous Shroud of Jesus Christ which is today kept in Turin Cathedral. The history and the condition of the Shroud are as adventurous as the founding of the Templar Order:

On May 28, 1356, St. Marie's Church was consecrated, but on September 19, 1356, just a few months after the Shroud is exhibited in the church in Lirey, Geoffroy de Charny died in the Battle of Poitiers. He was the King's standard-bearer of the *Oriflamme*, which we will come back to later when we talk about Abbot Suger of St. Denis. One year after de Charny's death, the first exhibition of the Turin Shroud in Lirey is documented by pilgrim medals that can still be admired today.

In April 1389, Geoffroy de Charny's son, Geoffroy II, ignored the protests of the Bishop of Troyes, Peter D'Arcis, and decided to continue to exhibit the Shroud. Antipope Clement VII in Avignon granted his blessing and had the Bishop silenced. In 1418, the commune of Lirey was no longer able to deal with the storm of pilgrims who were willing to commit murder for a scrap of the relic. As a result, the Shroud was brought to the fortress, not far from Montbard in Burgundy. In 1449, Margaret de Charny exhibited the Shroud in Belgium and in 1453 in Germolles near Mâcon. Margaret was the last of the de Charny family. Consequently, she bequeathed the Shroud to Duke Louis I of Savoy. The great belief in the genuineness of the relic during this period is illustrated by the fact that Margaret de Charny received the Castle of Varambon and significant sums of money in return. On June 11, 1502, the Shroud changed hands to Duke Louis I of Savoy who kept it in the St. Hippolyte Chapel, on the modern-day border to Switzerland. The Savoy family had no problem publicly exposing the alleged Shroud on their travels to emphasize their privileged position among France's nobility.

In 1502, the Shroud was hidden in a silver casket under the altar of the castle chapel of Chambry. On December 4, 1532, there was a disastrous fire. The relic remained unscathed apart from a few scorch marks. Two years later, nuns from the Poor Clares convent patched up the damaged parts. When the Savoy family moved to Turin, the Shroud was brought to the Cathedral Duomo di San Giovanni on September 14, 1578. This was for organizational reasons because Duke Emmanuel Philibert did not intend to settle permanently in Turin. For more then a century, the Shroud was kept in the Cathedral and only in 1694 was it stored in a specially crafted shrine. In May 1898, the Shroud was photographed for the first time by Secondo Pia. While developing the negative, he noticed the mysterious image of Jesus Christ. This development triggered a huge debate. The belief in a photographic miracle spread. Not until May 3, 1931, did it become apparent that this was not a photographic anomaly when Giuseppe Enrie photographed the Shroud and had the same experience as Secondo Pia.

The Catholic Church was very uneasy about the whole thing. In June 1969, Cardinal Pellegrino summoned a commission of experts in Turin to examine the Shroud. Subsequently, in 1973 and 1978, the Shroud was examined for pollen and other residue by the Swiss forensics expert Max Frei-Sulzer who was able to reveal the origin of the Shroud. In addition, 15 single threads were taken out of the Shroud to check for consistency. The study showed that the Shroud was very probably from Jerusalem or the surrounding area. In 1978, further samples of the Shroud were taken with adhesive tape for natural science studies. In 1983, the Savoy family left the Shroud of Christ to the Vatican who has since exhibited it in the Cathedral behind bulletproof glass and only allows public access to it at certain times. On April 11, 1997, the Shroud escaped the flames of a cathedral fire thanks to the courageous actions of a Turin firefighter. For the Great Jubilee of 2000, it was publicly exhibited and then once again locked away from the world for an indeterminate period of time. In 2010, the Shroud was exhibited again from April 10 to May 23. The next exhibition of the Shroud will be for the Great Jubilee of 2025.

That's the story of the Turin Shroud so far. But does it really show an authentic imprint of the body of Jesus Christ that possibly even contains his genetic information in the form of hair or blood residue? Let's take a closer look at the Shroud: It is 4.36 meters long, 1.10 meters wide and made of linen with a woven herringbone pattern that was more likely to have been woven in the Middle Ages – in the Orient, at the time of Christ, it would have been proof of a very rich owner such as the nobleman Joseph of Arimathea who, according to the Gospels, donated his tomb for the burial of Jesus. According to the studied fibers, it is from Israel, so definitely from the Orient. It shows the image of a naked, bearded man with long hair on the front and back who is between 5'9" to 5'11" in height, between 30 and 35 years of age and, judging by his build, weighs 165 and 180 pounds.

Examinations of the image reveal strange details on the body and face of the depicted man. For instance, there are up to 500 marks of castigation on upper arms, thighs and abdomen. His wrists also show scars that could have been caused by nails. Astonishingly, these details differ greatly from the standard iconography of the Middle Ages. The wounds on the man's head are more suggestive of a *hood of thorns* than a crown of thorns. Hoods of thorns covered the entire top of the head and were more widespread in the Orient than crowns of thorns which were only made up of a garland and, on the other hand, frequently featured in medieval art.[13]

On April 21, 1988, in the presence of the Archbishop of Turin, Anastasio Ballestrero, his scientific advisor Gonella and a representative of the British Museum a 10 mm by 70 mm sample was taken of the Shroud and cut into three pieces. After the samples were taken away in containers, they were microscopically examined and then cleaned of soiling and residue such as soot particles and dirt. The samples were burned and the residue examined by mass spectrograph to ascertain their individual chemical components and age in three different laboratories of the Universities of Oxford, Zurich and Arizona. Oxford, Zurich and Arizona carbon-date the Shroud to between 1200 and 1304 A.D.[14]

Since that time, the Turin Shroud has been regarded as a fake from the Middle Ages and various methods have been proposed as to how such a Shroud could have been created with the alleged image of Jesus. For instance, fabric paintings and imprints with heat-

---

13   Herbst, Karl, Kriminalfall Golgatha. Der Vatikan, das Turiner Grabtuch und der wirkliche Jesus, Düsseldorf: Econ Verlag, 1992, p. 83.

14   Damon, P. E., Donahue, D. J., Gore, B. H., Hatheway, A. L., Jull, A. J. T. et al., Radiocarbon Dating of the Shroud of Turin, in: Nature 337, No. 6208, 16th February 1989, p. 611ff.

ed metal reliefs have been considered that could explain the flat, one-dimensional face of the alleged Jesus, but they fail to explain many other facts. The authors Lynn Picknett and Clive Prince suspected Leonardo da Vinci of constructing a camera obscura and a chemical that reacts with light to burn a self-portrait of himself on to the linen of the Shroud out of protest against the Catholic Church. Similar to the painter Albrecht Dürer, Leonardo is said to have depicted himself as Jesus Christ. But in view of the fact that measurements show the Shroud to have been produced in 1304, this rules out Leonardo da Vinci, who wasn't born until 1452.[15] Undoubtedly, Leonardo da Vinci could have gone to the effort of using a linen cloth from Palestine that was produced around the time of Christ. But how could Leonardo have known the age of a linen cloth from Palestine? The theory of Lynn Picknett and Clive Prince can be ruled out alone due to the fact that, just like Keith Laidler, they fell for the fraud of French con man and inventor of the fictitious Prieuré de Sion, Pierre Plantard, and stated in their book that Leonardo da Vinci was supposedly a master of this invented order.

To date, no plausible proof has been provided on how someone could have fabricated a forgery as clever as the Turin Shroud. The strange concurrences with the Crucifixion of Christ were reason enough to subject the Shroud to closer examination. In 2004, scientists from the University of Padua in Italy discovered a similar face on the back of the Shroud that was even more blurry than the face on the front of the Shroud.[16]

The material of the Shroud is not only marked by fire and the water used to extinguish it, but also by creases. Human blood was also detected on the linen cloth, which was visible under the imprint of the human body. It is doubtful whether this is the blood of Jesus Christ. If we assume that the dead body of Jesus Christ was taken down from the Cross after just one day and then placed on the shroud, the blood flow caused by the castigation of the Roman legionnaires and the subsequent piercing of the hands by the nails

---

15   Picknett, Lynn and Prince, Clive, Die Jesus-Fälschung, Leonardo da Vinci und das Turiner Grabtuch, Bergisch Gladbach: Lübbe-Verlag, 1994, p. 124ff.

16   Fanti, G. and Maggiolo, R., The Double Superficiality of the Frontal Image of the Turin Shroud, in: Journal of Optics A Pure and Applied Optics 6, 2004, p. 491ff.

and lance of the Roman soldier Longinus would have already dried out and could not have left behind any such traces on the cloth.

Further proof for the forgery of the Turin Shroud is the fact that the pollen analysis of Max Frei-Sulzer was insufficient because the strips of adhesive tape only contained very little pollen, but a single strip of tape that did not come into contact with the cloth contained a lot of pollen. It is also rather dubious that a few years later Frei-Sulzer dubbed the infamous Hitler Diaries as authentic. The Israeli botanist Dr. Avinoam Danin from the Hebrew University of Jerusalem sees the pollen studies as confirmation that the Shroud is from Palestine and is thus authentic.

In 2003, the chemists Raymond N. Rogers and Anna Arnoldi claimed in the publication *Melanoidins* that the Shroud was woven long before the year 1300 and could definitely be authentic. Rogers and Arnoldi pronounced their doubts about the accuracy of the measurements of the Shroud sample taken in 1988. The study proves that a patch was examined that had been used to repair the cloth from the damage caused by the burn marks. Based on this, the fabric was said to have originated in the 16th century when the Shroud was already owned by the Dukes of Savoy. So the original fabric of the Shroud had not even been the subject of the examinations in the laboratories of the Universities of Oxford, Zurich and Arizona back in 1988.[17]

And this is how it's been going on for decades. Skeptics disprove believers, believers disprove skeptics, although in the last few years there have been more skeptics than believers. But what does all this have to do with the Templars?

In 2009, the Vatican newspaper *L'Osservatore Romano* published an extract from a book by Barbara Frale, a historian and paleographer at the Vatican Secret Archives. In her book, Frale claims that the Shroud, in addition to Greek and Latin characters, also has Aramaic characters below the head of Jesus Christ. She bases her thesis on the studies of French scientist Thierry Castex who used an image processing technique to discover supposedly Aramaic characters.

17   Roger, Raymond N. and Ardoli, Anna, Melanoidins, The Shroud of Turin: An Amino-carbonyl Reaction (Maillard reaction) May Explain the Image Formation, Volume 4, Ames J. M. ed., Office for Official Publications of the European Communities, Luxembourg, 2003, p. 106ff.

Frale states that she presented the pictures to two experts in Hebraic Studies without telling them what they were. Independently of each other, both scientists stated that the inscriptions were Aramaic. Furthermore, Barbara Frale claims that the Templar Order worshiped an image of Jesus Christ on a cloth. The trial records mentioned that such an image on a linen cloth was supposedly worshiped during the initiation rites. Frale argues that the first proven owner Geoffroy de Charny was a grandson of the Templar Grand Master Geoffroy de Charney and that the Templars took possession of the cloth in Greece after it was originally found in 1204 during the plundering of Constantinople and before then was brought there from Jerusalem.[18]

The Shroud was not in the possession of Hugues de Payns, Count Hugues I of Champagne and their Templar brothers because – just like Keith Laidler's thesis on the mummified head of Jesus Christ – it doesn't make any sense to search for relics of Jesus Christ under the Temple Mount. Likely hiding places would have been the Church of the Holy Sepulchre, Nazareth, Bethlehem, Bethany or Qumran by the Dead Sea. But there are no Templar excavation activities documented there. Moreover, Barbara Frale's theory is entirely based on the fact that the Inquisition, as we have seen, was instructed before the arrest of the Templars to question the Templars about heretic idols while subjecting them to torture. In some cases, the Templars confessed what the Inquisition wanted to hear. Whatever the Templar treasure was, it wasn't the Turin Shroud which is highly probably a clever forgery, created by using a linen cloth from the Palestine region that dated back to circa 70 A.D.

Someone taps me on my right shoulder and I start from my reflections. The old lady I mentioned earlier is standing next to me. "Isn't it amazing?" she says and, with her shaking hand, points to the cloths next to the altar with the negative image of Jesus Christ.

I respond: "Do you believe the Turin Shroud is genuine?"

"No," answers the lady.

"So why do you find it amazing?"

She crosses herself. "It's amazing how many people are willing to believe in a forgery."

Then she shuffles on and I watch her in amazement.

18   L'Osservatore Romano, 5 Aprile 2009, Città del Vaticano.

The Search for the Holy Grail

I'm sitting in a brasserie in the old town of Troyes, drinking a glass of Kronenbourg, and I'm disappointed about my new findings. Neither the mummified skull of Jesus Christ nor the Turin Shroud are possible candidates for the Templar treasure. That much is certain. So was the treasure merely made up of gold coins and bonds that King Philip the Fair had his militia take out of the Paris *Temple* in the night of October 13, 1307? Is the treasure merely a phantom, a ghostly fata morgana without any grain of historical truth?

I take a look around. The brasserie on the square of St. Pierre's Cathedral is on the corner of Rue Chrétien de Troyes. The street was named after the famous son of this town, the author of epic courtly poetic novels such as *Erec and Enide; Yvain, the Knight of the Lion; Cligès; Guillaume d'Angleterre* or *Lancelot, the Knight of the Cart*. But above all Chrétien de Troyes was famous for his first novel about the search of the knight *Perceval* for the Holy Grail in his unfinished work *Le Conte del Graal* or *Perceval, the Story of the Grail*. Could Hugues de Payns' Templars have found the Holy Grail in Jerusalem in the form of the cup that Jesus used at the Last Supper that the nobleman Joseph of Arimathea also used to catch Christ's blood at his Crucifixion? What is the Holy Grail? And who was Chrétien de Troyes?

The legend of the chalice as a Christian symbol that grants immortality only goes back to the Anglo-Norman poet Robert de Boron who died in 1212 – not a single word is mentioned about the "Grail" in the Bible. However, as we shall soon see, the Holy Grail is not a chalice at all. The search brings to light the first two medieval contemporary documents that prove that the Templars were in possession of a holy relic. Let's first take a look at the story of Chrétien de Troyes.

Chrétien de Troyes' *Perceval*

Not much is known about this poet. Chrétien was born 1140 in Troyes at a time when Theobald II, the nephew of the Templar founder Hugues I of Champagne, was reigning over the region. It is quite probable that Chrétien had a very thorough education. In any case, the literary references to Latin classics in his work would lead us to believe this.[19] The philologist Philipp A. Becker suspects that because of his name "de Troyes" Chrétien was a descendant of medium-ranking nobility. Chrétien de Troyes is believed to have been a son of Milo II, Lord of Bray and Montlhéry, and on his mother's side a great-grandson of William I the Conquerer.

But it is much more probable that Chrétien de Troyes was a clergyman of the Abbey of Saint-Loup of Troyes[20] which Bernard of Clairvaux reformed in 1134 by advising the abbot to henceforth embrace the strict Rule of Saint Augustine. A *Christianus*, monk of the Abbey of Saint-Loup, is mentioned in a document from the episcopal archive from the year 1173.[21] Chrétien de Troyes felt a very close affiliation with Judaism and the Jewish religion obviously influenced his work – maybe he even converted from a Christian cleric to Judaism[22] because the Abbey of Saint-Loup was right around the corner from the synagogue and the house of its greatest Talmud scholar at that time, Rabbi Rashi.

As a clergyman of the Abbey of Saint-Loup, it is very probable that in his younger years Chrétien came into contact with the teachings of Bernard of Clairvaux. Maybe Bernard even met Chrétien. What is certain is that the poet from Troyes served at the court of Countess Marie of Champagne, the daughter of King Louis VII of France and Eleanor of Aquitaine, and composed the poetic novel *Lancelot, the Knight of the Cart* for her. The dedication of his book to Marie of Champagne is proof of this fact. Marie of Champagne was a member of the Capetian dynasty. She was the half-sister of the English King Richard the Lionheart and English King John Lackland, but also through her marriage to Henry I of Champagne she was the daughter-in-law of Count Theobald II, who attended the Council of Troyes in 1129 and witnessed the founding of the Templar Order. It is to be assumed that, due to her father-in-law, Marie was initiated into Templarism and passed on this knowledge to Chrétien de Troyes.

19   Hofer, Stefan, Chrétien de Troyes, Leben und Werk, Graz-Cologne: Verlag Hermann Böhlau, 1954, p. 41.
20   Benton, John F., The Court of Champagne as a Literary Center, in: Speculum 36/4 (October 1961:551-591), p. 13.
21   Vigneras, L. A., Chrétien de Troyes Rediscovered, in: Modern Philology, 32, 1935, p. 341ff.
22   Holmes, U. T., A New Interpretation of Chrétien's Conte del Graal, Studies in Philology, XLIV, North Carolina, 1947, p. 475.

When Chrétien was working at Marie's court and she was his pa-
troness so that he would compose knightly epics for her, he not only
became familiar with the Abbot Bernard of Clairvaux and the Cistercian Clairvaux Abbey, but also with the Templar Order and the Jews
of that region. Circa 1180, Chrétien de Troyes began his great epic
Le Conte del Graal. Many place names indicate that the novel is set in
Brittany, in north-east France, in the regions of Champagne, Burgundy and Picardy. When Chrétien died in 1190, he had completed only
9000 lines of his unfinished work. In his prologue, Chrétien de Troyes dedicated his work to Count Philip of Flanders, the second son of
Count Thierry of Flanders (known in Flanders as Diederik van den
Elzas) and Sibylla of Anjou, the daughter of Count Fulk V of Anjou.
To recap: Fulk V was the count who in 1120 supported the founding
Templars Hugues de Payns and Count Hugues I of Champagne before becoming King of Jerusalem.[23]

Chrétien de Troyes had direct access to the stories about the
Knights Templar. The search of Hugues de Payns and his followers beneath the Temple Mount of Jerusalem must have been a very
important source of inspiration for Chrétien. So it's no wonder that
he composed a work that deals with the search of a knight for the
holiest of all treasures.

The true background of the story of the knight Perceval who is in
search of the Holy Grail was confided to Chrétien de Troyes by Philip
of Flanders in the form of a book. Perhaps the recordings of a Knight
Templar from Troyes. In his prologue to Perceval, Chrétien writes:

> Yes, there cannot be any doubt. Chrétien shall gain, since he has
> striven at the command the count has given and made endeavors
> manifold to rhyme the best tale ever told in any royal court: this tale
> is called the *Story of the Grail*. The count has given him the book;
> now judge what Chrétien undertook.[24]

At this time, the Counts of Flanders and Champagne and their
houses were friends. Philip of Flanders even asked for the hand
of Marie of Champagne – in vain. It appeared that Marie did not

23   Chrétien de Troyes, Perceval oder die Geschichte vom Gral, Stuttgart: Ogham
Verlag, 1991, p. 8.
24   Ibid., p. 8.

approve of Philip's daring lifestyle. Philip was born in 1143, became Count of Flanders at the age of 25 and went on a pilgrimage to the Holy Land in 1177. Circa 1180, he became a regent of France and the guardian of French King Philip II Augustus. Eight years later, Philip of Flanders went on a crusade to the Holy Land. And that was where all trace of him disappears.

When Chrétien left the court of Marie of Champagne to go into the service of Philip of Flanders, he didn't break off contact with her.[25] He also incorporated his personal impressions at court in the story.

So in his work *Perceval* Chrétien described the societal and political circumstances during the era of soulful troubadours, love-crazed minnesingers and daring knights who thrust themselves into life-threatening adventures. Just like a medieval report, he described the life of the worldly knight whom Bernard of Clairvaux condemned in his treatise to the Templars, *De laude novae militiae*, to ultimately turn the Arthurian knight Perceval into a religious warrior of God who recognizes God in the form of the Holy Grail.

The novel is split into the adventures of the knight Gawain and the knight Perceval. Gawain is also in search of the Grail, but right from the outset he is gifted with knightly attributes which make his search much less problematic than that of Perceval. Thus, the poet Chrétien de Troyes mixed the adventures of the clueless fool who becomes a God-fearing knight and discovers the secret of the Grail with the Arthurian legend that was first recorded by Geoffrey of Monmouth (1100-1154) around 1135 in his work *Historia Regum Britanniae*. Historians theorize that the real Arthur was a legendary king who fought against Britain's Angle and Saxon invaders circa 500 A.D. The character of King Arthur in the courtly poetic novels shows that at the time of Chrétien he was regarded as the perfect knight. Nevertheless, it is obvious from the French and Breton place names that Chrétien's novel *Perceval* is not set in Britain, but in France. Chrétien's language is Old French, the places are set in Brittany, the Massif Central, even Champagne and Burgundy.

In addition to the Arthurian legend, the novel describes the transformation of the young fool Perceval who leaves the loving

---

25   Sandkühler, Konrad, Afterword to Chrétien des Troyes' *Perceval oder die Geschichte vom Gral*, Stuttgart: Ogham Verlag, 1991, p. 224.

care of his mother when he meets five knights in a forest who answer his childlike questions by revealing that they are King Arthur's Knights of the Round Table. Henceforth, Perceval feels a strong urge to also become a Knight of the Round Table. As his mother has already lost Perceval's brothers in knightly combats and her husband died from grief for the death of his sons, she is overcome with sadness when her last son decides to go out into the world to experience *adventure* in the form of knightly combats.

Perceval wants to follow the five knights. His mother is horrified about his plan, but feels forced to sew her boy a coat and give him a lance to defend himself to prevent the worst from befalling him. Armed with her social counsel about life in the knightly world and how to behave in the presence of noblewomen, Perceval sets off – clueless and naive. After meeting a sleeping woman in a tent, kissing her against her will and then taking her wedding ring, thus misinterpreting the lessons of his mother, he meets a charcoal-burner who shows him the way to King Arthur's castle. When he arrives there, a knight in red armor comes galloping towards him. Perceval's desire to own such an armor overcomes him and he seeks to ask King Arthur whether he may be granted his request.

Perceval kills the Red Knight with his lance and, with the help of the squire Yonet, takes off his armor. Then he rides away and, after some time, reaches the castle of the knight Gornemant of Gohort. Here Perceval is given the necessary teaching on how to conduct himself as a knight: above all, Perceval shouldn't ask too many questions and constantly talk about his mother. But that's not so easy for him because Perceval is yearning for his mother.

After a couple of knightly battles, he arrives in a thick forest by a river that he cannot cross. Suddenly, he sees a boat with two men. He recognizes one of them as a fisherman. Perceval asks them where he can cross the river and the fisherman replies that there is no ferry or bridge or ford for 20 leagues upstream or downstream. As he cannot travel on, Perceval asks for shelter and the fisherman invites him to his home. He follows the description of the fisherman, rides up a mountain and, as he is getting angry with the fisherman for having misled him, he spies a tower down in a nearby valley. Chrétien de Troyes writes: "From here to Beirut you would not have found one more handsome or more finely placed; it was square and built of grey rock, flanked by two smaller towers. The hall stood before the tower, and lodges before the hall."[26]

Perceval praises the fisherman, no longer calling him dishonest or untruthful. He rides towards the castle and finds a lowered drawbridge. Four boys come to meet him, two of them disarm him, one leads his horse away and the fourth dresses him in a mantle of scarlet cloth. Then Perceval is led to the lodges and, as Chrétien de Troyes described: "... a man could have searched as far as Limoges without finding any as handsome." Two servants led him to a square hall which was "as long as it was wide."[27]

There he finds a man in bed, leaning on his elbow, who greets the newcomer. Surrounded by four columns, in a chimney there is a huge fire of blazing logs. The dimensions of the room become clear when Chrétien de Troyes described that "four hundred men could easily have sat around that fire and each would have had an excellent place." The lord regrets that he cannot get up because he is sick. A boy appears and presents to the lord a valuable sword made of incredibly light steel, which he subsequently gives to Perceval as a gift.

After Perceval and the lord talk to each other, a boy appears with a shiny iron lance with a drop of blood issuing from the tip of the lance's head and running right down to the boy's hand. Perceval doesn't dare ask where the blood is from because he fears that this question could be considered offensive. Then two boys appear with golden candlesticks that can hold at least 10 candles. The boys are followed by a beautiful maiden who is holding *a grail* between her hands. An ethereally bright light is streaming from it. Chrétien de Troyes wrote that "the grail ... was made of fine, pure gold; and in it were set precious stones of many kinds, the richest and most precious in the earth or the sea: those in the grail surpassed all other jewels, without a doubt." And the grail brings exquisite dishes and wines on the table and Perceval wonders where the dishes come from. But he decides to wait until

26   Chrétien de Troyes, Perceval oder die Geschichte vom Gral, Stuttgart: Ogham Verlag, 1991, p. 65.
27   Ibid., p. 65.

daybreak before asking his question. Then the lord excuses himself and is carried away to his bed chamber.

The next morning, Perceval finds the castle surprisingly empty. The lord and his servants have disappeared. But his horse is saddled up and the sword and lance are leaning against a wall. Perceval succeeds in escaping from the castle with his horse. He follows tracks leading into a forest. There he encounters a maiden (Old French: "pucele") who asks him where he came from. When Perceval tells her the story of the sick lord and the grail, she is furious that he didn't ask about the secret of the grail because only this question could have cured the lord. When she asks him for his name, he answers: "Perceval the Welshman." Because he didn't ask the question, Perceval will now have to suffer the death of his mother.

After further fights, Perceval meets King Arthur's knights, led by Gawain, who reveals himself to be the Red Knight. An ugly woman curses him because he didn't ask the question about the grail. Perceval decides to find out the secret of the Grail. After five years of *adventures* and forgetting God, because the death of his mother and the brutality of the knightly combats have made Perceval lose his faith in God, Perceval meets unknown knights on Good Friday. They instruct him to lay down his arms on the day of Christ's Crucifixion. As atonement he should meet with a hermit in a forest and confess his actions. "In a little chapel he found the hermit," writes Chrétien de Troyes, "and a priest and a clerk – this is the truth – who were beginning the highest and sweetest service that can be held in a holy church."

Perceval confesses his godlessness to the hermit. The hermit proves to be Perceval's uncle. He tells him that Perceval's mother had died of grief because he left her and he, the hermit, the ailing lord and his mother are siblings. The fisherman on the river who showed Perceval the way was the son of the sick king and lord. "And don't imagine that he's given pike or lamprey or salmon; he's served with a single host which is brought to him in that grail. It comforts and sustains his life – the grail is such a holy thing. And he, who is so spiritual that he needs no more in his life than the host that comes in the grail."[28]

---

28   Ibid., p. 133f.

As penance for his sins, his uncle instructs him to go in and pray whenever he's in a place where there's a minster, a chapel or a parish church. "Love God, believe in God, worship God."

Chrétien de Troyes *Perceval* is already very mysterious, but it gets even stranger when his uncle whispers a prayer in his ear that apparently nobody else is meant to hear. Chrétien wrote: "Many of the names of Our Lord appeared in this prayer, including the greatest ones, which the tongue of man should never utter in fear of death. And when he had taught him the prayer he forbade him ever to utter those names except in times of great peril." Perceval responded that he would obide by his command. This is where Chrétien de Troyes' tale of Perceval's search for the Holy Grail ends.

The religious symbolism suggests that the lance and Grail form an inseparable unity. Furthermore, we now know that the Grail is an artifact that provided plentiful food and drink and is made of the purest gold. However, its form is still uncertain. But only he who finds the secret of the Grail can see God. Chrétien was not referring to Jesus Christ here, but to God. Perceval's uncle commands him to learn a prayer that names the many names of God and commands him to never reveal this prayer to anyone except on pain of death. In Christianity there is only one name for God: God or Lord. But in Judaism, on the other hand, there are many: Yahweh, Zebaoth, Adonaj, Elohim, HaShem, Elah, etc. Perceval's uncle commands him to go to church, but his true belief is in the secret prayer that contains the many names of God.

Officially, Perceval is supposed to act like a Christian, but unofficially believe like a Jew: namely in God or Yahweh. This confirms Chrétien's relationship to Judaism in his home town of Troyes, which was populated by a small Jewish community in which a few Christians converted to Judaism. Maybe even Chrétien himself. The references in his work to only pray to God lead us to believe this.[29] Chrétien de Troyes' Perceval with its Jewish motifs ultimately gained international acclaim.

---

29   Holmes, U. T., A New Interpretation of Chrétien's Conte del Graal, Studies in Philology, XLIV, North Carolina, 1947, p. 473f.

Wolfram von Eschenbach's *Parzival*

German poet Wolfram von Eschenbach was familiar with Chrétien de Troyes' *Perceval* when he published his own epic poem *Parzival* in 1210. He translated Chrétien's story into Middle High German, embellished it with his own sub-plots and characters and expanded the novel to a full 16000 lines. It cannot be exactly proven whether Wolfram and Chrétien ever met personally, but the similarity of both authors' topics leads one to suspect this. What is certain is that Wolfram's Parzival contains numerous striking Jewish motifs that were previously overlooked by literary studies and that will help us in our search for the Templar treasure.

But who was Wolfram von Eschenbach? Not much is known about him. He was born 1160 and was from the small town of Eschenbach in Upper Franconia, which is today known as Obereschenbach near Ansbach. Hermann I, Landgrave of Thuringia, a well-known aesthete and patron of Middle High German literature, was his patron.[30] Wolfram von Eschenbach was himself a knight, familiar with the customs at the Landgrave's court and witty in terms of his brilliant double entendres. Thus, at the beginning of his work he playfully practiced false modesty by claiming that he is not capable of reading and writing, but is merely a nincompoop and his story of Parzival is in no way based on erudition. It quickly becomes obvious that this cannot be the case when the readers see themselves confronted with profound astronomical, geographical, societal, literary and religious aspects during Parzival's adventures. This knowledge leads us to conclude: Wolfram von Eschenbach was a highly intelligent and very well read individual.

Wolfram must have experienced great joy in encoding the names of places and characters: For instance, Wolfram named the Grail bearer *Repanse de Schoye*. During Wolfram's era, so-called "responsa" – in Hebrew *Sche'elot Uteschuwoth* – involved a response to legal questions on the *Halakha* addressed to a Jewish council of rabbis.[31] The Hal-

---

30   Barber, Richard, Der Heilige Gral, Geschichte und Mythos, Düsseldorf: Verlag Artemis&Winkler, 2004, p. 102.
31   Mutius, Hans-Georg von (ed.): Rechtsentscheide Raschis aus Troyes (1040-1105). Quellen über die sozialen und wirtschaftlichen Beziehungen zwischen Juden und Christen, Frankfurt am Main, 1986 (Judentum und Umwelt 15); cf. Elon, M., Ha-Mischpat ha-libri, 3rd edition, 1988, p. 1213ff.

akha is the orally transmitted legal part of the Torah, the Five Books of Moses, and provides rules on the religious life of Jewish believers.[32] It is a code of behavior towards other religions such as Christianity. So a responsa asked whether or not a certain act of faith was permissible. Wolfram encoded the name of the Grail bearer *Repanse de Schoye* with the Latin word *repono* for "bury," "keep" or "store." Choye – in *Parzival* known as Schoye – is a small town in the department of Haute-Sâone that is located 16 miles to the north-west of Besançon. Not far from Choye is the former Cistercian Abbey of Acey, which was consecrated in 1136 by Bernard of Clairvaux. So to be precise *Repanse de Schoye* could be an allegory for something that was or is stored in Schoye, but is of Jewish origin and, above all, has something to do with Bernard of Clairvaux. Is this a clue from Wolfram von Eschenbach about the Jewish nature of a Grail that is kept by a monk-like society such as the Cistercians of Bernard of Clairvaux? Another example among many for Wolfram's code names can be found in the epilogue to *Parzival*. Here the Franconian poet loudly denounces the false story of Parzival's search for the Holy Grail. According to Wolfram, in reality the story has to be told differently – just as he told it:

> If Chrétien of Troyes, the master, hath done to this tale a wrong.
> Then *Kiot* may well be wrathful, for he taught us aright the song,
> To the end the Provençal told it – How Herzeleide's son the Grail
> Did win, as was fore-ordained when Anfortas thereto did fail. [33]

In contrast to Chrétien de Troyes who found his original source for the tale of the Grail *Perceval* in a book of Count Philip of Flanders, Wolfram von Eschenbach's source was supposedly *Kyot the Provençal*. German scholars and philologists mostly identify him with the poet *Guiot de Provins*.[34] But *Provins* should not be confused with the region of Province: Provins is a town in Champagne, to the south-east of Paris. Guiot de Provins was a Templar sympathizer and even composed a few songs and texts such as his famous *Bible*

32   Kern-Ulmer, Brigitte, Rabbinische Responsen zum Synagogenbau: Die Responsentexte, Hildesheim: Georg Olms Verlag, 1990, p. 2f.
33   Wolfram von Eschenbach, Parzival, Munich: Langen Müller, 2001, p. 420.
34   Barber, Richard, Der Heilige Gral, Geschichte und Mythos, Düsseldorf: Verlag Artemis&Winkler, 2004, p. 203f..

about morality in the High Middle Ages.[35] As it is, a Provençal author would have composed his work in Occitan and not in Old French, like Guiot de Provins. Thus, as renowned historian Richard Barber believes, Wolfram seems to have encoded the very respectable name of the poet Guiot de Provins with "Kyot the Provençal" and used it in his work. Wolfram tells us that this *Guiot de Provins* found his story of the Holy Grail in a manuscript of the Jewish astronomer *Flegetanis* in the Spanish city of Toledo. This Flegetanis was a descendant of King Solomon on his mother's side and of the Muslim "heathens" on his father's side – based on this he was a native of Jerusalem or Palestine.[36] Wolfram writes the following about the Jew Flegetanis: "He wrote about the Grail's history. He was a heathen on his father's side, this Flegetanis, who still prayed to a calf as though it were his God."

Here Wolfram is referring to the Second Book of Moses (Exodus), which describes how the Israelites prayed to a golden idol in the form of a calf.[37] But we'll come back to that.

So this *Flegetanis* was the son of a man named Solomon and descended from a centuries-old Jewish family whose forefathers went back to long before the birth of Christ and probably to the construction of the Temple of Solomon.[38] Toledo had been snatched away from the Muslim Moors during the Reconquista. This is the only way to explain why Wolfram still describes Flegetanis as a heathen although his forefathers worshiped the Golden Calf. But maybe Wolfram also studied an old Jewish manuscript in Arabic with the title *felek thâni*, which is roughly translated as "the outer sphere." The Jews of Toledo always used the Arabic language for both religious texts and documents.[39]

Even if Flegetanis is merely invented, Wolfram's knowledge of Judaism in the Spanish city of Toledo from the 11th to the 13th century, which is revealed in his work, demonstrates his astonishing erudition. Furthermore, the many code names suggest that Wolfram at least had a Jewish source who provided him with information on

---

35   Barber, Malcolm, Die Templer, Düsseldorf: Patmos Verlag, 2005, p. 203f.
36   Barber, Richard, Der Heilige Gral, Geschichte und Mythos, Düsseldorf: Verlag Artemis&Winkler, 2004, p. 112
37   Second Book of Moses (Exodus) 32,1-4
38   Kolb, Herbert, Munsalvaesche, Studien zum Kyotproblem, Munich: Wilhelm Fink Verlag, 1963, p. 129.
39   Ibid., p. 150.

the secret of the Grail – maybe from the *felek thâni* manuscript. Consequently, both Chrétien's *Perceval* and Wolfram's *Parzival* are partly based on true events. They are a dramatic blend of *fact* and *fiction*.

But why should a Franconian poet and knight include Jewish allegories on the secret of the Grail in his text in the form of the Grail bearer *Repanse de Schoye* and other code names? Because Wolfram hints in his epilogue that Chrétien de Troyes "hath done to this tale a wrong," we can assume that he was aware of the Jewish content of this story. Contrary to the assumption that Chrétien de Troyes' *Perceval* and Wolfram von Eschenbach's *Parzival* are adaptations of Celtic-Christian myths, the Jewish elements are definitely no coincidence, and cannot be overlooked.

First of all, Wolfram's *Parzival* has a similar narrative structure to Chrétien's *Perceval*. There is a plot divided in two about the adventures of Perceval/Parzival and the knight Gawain/Gauwain. Wolfram's Gawain is also a noble knight who from the outset is equipped with courtly virtues. Both Parzival and Perceval are the sons of a knightly family of nobility. But what Chrétien de Troyes misses is practiced to the extreme by Wolfram von Eschenbach: the introduction of new names and characters. Thus, Wolfram von Eschenbach named Parzival's father Gahmuret from the noble family of Anjou – perhaps a reference to Chrétien de Troyes' patron for the novel *Perceval* – Philip of Flanders, who was a grandson of Fulk V of Anjou, a king of Jerusalem and an unofficial Templar. Gahmuret rides out into the world to acquire fame and fortune. He goes to the present-day Iraq and Arabia where he fearlessly fights bloody battles. He falls in love with the dark-skinned beauty Belacane, the Queen of Sasamanc. Belacane gives birth to Gahmuret's son Feirefiz whose skin is mottled black and white, perhaps due to a fungal disease or a skin pigmentation disorder as these occasionally occur today. When Gahmuret returns to the West, he succumbs to the seduction of Herzeloyde, the Queen of Wales. She is Parzival's mother who – like Chrétien de Troyes' version – does not want to let the naive boy leave home and dies from grief for the loss of her son.[40] The nameless knight in Chrétien de Troyes' manuscript, who instructed Parzival on courtly customs and knightly combat in

40   "Herzeloyde" is W. von Eschenbach's code name for "Herzeleid" (Heartbreak).

Wolfram's work, is called Gurnemanz instead of Gornemant of Gohort. Parzival has him to thank for his survival in knightly combat.

When Parzival reaches a lake and finds out from an elegantly
clothed fisherman that there is no accommodation for 30 miles,
Wolfram von Eschenbach also has the fisherman point out the way
to his home that proves to be the Grail castle. But the fisherman
himself was the King and Lord of the Grail castle – in Chrétien de
Troyes' version the lord was the son of the Fisher King.

Wolfram named the Grail castle *Munsalvaesche*. It has many
towers, a temple and an adjacent palace.[41]

This description is practically identical to the architecture of
the Knights Templar whose houses were also built next to round
churches.[42] Chrétien de Troyes, on the other hand, didn't give the
Grail castle a name. German and Medieval scholars have both been
puzzled for a long time about what *Munsalvaesche* might mean. It
may be possibly a code name for *Wildenberg* Castle which is derived from Mun (mount) and sauvage (savage or wild).[43] Wolfram
von Eschenbach named this castle *Wildenberc*, and its ruins can still
be found today in the Odenwald where, according to the legend, a
part of Parzival may have been written. But if Wolfram had already
refered to *Munsalvaesche* Castle in *Parzival* as Wildenberc, there
would be no reason to give it the code name Munsalvaesche.

During the course of the Jewish-Talmudic interpretation of
Parzival, which is practically inevitable when you read Parzival,
it makes sense to assume that you should translate *Munsalvaesche*
with *Mont des saintes vaches*: Mount of holy cows. King Solomon
had his Temple in Jerusalem built on Jerusalem's Temple Mount –
Har HaBayit. Clearly this is once again Wolfram referring to Judaism and even to the Temple of Solomon: the Book of Kings states
that in the Temple courtyard there was a cast bronze basin for the
ritual washing of the high priests, which stood on 12 bulls. At first
glance, it doesn't appear to make sense to search for a mountain in
France with holy cows. But, as we will see, Wolfram was an atten-

---

41   Parzival, 226,18.
42   Kolb, Herbert, Munsalvaesche, Studien zum Kyotproblem, Munich: Wilhelm
Fink Verlag, 1963, p. 104.
43   Kordt, Christa-Maria, Parzival in Munsalvaesche, Herne: Verlag für Wissenschaft
und Kunst, 1997, p. 210f.

tive observer and his encoded descriptions in Parzival contained more truth than we might believe. In actual fact, there really *is* a *Mount of Holy Cows* in France.

But what do all these encoded Jewish references in *Perceval* and *Parzival* actually mean? Let's take a closer look at Wolfram's *Parzival*: The Grail castle is guarded by a brave horde that Wolfram von Eschenbach calls *Templeisen*.[44] He was undoubtedly thinking of the Templar Order when he wrote about them – those warrior monks whom Bernard of Clairvaux praised in his treatise *De laude novae militiae*. Thus the transformation of Parzival who develops from a dumb simpleton to a knight experienced in battle who recognizes God through the Grail confirms that Chrétien de Troyes and Wolfram von Eschenbach must have studied the beliefs of the Cistercians and the Templar Order or even been in contact with them. As an experienced knight, Wolfram would have seen the Templars as a paragon of his era because he traveled through Thuringia and today's Saxony-Anhalt where the Templars were held in high esteem and ran influential commanderies – one of these was the commandery of Mücheln in Saxony-Anhalt, where a Templar chapel can still be visited.[45]

The tidings that Hugues de Payns' Templars had obviously searched for a missing relic in Jerusalem would have reached him through the Templar founder Count Hugues I of Champagne, his nephew Theobald II, Marie of Champagne and ultimately Chrétien de Troyes. Consequently, Parzival – in search of the discovery of the true nature of the Grail – also becomes a Templeise and master of the Grail temple – similar to an abbot watching over an abbey.[46]

The Templeisen guard the Grail in a square, windowless room which Wolfram only describes at the end of his work as a "temple." This is obviously referring to the Temple of Solomon in Jerusalem with its three divisions. The "temple" resembles the description of a crypt, an underground, windowless lower church that can only be found in religious buildings such as cathedrals. Wolfram's description of the Grail castle *Munsalvaesche* on the mountain is thus none other than an allegorical depiction of the Temple of Solomon

44   Parzival, 468, 24-25.
45   Snelleman, Willem, Das Haus Anjou und der Orient in Wolframs "Parzival," Nijkerk: Callenbach, 1941, p. 138.
46   Ibid., p. 131.

of Jerusalem – on the ruins of which the former Al-Aqsa Mosque was built and which served as Hugues de Payns' and his followers' headquarters.[47] But there is a big difference: The Jerusalem that Chrétien and Wolfram describe is in Europe, to be precise: in the north of France, the land of large Gothic cathedrals.

How is the Grail obtained in Wolfram von Eschenbach's *Parzival*? The Fisher King who shows Parzival the way to the castle proves to be the Grail king Anfortas who was wounded *in the side* by a lance in battle and has been wasting away for years. Only by the nourishment provided by the Grail and his belief in God can he stay alive. Anfortas is Parzival's uncle. The lance bleeding from its tip, which Wolfram describes, is carried into the room by a procession of squires. Subsequently, four beautiful maidens place a thin table made of a slab of garnet-hyacinth before the Lord and "the rich host ate above it." They are followed by two princesses who are carrying two silver knives which they place on the table. After numerous maidens have laid the table, the virgin queen appears and "So bright the maiden's face and mien, All thought the dawn was breaking."[48] Wolfram then describes the Grail for the first time: Upon a green Achmardi the Grail queen bears "the pride of Paradise. Root and branch, beyond all price." "It is called lapsit exillîs," writes Wolfram. "… the stone is also called the Grail."[49] The Grail had to be born by a pure, innocent hand: that of the chaste Grail queen Repanse de Schoye.

So the Grail is a stone, but is made of wood – hence root and branch. Wolfram seems to have been anything but a clueless fool. He was undoubtedly fluent in Latin. "Lapis" is Latin for "stone." A popular interpretation among German scholars and philologists for Wolfram's description "lapsit exillîs" is "lapis ex coelis," which means "the stone from heaven." But there is no justification for this translation as "lapis exillîs" can only be literally interpreted. So Wolfram's description of the Grail as "lapsit exillîs" means "thin stone" or "meager stone." (lapis exilis) When we take into account the previously transpired Jewish attributes of the Grail story, the Holy Grail consists of a thin stone slab.

---

47   Kolb, Herbert, Munsalvaesche, Studien zum Kyotproblem, Munich: Wilhelm Fink Verlag, 1963, p. 129.

48   Wolfram von Eschenbach, Parzival, Munich: Langen Müller, 2001, p. 121

But how can a stone slab provide infinite food? As we have seen, the Grail isn't remotely connected to the myth of a cup – that supposed chalice of the nobleman Joseph of Arimathea that he used to catch Christ's blood at his Crucifixion.[49] Alone the simple fact that neither Chrétien de Troyes nor Wolfram von Eschenbach described the Holy Grail as a chalice refutes this interpretation of the Grail. Chrétien described the Grail as *such a holy thing* ("tant sainte chose est li graals"). Let's remind ourselves that Wolfram von Eschenbach called "the master." Chrétien de Troyes a fool who was not quite truthful in his story. The Grail's name comes from the Old French word "grêle" for "thin" or "meager"[50] and appears to be a thin stone slab that is protected by a wooden holder that is covered in pure, radiant gold.[51] Wolfram calls this wood *root and branch*. So we are referring to wood that is covered in gold.

In Parzival God speaks to a select crowd through the stone: The dwelling or settling of God in his select people, his presence, is known in Judaism as *schechinah*. God lived in the Temple of Jerusalem in which King Solomon kept the Ark of the Covenant. At the end of the 11th century, this doctrine was already very well-known in Champagne and Troyes due to the Talmudic school of Rabbi Rashi, even among Christians. The *schechinah*, God's presence, manifested itself in the Temple of Solomon; it showed itself in the form of the Ark of the Covenant which contained the Mosaic stone tablets with the Ten Commandments, Aaron's rod and the jar of manna. Therefore, based on the description from

---

49   German scholar Hans-Wilhelm Schäfer believed to have sighted the Holy Chalice in the Valencia Cathedral. He claimed the Grail king Anfortas is identical to King Alfonso I of Aragon. The chalice, which was kept in the Monastery of San Juan de la Peña and has been exhibited in Valencia Cathedral since 1437, bears an inscription that Schäfer interpreted as AL-LABSIT AS-SILIS – supposedly Wolfram's lapsit exillîs. But this is inconclusive in Arabic, neither as Latin terminology in Arabic characters nor as Arabic terminology in Latin characters (because many Arabs at that time also wrote in Latin characters). There is also a lack of major semiotic features that clearly identify the script as Arabic. The Spanish archeologist Antonio Beltrán Martínez proved that the inscription means li-Izahirati: "For whom flourishes." Cf. Beltrán Martínez, Antonio, Estudio sobre el santo Cáliz de la Catedral de Valencia, Valencia 1969, 2nd edition 1984. In part because of this the Santo Cáliz from Valencia Cathedral is definitely not the Holy Grail from Chrétien's "Perceval" and Wolfram's "Parzival." As it is, Jesus Christ supposedly abstained from any splendor at the Last Supper and merely used the wooden cup of a carpenter.

50   Barber, Richard, Der Heilige Gral, Geschichte und Mythos, Düsseldorf: Verlag Artemis&Winkler, 2004, p. 209.

51   Another translation derives "graal" from the Latin word "gradale" for "dish." But this translation has little etymological basis. Cf. Kolb, Herbert, Munsalvaesche, Studien zum Kyotproblem, Munich: Wilhelm Fink Verlag, 1963, p. 144f.

Perceval and *Parzival*, "lapsit exillîs" is something completely Jewish: the stone tablets with the Ten Commandments that Moses received from God on Mount Horeb and that were carried around by the Israelites in the Ark of the Covenant.[52] God lives in the Grail in the sense of the Jewish *schechinah* and in the Grail community of the Templeisen.[53]

Just like Chrétien de Troyes' *Perceval*, Wolfram von Eschenbach's protagonist Parzival also has to ask the magic question about for whom the Grail is providing this cornucopia of food and drink. According to the Bible, the Ark of the Covenant contained the stone tablets with the Ten Commandments of God that Moses recreated when he shattered them. Furthermore, they contained Aaron's rod, a sprouting stave that thus showed that the tribe of Levi had been selected for the office of high priests, as well as a pot of manna.[54] The Isralites ate the manna when they were wandering through the Sinai Desert for 40 years, in search of the Promised Land, but we'll come back to that in the next chapter. The heavenly manna is likely the food that the Grail provided in unlimited amounts to the Grail community of the Templeisen – the Templars.

In the end, Parzival succeeds in asking the magic question of whom the Grail is feeding – and Anfortas is healed. Parzival finds out that he is the keeper of the Grail. His half-brother, the heathen Feirefiz, can only see the Grail if he is baptized.[55] Feirefiz has to declare his faith in God's Ten Commandments to be able to see God and thus the Grail.

Parzival and Bernard of Clairvaux

Now we must ask the question of whether Parzival really existed. Let's take a closer look at the name *Perceval/Parzival*. From a linguistic viewpoint, the name Perceval is a compound of *perce* and *val* and means "pierce the valley." In the nominative Perceval would be written as *Percevaux*, which is very similar to the

---

52   Mergell, Bodo, Der Gral in Wolframs Parzival, Halle: Max Niemeyer Verlag, 1952, p. 41.

53   Kolb, Herbert, Munsalvaesche, Studien zum Kyotproblem, Munich: Wilhelm Fink Verlag, 1963, p. 168.

54   In the Old Testament, Aaron's rod and the pot of manna are placed in front of the Ark of the Covenant. The New Testament, however, describes how they are placed in the Ark of the Covenant.

55   Wolfram von Eschenbach, Parzival, Munich: Langen Müller, 2001, p. 412

term "Clairvaux" – valley of light.[56] It is also significant that in Old French *Perceval* is synonymous with *Claraval*, i.e. Clairvaux.[57]

If the Cistercian abbot Bernard saw himself as the keeper of the Grail who called upon the Templars in his treatise to search for the relic under the Temple of Solomon, it makes sense to suspect that the Templar treasure consisted of the Ark of the Covenant with the divine tablets of the covenant law. In that case, Parzival's uncle Anfortas would be none other than André de Montbard who founded the Templar Order together with Hugues de Payns. The fifth Templar Grand Master André de Montbard was Bernard's uncle.

And if we take a closer look at Parzival's family, we come across equally interesting findings: Parzival's aunt Schoysiane marries a certain Kyot of Katelangen. Katelangen was incorrectly identified as Catalonia in Spain. But what is meant here is *Catalaunum*. It is on the Catalaunian Fields that a battle took place in 451 A.D. between the Visigoths and the Huns – these are in Champagne between Châlons and Troyes. The name of the town of Châtillon is derived from the Catalaunian Fields. Fontane, in the direct vicinity of Châtillon, is the birthplace of Bernard of Clairvaux. Wolfram's place names in Parzival are thus more in the east and north of France, all the more so because Chrétien de Troyes' version was his main source of inspiration. If Perceval is a metaphor for Bernard of Clairvaux and Anfortas, the Templar founder, is the counterpart of André de Montbard, then *Kyot of Katelangen* is none other than Hugues de Payns. His wife Catherine, a close relative of Bernard (and thus of Perceval/Parzival), was related to the Montbard family.

So let's recap: Wolfram von Eschenbach based his work Parzival on contemporary real events.[58] His role model seems to have been

56   According to the assessment of Dr. Frank Paulikat from the Institut der romanischen Sprachwissenschaften (Institute of Romance Language Studies) of Augsburg University. Personal correspondence from June 16, 2009.
57   Barthel, Manfred, in: Charpentier, Louis, Macht und Geheimnis der Templer, Olten: Walter Verlag, 1986, p. 15. But "percer" also means "pierce." "Val" could be a corruption of "épaule" for "shoulder blade," but is derived from the Latin word "scapula." A scapular is a shoulder wrap over the habit of a monk. The Cistercians wear it below the belt. So, based on this, "Perceval" would be a monk who got pierced with a lance through the shoulder blade. The result would be a red blood spot on the white habit of the Cistercian monk – the Knights Templar wore a red cross pattée on the left shoulder of their white surcoats.
58   Snelleman, Willem, Das Haus Anjou und der Orient in Wolframs "Parzival,"

Bernard of Clairvaux. And there's another pretty fascinating fact in this context: *Clairvaux Abbey housed the greatest collection of cross and divine relics in Christendom.*[59] In 1504, it had a total of 142 relics.[60] In 1135, Bernard of Clairvaux thanks the Patriarch of Jerusalem for the receipt of a fragment of the Cross of Christ.[61] In 1164, the Templar Artaud brought a cross relic to Clairvaux Abbey. It was part of a gold- and precious stone-decorated shrine with several relics that was donated by the King of Jerusalem.[62] When Artaud joined Clairvaux in 1205, he donated further relics, as did other Templars. Bernard of Clairvaux and the subsequent abbots attached great value to constantly expanding Clairvaux's collection of relics. Thus, the Abbey was also in possession of the Lance of Longinus – that lance which in the Bible the Roman legionnaire Longinus stuck in the ribs of the crucified Jesus Christ to make sure the Savior was dead.[63] In terms of the Grail legend, this is particularly interesting because both Chrétien and Wolfram mention a lance.

In the Cistercian Lichtental Abbey, there was a unique 16.6 cm x 11.6 cm x 15 cm box with rich iconography that was borne by leonine figures who depicted the tribes of Judah. The inscription of the shrine contains the word *Arca* – a clear reference to the Ark of the Covenant of the Israelites because in the Latin Bible (Vulgate) this is called *Arca Foederis*. Today, the box from the early 14th century can be admired in the Pierpont Morgan Library in New York. The Lichtental box is proof that the Ark of the Covenant was of great significance to the Cistercians.

Philip of Flanders, the patron of Chrétien de Troyes, also owned several valuable relics, such as Jesus' manger, the Holy

---

Nijkerk: Callenbach, 1941, p. 198.

59 Lahore, Chr. (Ed.), Le trésor de Clairvaux du XIIe au XVIIIe siècle, Troyes, 1875, p. 114f.

60 Inventar von 1504, No. 10, Jubainville (ed.), p. 500; cf. Frolow, Anatole, La rélique de la vraie Croix. Recherches sur le développement d'un culte, Paris, 1961 (Archives de l'Orient chrétien 7), p. 389f.

61 Bernhard von Clairvaux, Sämtliche Werke, Volume 2, Innsbruck: Tyrolia-Verlag, 1995, Letter 175.

62 Inventar von 1504, No. 2, Jubainville (ed.), p. 497; cf. Frolow, Anatole, La rélique de la vraie Croix. Recherches sur le développement d'un culte, Paris, 1961 (Archives de l'Orient chrétien 7), p. 418f.

63 Inventar von 1504, No. 1, Jubainville (ed.), p. 496; Inventar von 1405, no. 1; cf. Frolow, Anatole, La rélique de la vraie Croix. Recherches sur le développement d'un culte, Paris, 1961 (Archives de l'Orient chrétien 7), p. 409f.

Sponge, parts of Christ's Cross, and also a vial with the blood of Christ.[64] After Philip's death in 1191, his entire treasure of relics and his mortal remains were brought to Clairvaux. Many treasures were destroyed during the French Revolution, unless they had first been brought to another place.

Based on all these findings, it is obvious that Chrétien de Troyes and Wolfram von Eschenbach were inspired by real relics in Clairvaux Abbey. If the *Templeisen* owned the "grâl," i.e. the Ark of the Covenant with the tablets of the covenant law, Chrétien de Troyes and Wolfram von Eschenbach got the inspiration for their courtly poems *Perceval* and *Parzival* from an actual historical event.

The knowledge about the Templar treasure was passed from the counts of Champagne to Chrétien de Troyes and ultimately Wolfram von Eschenbach. The actions of Bernard of Clairvaux, whose works were translated into Old French as early as the 12th century, were thus the trigger for the literary development of the Grail legend.[65]

Back to Troyes and back to the present. Meanwhile, I am sipping my second beer. I go through my notes and the new and fascinating findings:

- Chrétien de Troyes' *Perceval* and Wolfram von Eschenbach's *Parzival* are medieval, literary embellishments of a true historical event.

- Starting with the founding of the Knights Templar by Hugues de Payns, André de Montbard and their followers, the knowledge about the Templar treasure was passed from the counts of Champagne to Chrétien de Troyes and Wolfram von Eschenbach.

- Katelangen is not the Spanish Catalonia, but the Catalaunian Fields (Catalaunum) not far from Troyes.

- Marie of Champagne, a descendant of Templar founder Count Hugues I of Champagne, was the daughter of King Louis VII of France.

64   Adolf, Helen, A Historical Background for Chrétien's Perceval, PMLA, Vol. 58, No. 33, Sep., 1943, p. 601.
65   Mergell, Bodo, Der Gral in Wolframs Parzival, Halle: Max Niemeyer Verlag, 1952, p. 99.

- Perceval's real-life counterpart is the Cistercian abbot Bernard of Clairvaux.

- Anfortas is the Templar founder and uncle of Bernard, André de Montbard.

- Hugues de Payns' literary pendant is Kyot of Katelangen.

- The fact that women rank among the selected keepers of the Grail, above all Repanse de Schoye, indicates that the Cistercian Order is meant here because it was the first order to accept women.

- Wolfram's description of the Grail as a stone demonstrates striking Jewish-Talmudic attributes of the Ark of the Covenant with the Mosaic tablets of the covenant law.

- The depiction of the *Templeisen,* a selected Grail brotherhood and code name for the Templars, resembles the Jewish *schechinah,* the presence of God.

- The Grail castle *Munsalvaesche* with its temple used to store the Grail resembles the Templar architecture. It has strong characteristics of a cathedral crypt and could be translated with *Mount of holy cows* in the sense of the Temple of Solomon: in the courtyard of the Temple of Solmon, 12 bulls supported the *cast bronze basin* for the ritual washing of the high priests.

- The origin of the Grail legend of Perceval and Parzival can be found in Champagne: so in the north of France. The Grail castle *Munsalvaesche* is situated in north or north-east France, which is probably also the location of the Templar treasure.

I close my notebook, put my pen in my shirt pocket and rummage around in my backpack for a book. I glance at the title: *The Mysteries of Chartres Cathedral,* written by a certain Louis Charpentier. In this book the author claims that Hugues de Payns' Templars found the Ark of the Covenant during their stay beneath Jerusalem's Temple Mount – and brought it to France.

Charpentier's claim is pretty daring and I am tempted to check the plausibility of his hypothesis. That is why I first have to find out whether the Ark of the Covenant really existed from an archaeological perspective and whether it was possibly still hidden in Jerusalem between 1105 and 1187.

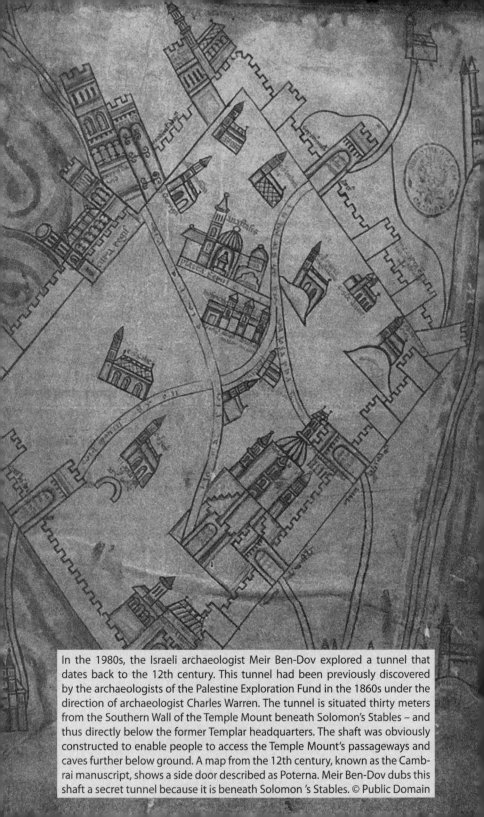

In the 1980s, the Israeli archaeologist Meir Ben-Dov explored a tunnel that dates back to the 12th century. This tunnel had been previously discovered by the archaeologists of the Palestine Exploration Fund in the 1860s under the direction of archaeologist Charles Warren. The tunnel is situated thirty meters from the Southern Wall of the Temple Mount beneath Solomon's Stables – and thus directly below the former Templar headquarters. The shaft was obviously constructed to enable people to access the Temple Mount's passageways and caves further below ground. A map from the 12th century, known as the Cambrai manuscript, shows a side door described as Poterna. Meir Ben-Dov dubs this shaft a secret tunnel because it is beneath Solomon's Stables. © Public Domain

Chapter Three

God's Ark

I'm going after a find of incredible historical significance.

— Dr. Henry Jones Jr.

The Covenant with God

The history of the Ark of the Covenant begins with Moses whom God appears to in Egypt as a burning thorn bush.[1] God instructs him to bring the people of Israel out of Egypt to the land of the Canaanites, Hittites, Amorites, Perizzites, Hivites and Jebusites – in short, the country that is today known as Israel. Before then, the Israelites had spent more than 400 years in Egypt, serving the pharaohs as slaves.[2] It became time to escape this tyranny, and when Moses asks why he should be the one to lead the people, God replies that he has heard the cries of the tortured slaves of the Egyptian pharaoh and has decided to make them his people. God says he will be with Moses. When Moses asks about God's identity, God reveals: "I will be what I will be." Other Biblical translations render this as: "I am who I am," and Moses is told to tell the Israelites, "The Lord, the God of your fathers – the God of Abraham, the God of Isaac and the God of Jacob – has sent me to you."

Today's historians are still uncertain about whether the Pharaoh mentioned was Ramses II, who ruled between 1295 and 1275 B.C.[3] However, the era of Ramses II's reign would suggest that this is the case.[4] Moses talks to Pharaoh and tells him that the God of

1   Second Book of Moses (Exodus) 3:1-15.
2   Second Book of Moses (Exodus), 12:40, cf. Flavius Josephus, Antiquities of the Jews, Book 2, Chapter 13.
3   Cf. Finkelstein, Israel und Silberman, Neil, Keine Posaunen vor Jericho, Munich: DTV, 2001, p. 61.
4   Andrews, Richard, Tempel der Verheißung. Das Geheimnis des heiligen Berges

the Hebrews has appeared to them. However, Pharaoh Ramses II gives him the cold shoulder. He will not let the Hebrews go. After all, they are working for him for free. Subsequently, God punishes Pharaoh and Egypt with 10 terrible plagues. But Pharaoh is unimpressed by the poisoned Nile, the invasion of frogs, the lice and flies, the disease on livestock, the incurable boils, the hail, the locusts and even the frightening darkness. As a result, God curses Egypt with an even crueler plague: the death of the first-born of all Egyptian humans and animals. Yahweh, the LORD, sends these plagues as proof that he is far greater than all the multiple gods of the Egyptians.[5] God delivers a tough blow at midnight. It is only then that Pharaoh admits his powerlessness over the one God and asks Moses and the Israelites to make haste to leave his land in order to end the cruel punishment of Egypt by Yahweh. The Israelites make their exodus to the Sinai Desert on the feast of Passover.

God encounters the Israelites in various forms during their exodus from Egypt: as a pillar of cloud by day, as a pillar of fire by night "to give them light, so that they could travel by day or night." When they become hungry and the people grumble against Moses and Aaron, God rains down bread and quail from heaven – at twilight there would be meat and in the morning bread. The people of Israel call the bread "manna." It is "white like coriander seed and tastes like wafers made with honey." Moses orders Aaron to put the manna in a jar to be kept as proof of the presence of God for the generations to come.[6] The Israelites eat manna and wander through the Sinai Desert for forty years. It is a long and arduous march. God leads the Israelites in the metaphysical guise of a force of nature to show them the way.[7] He does not let them on the road through the Philistine country to avoid demoralizing them by war and violence, but instead leads them through the desert road to the Red Sea. It seems as if Moses himself doesn't know where they are going. They were "600,000 soldiers on foot, besides their families."[8]

---

von Jerusalem, Bergisch-Gladbach: Lübbe-Verlag, 1999, p. 42.
5   Second Book of Moses (Exodus) 12:11-50.
6   Second Book of Moses (Exodus) 16:31-33.
7   Second Book of Moses (Exodus) 13:21.
8   Second Book of Moses (Exodus) 12:37.

They reach Mount Sinai. Now, after all his efforts, Moses is finally standing on Mount Horeb (Sinai). The 12 tribes of the Israelites
set up camp at the foot of the mountain.[9] Moses, from the tribe of
Levi, hears God's voice echoing down to him from heaven. Moses
was told to tell the Israelites that the exodus from Egypt was only
possible by God's help "just as a mighty eagle carries its young." In
other words: Without him they would never have gotten that far
and so they should stop moaning and carry on until they reached
the "land flowing with milk and honey."[10] But God becomes more
explicit when he makes a tempting proposal that Moses and the Israelites can hardly refuse: "Now if you will faithfully obey me, you
will be my very own people. The whole world is mine, but you will
be my holy nation and serve me as priests. Moses, that is what you
must tell the Israelites."[11]

Moses obeys, gathers the elders, tells them about God's propos-
al and they agree. They will do as Yahweh orders. Henceforth, the
Israelites are God's chosen people. They have made a covenant with
Yahweh. The mountain is blocked off. Only Moses and his brother
Aaron should climb it. The priests should avoid even glancing at
Yahweh because otherwise God would break out against them.

On the third day, God appears again. Smoke "like smoke from
a furnace" billows up from the trembling mountain as God descends on it "in fire" and a sound of the trumpet echoes through
the Sinai Desert.

Moses goes up Mount Horeb (Sinai) again, Aaron stays at the
bottom. Moses talks to God and the LORD answers. He gives him
the Ten Commandments: "I am the Lord your God, who brought
you out of Egypt, out of the land of slavery. You shall have no other
gods before me. You shall not make for yourself an image in the
form of anything in heaven above or on the earth beneath or in the
waters below. You shall not bow down to them or worship them!"

God openly threatens: "for I, the Lord your God, am a jealous
God, punishing the children for the sin of the parents to the third
and fourth generation of those who hate me, but showing love to

9   Second Book of Moses (Exodus) 24:4.
10   Second Book of Moses (Exodus) 3:8.
11   Second Book of Moses (Exodus) 19:3-6.

a thousand generations of those who love me and keep my commandments."

This is followed by civilizational principles that are today ingredients of every democratic society: "You shall not murder. You shall not commit adultery. You shall not steal. You shall not give false testimony against your neighbor. You shall not covet your neighbor's house. You shall not covet your neighbor's wife, or his male or female servant, his ox or donkey, or anything that belongs to your neighbor."[12] These words are emphasized by the mighty crashing of thunder and lightning. Subsequently, God imparts further laws and counsel: "If you buy a Hebrew servant, he is to serve you for six years. But in the seventh year, he shall go free. Anyone who strikes a person with a fatal blow is to be put to death. If a bull gores a man or woman to death, the bull is to be stoned to death, and its meat must not be eaten. Six days do your work, but on the seventh day do not work." And so on and so forth.

But God wants to give these Ten Commandments in writing, so he calls Moses up again to Mount Horeb (Sinai). His aide, Joshua, accompanies him. "Come up to me on the mountain and stay here, and I will give you the tablets of stone with the law and commandments I have written for their instruction."[13]

For six days the cloud covers the mountain. On the seventh day the glory of the lord appears like a consuming fire. Moses enters the divine cloud and stays on the peak of the mountain for forty days and forty nights. During this time, God reveals to Moses basic ritual objects that he and his people should create for Yahweh. The Israelites should build Yahweh a sanctuary. Moses and his people should make this sanctuary like the pattern God shows them in which God will "dwell" among the Hebrews. The following is an exact description of the construction of a box in which the Ten Commandments are to be stored:

> Have them make an ark of acacia wood – two and a half cubits
> long, a cubit and a half wide, and a cubit and a half high. Overlay
> it with pure gold, both inside and out, and make a gold mold-

---

12   Second Book of Moses (Exodus) 20:1-18.
13   Second Book of Moses (Exodus) 24:12.

ing around it. Cast four gold rings for it and fasten them to its four feet, with two rings on one side and two rings on the other. Then make poles of acacia wood and overlay them with gold. Insert the poles into the rings on the sides of the ark to carry it. The poles are to remain in the rings of this ark; they are not to be removed. Then put in the ark the tablets of the covenant law, which I will give you. Make an atonement cover of pure gold – two and a half cubits long and a cubit and a half wide. And make two cherubim out of hammered gold at the ends of the cover. Make one cherub on one end and the second cherub on the other; make the cherubim of one piece with the cover, at the two ends. The cherubim are to have their wings spread upward, overshadowing the cover with them. The cherubim are to face each other, looking toward the cover. Place the cover on top of the ark and put in the ark the tablets of the covenant law that I will give you. There, above the cover between the two cherubim that are over the ark of the covenant law, I will meet with you and give you all my commands for the Israelites.[14]

God communicates with the Israelites through the Ark of the Covenant. But to make offerings to God, he instructs Moses and the Israelites to build an offering table for the bread of the Presence (shewbread), a seven-branched lampstand, the Altar of Burnt Offering and a Tabernacle as a type of mobile temple. This Tabernacle is stored in a rectangular 46-meter long and 23-meter wide courtyard that is divided in two and separated from the Israelite camp by fence posts with animal hair curtains. The Tabernacle itself is 13.7 meters long and 4.6 meters wide. Three frames are made of acacia wood, attached over the curtains embellished with woven cherubims. The covering of the Tabernacle is made of goat hair, ram and badger skins. The Altar of Burnt Offering stands in the middle of the east end of the courtyard. The Tabernacle with the Ark of the Covenant stands in the west end of the courtyard. This is also divided into three zones: the courtyard, the Holy Place and the Holy of Holies. This division is emphasized by the fact that the objects in the courtyard are made of copper, but those in the Holy Place and the Holy of Holies are made of gold. In the Holy Place the golden

14   Second Book of Moses (Exodus) 25:10-22.

sacred objects such as the Menorah and the table of the bread of the Presence (shewbread) are kept. Only the high priest can enter the Holy of Holies. Moses now has to tell his brother Aaron that he is God's priest. Consequently, only Aaron may enter the 9.1-meter long and 4.6-meter wide Holy of Holies.[15]

Aaron and his sons are to have special garments made for them with gold, blue, purple and scarlet yarn and fine linen. The breastpiece of Aaron's garment should have 12 precious stones arranged in four rows of three, for the 12 tribes of Israel: carnelian, chrysolite and beryl; turquoise, lapis lazuli and emerald; jacinth, agate and amethyst; topaz, onyx and jasper.[16] Aaron and his sons should wear their special golden garments whenever they enter the Holy Place and first wash themselves in the bronze basin. The descriptions go into the minute details, but it appears that such exact data and instructions could only be testimony of an authentic event in Biblical history – and no invention.

Then the Lord tells Moses that he has chosen Bezalel of the tribe of Judah and Oholiab of the tribe of Dan to make the Ark of the Covenant, the seven-branched Menorah, the table of the bread of the Presence (shewbread), the altar of incense, the Altar of Burnt Offering, the bronze basin for washing, the tent of meeting and all its utensils for the services and the garments for Aaron and his sons. After this speech, he hands Moses the tablets with the Ten Commandments.

When Moses descends from Mount Horeb (Sinai), to his disappointment he recognizes that the Israelites are praying to a Golden Calf. In Moses' absence, they had asked Aaron to create for them such an idol because they mistrusted God's authority and were searching for a new god. Angry about this blasphemy, Moses breaks the tablets to pieces, melts down the Golden Calf and grinds it to powder which he makes the Israelites drink before having 3000 of them massacred.[17]

He pitches a tent outside the camp and, to the Israelites' astonishment, God's pillar of cloud appears. Yahweh, the Lord, talks to

15   Hamblin, William J. and Seely, David R., Salomos Tempel, Mythos und Geschichte des Tempelberges in Jerusalem, Stuttgart: Belser Verlag, 2007, p. 19f.
16   Second Book of Moses (Exodus) 28:1-43.
17   Second Book of Moses (Exodus) 32:19-20.

Moses when he wants to see God's countenance: "You cannot see my face, for no one may see me and live."

Then God instructs Moses to chisel out two new stone tablets and to climb up Mount Horeb with them. In the early morning, God appears again and makes a final covenant with Moses and the Israelites. When Moses comes down from Mount Sinai with the two tablets of the covenant law in his hands, his face is radiant because he has spoken with the Lord. He tells the Israelites about the new commandments.[18] The Book of Exodus now describes the crafting of the sacred objects. The Ark of the Covenant is crafted by Bezalel.[19]

After all sacred objects have been completed, Moses inspects the work of the artists and appears to be highly satisfied because he blesses Bezalel, Oholiab and their helpers. The tent of meeting for the Ark of the Covenant and all sacred objects are set up. Exodus 40:20 tells of the first time Moses places the tablets of the covenant law in the Ark of the Covenant and arranges the remaining sacred objects and offerings as God had ordered.

Suddenly, God's cloud covers the Tabernacle. Moses has to leave this place because the "glory of the Lord filled the tabernacle." Whenever the cloud lifts from above the Tabernacle, the Israelites set out to continue on their way to the Promised Land. But if the cloud does not lift, they do not set out. At night, it transforms into a pillar of fire.

This is the end of the story of the exodus of the Israelites from Egypt. At the same time, it is the beginning of thousands of years of fascination with the most puzzling archaeological artifact of Biblical history.

Let's take a closer look at the Ark of the Covenant.

The Ark of God

Based on the description in the Book of Exodus, this divine box was two and a half cubits in length, one and a half cubits in width and one and a half cubits in height. At the time of Moses, the regal Egyptian cubit was equal to five handspans or 20 fingers,

---

18   Second Book of Moses (Exodus) 34:1-35.
19   Second Book of Moses (Exodus) 37:1-9.

so a length of approx. 52.5 cm.[20] Thus, with a length of 131.25 cm, a height of 78.75 cm and a width of 78.75 cm, the Ark was not a handy Ikea piece of furniture and had to, wherever possible, be carried on the shoulders of four strong men with a lot of stamina.

The Ark was probably made of the wood Acacia raddiana, which is mainly found in the stony, sandy desert of the Middle East and, in particular, in the Negev Desert and west of the Dead Sea. This tree is a type of acacia that can reach heights of up to eight meters. The wood is very resistant to strong temperature and moisture fluctuations.[21] The Jewish historian Flavius Josephus goes into a little more detail in his description of the wood:

> There was also an ark made, sacred to God, of wood that was naturally strong, and could not be corrupted. This was called Eron in our own language. Its construction was thus: its length was five spans, but its breadth and height was each of them three spans. It was covered all over with gold, both within and without, so that the wooden part was not seen. It had also a cover united to it, by golden hinges, after a wonderful manner; which cover was every way evenly fitted to it, and had no eminences to hinder its exact conjunction. There were also two golden rings belonging to each of the longer boards, and passing through the entire wood, and through them gilt bars passed along each board, that it might thereby be moved and carried about, as occasion should require; [...] Upon this its cover were two images, which the Hebrews call Cherubims; they are flying creatures, but their form is not like to that of any of the creatures which men have seen.[22]

The author of Exodus possessed detailed knowledge of carpentry that was only known to Egyptian cabinet-makers and goldsmiths at the courts of pharaohs. Based on the reports, it is very probable that the Ark was gilded with layers of gold leaf. The four rings for the poles were cast from gold. Undoubtedly, this was also

---

20   Jánosi, Peter, Die Pyramiden, Mythos und Archäologie, Munich: C.H. Beck, 2004, p. 123.
21   Zwickel, Wolfgang, Der Salomonische Tempel, Mainz: Verlag Philipp von Zabern, 1999, p. 106.
22   Flavius Josephus, Antiquities of the Jews, Book 3, Chapter 6.5.

mixed with another harder metal because gold alone is very malle-able. This could conceivably have been brass, which was already manufactured in Mesopotamia. The question of the stability of the poles is a purely physical matter: The acacia wood had to be thick enough for a wooden box of at least 150 kilograms to be carried with it without the poles bending or even breaking. So a sensible length would have been 3.5 meters.[23]

Unfortunately, this Ark of the Covenant is merely a model from the movie "Indiana Jones and the Raiders of the Lost Ark." However, Steven Spielberg and George Lucas followed the Biblical descriptions of the Ark in the Book of Exodus to the letter. The Ark must have looked something like this. © Tobias D. Wabbel

And now we must question whether the Ark could even be car-ried, considering all the heavy material that was used for its con-struction. Simple mathematical calculations on the density of gold and the weight of acacia wood provide us with astonishing results: With a wood thickness of 3 cm, the Ark would weigh 150 kg with-out poles and gold rings, if the gold coating was only 0.1 millime-ters. But if the wood of the box frames were only 2 cm thick, a gold coating of up to 0.5 millimeters would have been possible. How-ever, this doesn't take into account the poles and the cherubim of

23   Graffe, Georg, Terra-X: Die Jagd nach der Bundeslade, Jerusalems verlorener Schatz, Augsburg: Weltbild Verlag, 1999, p. 75.

hammered gold. Thus, with poles and cherubim, the Ark would be much heavier than 150 kilograms, which means it could barely be carried. The high weight and the desert heat would have forced even four strong men to their knees after just a few hundred meters. So, it can be assumed that the Ark of the Covenant was pulled by oxen on a cart. The poles were to unload the golden box from the cart. But the thickness of the gold of 0.1 – 0.5 mm would still offer sufficient insulation from external environmental factors. The choice of acacia wood leads us to conclude that the Ark was designed to last a very long time. Flavius Josephus emphasizes that the wood could not be corrupted. Acacia wood lasts at least 500 years underwater and in a dry climate more than 1500 years. If the wood is insulated by gold, it is likely to last many thousands of years.

Many things suggest that the Israelites' Ark of the Covenant was inspired by Egyptian art: In November 1922, archaeologist Howard Carter discovered the Tomb of King Tutankhamen. In addition to the sarcophagus and the many burial objects and treasures, Carter also found a wooden chest with carrying poles in the antechamber.[24] The chest from the tomb of Tutankhamen is smaller than the Biblical Ark of the Covenant, but of a comparable construction. It contained stone and glass vessels, ceramics, four painted limestone plates, stone knives and the remains of organic materials. Beneath the chest's floor bronze rings are attached to pieces of board through which the carrying poles are pushed to shift the weight to four people during transportation. The chest has a gable lid, is decorated on the sides with goldleaf and crafted of dark cedar wood. Although cedar wood is not as resistant as acacia wood, the chest from the tomb of Tutankhamen survived thousands of years – very probably because the tomb of Tutankhamen was untouched and kept airtight for more than 3200 years since it was sealed. Now let us imagine that the Ark of the Covenant was covered in 0.5 millimeters gold so that it would have easily survived unscathed up to the present day.

God instructed Moses to attach two *cherubim* to the lid – *kapporeth* – of the Ark of the Covenant, the "atonement cover." So at

---

24   Wiese, André and Bordbeck, Andreas, Tutanchamun, Das goldene Jenseits, Exhibit No. 87: Box with carrying poles, Katalog der Kunst- und Ausstellungshalle der Bundesrepublik Deutschland, Bonn, 2005, p. 342.

every end there were two hybrid creatures with the heads of lions and the wings of eagles. Their wings were stretched upwards and cover the entire atonement cover although their faces are turned towards each other. The word cherubim comes from Babylonian and is derived from the Assyrian word "ilu kāribu," which means, roughly translated, "winged bull" and signifies a heavenly being that passes on the prayers of people to God. So a cherub is a winged messenger with the body of a bull, although it is not instantly visible whether the cherubim has either the face of a lion or an eagle.[25] According to the Talmud expert Rabbi Rashi of Troyes, on the atonement cover of the Ark of the Covenant stood two hybrid creatures opposite each other, one of which had the face of an eagle and the other the face of a lion.[26] Between them was the manifestation of God above the atonement cover.

The cherubim can be interpreted as polytheistic remnants that Moses had mounted on the Ark of the Covenant to appease the renegade Israelites who worshiped a Golden Calf during his absence. So we can assume from this that the introduction of the God Yahweh to the Israelites definitely didn't go as smoothly and speedily as the Bible would have us believe. The development of the belief from polytheism to monotheism and the respect of one single creator and almighty lord of the universe will have taken decades or even centuries. The cherubim on the Ark of the Covenant were a compromise between polytheism and monotheism.

Nothing else is known about the internal decorations of the Ark of the Covenant. We don't know whether it had carvings or engravings or other kinds of iconography that would lead us to further conclusions because the Bible is silent on this matter. However, to protect the stone tablets from vibrations during transportation, it can be assumed that the Ark was padded from inside by balls of fabric or fur on which the tablets of the covenant law rested. The lid will have been attached to the chest by hinges to prevent the atonement cover from falling to the ground by a shifting of its weight.

In the books of the Old Testament we come across further interesting hints. For instance, we read in the Fourth Book of Moses

25   Haran, M., The Ark and the Cherubim, Their Symbolic Significance, in: Biblical Ritual, Israel Exploration Journal IX, 1959, p. 30-38; p. 89-94.
26   Yaniv, Bracha, The Cherubim on Torah Ark Valances, in: Assaph, Studies in Art History, Volume 4, 1999, p. 163.

(Numbers) 17:24, that Moses' brother Aaron placed the sprouting stave in front of the Ark of the Covenant. This was just after Moses had appointed Aaron a high priest.[27] Aaron was selected when the representatives of the 12 tribes of Israel placed 12 staffs on the Ark of the Covenant. Only Aaron's staff sprouted – the sign for the divine task of the tribe of Levi.[28] But in accordance with the Epistle to the Hebrews of the New Testament, the pot of manna, Aaron's rod and the tablets of the covenant law were not kept *in* the Ark.[29]

Whether Bezalel or Moses himself crafted the Ark is unclear because according to the Fifth Book of Moses (Deuteronomy):

> So I made the ark out of acacia wood and chiseled out two stone tablets like the first ones, and I went up on the mountain with the two tablets in my hands. The LORD wrote on these tablets what he had written before, the Ten Commandments he had proclaimed to you on the mountain, out of the fire, on the day of the assembly. And the LORD gave them to me. Then I came back down the mountain and put the tablets in the ark I had made, as the LORD commanded me, and they are there now.[30]

In this part of the Bible we encounter a significant discrepancy on who the author of the Five Books of Moses really was. In the 12th century, the Jewish Talmud expert Moses Maimonides assumed that Moses himself was the author. Maimonides believed that the Torah was the holy truth with unshakable foundations.[31] But the story that describes Moses' death refutes this – because how can a dead man write about his own demise? This discrepancy is very striking when you examine the following lines: "And Moses the servant of the Lord died there in Moab, as the Lord had said. He buried him in Moab, in the valley opposite Beth Peor, but to this day no one knows where his grave is. Moses was a hundred and twenty years old when he died."

---

27   Second Book of Moses (Exodus) 29:4-35.
28   The names of the 12 tribes of Israel were: Reuben, Simeon, Levi, Judah, Dan, Naphtali, Gad, Asher, Issachar, Zebulun, Joseph, Benjamin.
29   Hebrews 9:4-5.
30   Fifth Book of Moses (Deuteronomy) 10:5.
31   Grierson, Roderick and Munro-Hay, Stuart, Der Pakt mit Gott, Auf der Suche nach der verschollenen Bundeslade, Bergisch-Gladbach: Lübbe-Verlag, 2001, p. 40.

God's Ark

We primarily notice that the Bible is composed of several sources that document Biblical matters from several perspectives. As a result, there was no sole author of the Five Books of Moses. Instead, the Pentateuch seems to be a kind of anthology. The Biblical publisher had a great struggle to combine the various sources into a plausible context that was free from contradictions. From these discrepancies we can see that they were not entirely successful. Furthermore, we can deduce that the Biblical texts were hardly edited at all. This is suggested by the fact that the Ark of the Covenant in the Book of Exodus was covered with gold, decorated with cherubim and crafted by Bezalel. In the Fifth Book of Moses (Deuteronomy), however, we read that the Ark was not gilted, there were no cherubim at all, it was a standard box of acacia wood – and Moses crafted it himself.

Secondly, we can conclude from this that possibly two arks of the covenant were in existence. The Ark that Moses might have had constructed was perhaps intended for the first tablets of the covenant law, but it was not destroyed when the second, more impressive Ark was created. The second Ark was for the second pair of tablets of the covenant law that Moses chiseled anew after he had punished the renegade worshipers of the Golden Calf by having them killed. However, it is very probable that there was only one single Ark of the Covenant because, as we have seen, it took a long time for the monotheistic belief in Yahweh to establish itself among the Israelites. The cherubim are proof that Moses was searching for a compromise between the idol worshipers and his Israelites who believed in God to prevent an open conflict from breaking out. In this sense, the Ark of the Covenant was not only a sign of God's presence, but also a peace settlement in the form of a wooden, gold-covered chest.

However, different sources lead us to suspect that the exodus from Egypt, the construction of the Ark of the Covenant, the Tabernacle and the other sacred objects were documented by various historians. It is a strong indicator of the fact that the Five Books of Moses are relating true events.

From a historical viewpoint the exodus is proven and identifies the tribes of Israel as slaves who were captured during Egyptian

campaigns of conquest and had to perform forced labor for pharaohs in the Nile Delta. For instance, the Israel Stele from the fifth
year of the reign of Pharaoh Merneptah (circa 1208 B.C.), which
was discovered in 1887 by the English archaeologist Sir Flinders
Petrie in the mortuary temple of Merneptah in West Thebes, documents the revolt of the tribes of "Israel" that was quashed by the
pharaoh.[32] The Amarna correspondence with Canaan from the
time of the pharaohs Akhenaten and Tutankhamen proves that the
Israelites were kept as slaves in Egypt and were dubbed *habiru*[33],
which changed to the word *apiru* for "Hebrews."[34] In the Fifth Book
of Moses (Deuteronomy) we then read that the Ark of the Covenant passes to the tribe of Levi whose members henceforth carry
and guard the divine shrine.[35]

The Odyssey of the Ark of the Covenant

The Israelites reach the land of Canaan circa 1295 B.C., led by
Joshua, whom Moses had designated as his successor to head
the tribe before his death.[36] The settlement area is rather small for
the Israelites as they are settling in Canaan, a land that has already
been settled by the Amorites and Hurrians from Mesopotamia, as
well as the Aramaic and Hebrew tribes. As military inferior nomads,
the Israelites are forced to get along with these groups of peoples,
and also with the invading Philistines on the west coast. They avoid
warring disputes as they are unable to carry out any real resistance
against an organized army.

The settlement of Canaan is rather peaceful. The tribes of Israel
live on the edges of the settlements, mostly in the unsettled, moun-
tainous tracts of land where they will not provoke anyone.[37] However, they quickly develop an active trade with the towns and learn
the language of the Canaanites. Their economic success fosters the

32   Hoffmeier, James K., Israel in Egypt, The Evidence for Authenticity of the Exodus Tradition, Oxford: Oxford University Press, 1997, p. 28.
33   Veen, Peter van der, Die el-Amarna-Habiru und die frühe Dynastie in Israel, in:
Veen, Peter van der und Zerbst, Uwe (ed.), Biblische Archäologie am Scheideweg?, Holz-
gerlingen: Hänssler Verlag, 2002, p. 359.
34   Vaux, Roland de, Histoire ancienne d'Israël, Volume I, Paris: Lecoffre, 1971,
p. 106ff.
35   Fifth Book of Moses (Deuteronomy) 10:8.
36   Fifth Book of Moses (Deuteronomy) 31:7.
37   Clauss, Manfred, Das alte Israel, Munich: C.H. Beck, 1999, p. 14ff.

growth of their military courage. After decades of settlement and adjustment, an Israelite army grows and attacks more and more Canaanite towns.

Circa 1230 B.C. marks the fall of Hazor, the capital of the kingdoms of Canaan.[38] Archaeological excavations confirm the destruction of the city during this period.[39] Over the next two hundred years, the Israelites conquer further villages and towns and new settlements develop in the kingdom of eastern Judah, but also in the hills of the kingdoms of Benjamin and Ephraim, which are situated to the north of present-day Jerusalem. This strong settlement of Israel after the capture of Hazor by Joshua is also for the part archaeologically confirmed. In the warring disputes against the Canaanites, the Israelites prefer to use guerilla tactics and avoid open, head-on attacks of fortresses.

It is at this time that we once again hear about the Ark of the Covenant. In the Book of Joshua, we read that God selects Joshua for a similar position as Moses and Joshua instructs the Levites to cross the Jordan River with the Ark:

> So when the people set out from their tents to cross the Jordan with the priests carrying the ark of the covenant before the people, and when those who carried the ark came into the Jordan, and the feet of the priests carrying the ark were dipped in the edge of the water (for the Jordan overflows all its banks all the days of harvest), the waters which were flowing down from above stood and rose up in one heap [...] So the people crossed opposite Jericho. And the priests who carried the ark of the covenant of the LORD stood firm on dry ground in the middle of the Jordan.[40]

This is one of the first reports about the wonderful capabilities of the Ark of the Covenant: The sacred box wherein God dwells is capable of putting the forces of nature out of action. Just a few chapters later, we are even more astonished when we read about how the Israelites conquer the city of Jericho. They manage to do so by marching around the city seven times with the Ark of the Covenant.

---

38   Joshua 11:10.
39   Ben-Sasson, H.H., Geschichte des jüdischen Volkes, von den Anfängen bis zur Gegenwart, Munich: C.H. Beck, 2004, p. 67ff.
40   Joshua 3:14-17.

The seven priests carrying the seven trumpets went forward, marching before the ark of the LORD and blowing the trumpets [...] On the seventh day, they got up at daybreak and marched around the city seven times in the same manner [...] the wall collapsed; so everyone charged straight in, and they took the city.[41]

Once again, we experience how the Ark of the Covenant seemingly defies the laws of nature and unleashes God's wrath. From 1200 to 1050 B.C. the armies of the Israelite tribes are ruled and commanded by the judges Ehud, Deborah, Gideon, Jephthah, Ibzan, Elon, Abdon and Samson. However, this form of government is incomparable from a political standpoint because it is based on the call for a leader in times of need and hardship – a form of government that is based on sheer charisma. The judge is appointed without taking into account their social origins or status. The tribe members who are in trouble push for the person whom they deem strong enough to lead them out of the crisis. Interestingly, in the patriarchal world of the Israelites, this could also be a woman like Deborah. The first judge, Ehud, dies and the Israelite people turns away from their belief in Yahweh. Deborah prevails upon Barak, the head captain of the Israelite army, and together they decide that it is God's will to vanquish Jabin, the king of Canaan, who rules over the people of Israel in Hazor. Deborah wins the battle.[42] However, from an archaeological standpoint, this battle does not appear to correspond to the Biblical details because after 1230 B.C. Hazor was no more than a village and it is thus improbable that Jabin even reigned there.[43]

The heathen Philistines are now settling on the west coast and invade Canaan circa 1050 B.C. The Israelite troops gather at Eben-Ezer. There and in the neighboring Aphek it comes to a bloody battle. But the Philistines are victorious, plunder Shiloh, the religious center of the Israelites, and steal the Ark of the Covenant from the Holy of Holies of the Tabernacle – in spite of the divine power emanating from the Ark of the Covenant: As the Old Testament

41   Joshua 6:6-20.
42   Judges 4:1-24.
43   Ben-Sasson, H.H., Geschichte des jüdischen Volkes, von den Anfängen bis zur Gegenwart, Munich: C.H. Beck, 2004, p. 88f.

relates: "And the Philistines fought, and Israel was smitten, and they fled every man into his tent: and there was a very great slaughter; for there fell of Israel thirty thousand footmen." [44]

Here we witness another strange incident. The Philistines bring the Ark from Eben-Ezer to Ashdod to the temple of their idol Dagon. When the Ark is placed in the temple of Dagon, however, its divine power makes the idol fall on its face to the earth. Ultimately, the idol breaks. It is destroyed by the Ark and the presence of Yahweh. A metaphor for the victory of monotheism over the heathen polytheism of the Philistines. The heathen priests are now afraid of the Ark. This fear is not unfounded because it is reported that the city of Ashdod and its surroundings are stricken by a mysterious scourge that causes tumors and is said to emanate from the Ark. The lords of the Philistines gather to discuss the fate of the Ark of the Covenant. Finally, they make the decision that they have to give the Ark back to the Israelites as fast as possible: "And they answered, 'Let the ark of the God of Israel be carried away to Gath.' So they carried the ark of the God of Israel away." [45]

When the Ark arrives in Gath, the people there are also infected by the mysterious divine illness and break out in tumors. As a result, the Ark is brought away from there as soon as possible and sent to Ekron. [46] But there it wreaks the same havoc. The Philistines recognize that it doesn't make sense to store the Ark in different places because in every place the same puzzling scourge of tumors breaks out. For seven months, the Ark was sent back and forth in the land of the Philistines as we would today treat a load of radioactive waste that nobody wants.

Ultimately, they load the Ark onto a cart pulled by two milk cows and send it down to the Israelite city of Beth Shemesh where the Levites receive the divine shrine. [47] As punishment that the inhabitants of Beth Shemesh curse the presence of the Ark, Jahweh, the LORD, kills 70 men, but it is unknown how. Consequently, the Ark of the Covenant is transported to Kiriath Jearim where it is

44   1 Samuel 4:1-11.
45   1 Samuel 5:8.
46   1 Samuel 5:1-12.
47   1 Samuel 6:1-17.

kept in Abinadab's house on the hill and guarded by his son Eleazar for 20 years.[48]

Under the rule of the last judge Samuel, the Israelites finally succeed in driving out the Philistines.[49] The Ark is brought back to Shiloh in the Holy of Holies.

Circa 1004 B.C. the Benjamite Saul is anointed King of Judah by Samuel.[50] Saul was victorious in the battle of Jabesh Gilead against the Ammonites and was thus chosen by the people as king. Later, he had to compete with the shepherd boy and subsequent Philistine mercenary David. David serves under Saul as an armor-bearer. The Bible reports that he played the lyre for Saul, "Then relief would come to Saul; he would feel better, and the evil spirit would leave him."[51] David vanquishes the Philistine Goliath with a sling and a stone, resulting in Saul making him a commander in his army.[52]

Saul gets angry with David because he achieves greater military success than himself. He believes that David wants to dispute his right to his throne and his rule over the lands of Judah and Benjamin. Ultimately, Saul's own family turns against him because they sympathize with David who intends to found another kingdom in the north. It couldn't get any worse for King Saul when his daughter Michal falls in love with David and they get married. Saul's son Jonathan betrays his father by warning David about him.[53] Saul gets depressed and becomes David's bitter enemy. In a battle against the Philistines he dies by his own sword and paves the way for the reign of David, his son-in-law.

The same year, revolt breaks out in a Jebusite village at the fortress of Zion under the onslaught of the army of David who has become the new regent after the suicide of King Saul of what is now the unified kingdom of Israel.[54]

The place is Jerusalem. It is 1000 B.C.

---

48   1 Samuel 7:1-2.
49   1 Samuel 16:13.
50   1 Samuel 10:1.
51   1 Samuel 16:21-23.
52   1 Samuel 17:12; 18:27.
53   1 Samuel 19:2-3.
54   2 Samuel 5:5.

The Temple of Solomon

The Bible reports that David gathered 30,000 men from his army to travel to Baalah in Judah. After 20 years, David has the Ark of the Covenant taken away from the house of Aminadab. He dances with joy before the Ark to songs and harps, lyres, timbrels, cymbals and trumpets. On the way to Jerusalem, one of Aminadab's sons, Uzzah, touches the Ark of the Covenant "because the oxen stumbled." The Lord's anger burns against Uzzah, and he strikes him down with a deadly blow. Out of fear of God and grief that Yahweh violently took Uzzah from him, David leaves the Ark of the Covenant in the house of Obed-Edom where it remains for three months. But then the Lord blesses the household. David stops procrastinating and has the Ark of the Covenant brought to Jerusalem, which at that time is a small town that is only populated by a few hundred inhabitants.[55] But David doesn't have the Ark brought to the town's temple, but instead to the Tabernacle, which was apparently erected at the Gihon spring.[56] David's tactic here is rather clever. He doesn't force the "one" God Yahweh on the population of Jerusalem, but in the form of the Ark of the Covenant and the Tabernacle ranks him side by side with the other gods who are worshiped. Thus, Yahweh is introduced to Jerusalem and Judah in a gradual process.[57]

With his second wife Bathsheba, David has a son Solomon whom he names his heir to the throne. The Bible story of King Solomon is unexpectedly short in view of the fact that his legacy would influence the fate of Israel and the Middle East for the next three millennia and beyond. After describing how the high priest Zadok anoints David's son Solomon king, there is a strange leap in time because the following sentence sounds like it was plucked right out of a school essay that was cut short: "So Solomon sat on the throne of the Lord as king."[58]

The Bible describes how Solomon marries the daughter of the Egyptian pharaoh. We find out something about the size of his kingdom which extends from the Euphrates to Gaza.[59] His army

---

55   2 Samuel 6:1-23.
56   1 Kings 1:33-39.
57   Zwickel, Wolfgang, Der Salomonische Tempel, Mainz: Verlag Philipp von Zabern, 1999, p. 23ff.
58   1 Kings 1:46.
59   1 Kings 5:4.

consists of four thousand stalls for horses and chariots and twelve thousand horsemen. We learn of his highly reputed wisdom which is said to be greater than that of the Egyptians, and which can undoubtedly only be ascribed to clever state propaganda in the style of the Assyrian kings.[60] Hiram, King of Tyre, who had always been on friendly terms with King David, finds out about this news.

It appears that King Solomon's plans to replace the mobile Tabernacle of acacia wood with a temple for the Ark of the Covenant have continued to flourish because Hiram fulfills Solomon's request for cedar and juniper wood. Solomon repays him with unlimited amounts of pressed olive oil and twenty thousand cors of wheat. King Hiram I of Tyre praises the plans of King Solomon to build a temple for the LORD in a letter.[61]

As support he sends the chief architect Hiram-Abiff (Huram), the son of a widow from the tribe of Naphtali and of a father who worked as a bronzesmith in Tyre.[62] The literary description of the construction project is very elegant.

> In the four hundred and eightieth year after the Israelites came out of Egypt, in the fourth year of Solomon's reign over Israel, in the month of Ziv, the second month, he began to build the temple of the Lord.

We read that it simply *happens*, that construction material is requested and slave laborers – seventy thousand men to bear burdens, eighty thousand to quarry stone and three thousand six hundred to oversee them – build a temple. The construction takes seven years.[63] The Book of Chronicles tells us more about the situation: It is built on Mount Zion, which is today the location of the Dome of the Rock – in Arabic: Qubbet as-sakhra – which with its golden dome is the modern-day landmark of Jerusalem. The entrance is in the east, the Holy of Holies in the west. The entire complex is sectioned off by a wall. The following is a detailed description of the Temple:

---

60   Finkelstein, Israel and Neil A. Silberman, David und Salomo, Archäologen entschlüsseln einen Mythos, Munich: C.H. Beck, p. 157f
61   2 Chronicles 2:11-12.
62   1 Kings 7:13-14.
63   1 Kings 6:38.

 God's Ark

The portico at the front of the temple was twenty cubits long across the width of the building and twenty cubits high. He overlaid the inside with pure gold. He paneled the main hall with juniper and covered it with fine gold and decorated it with palm tree and chain designs. He adorned the temple with precious stones. And the gold he used was gold of Parvaim. He overlaid the ceiling beams, doorframes, walls and doors of the temple with gold, and he carved cherubim on the walls. He built the Most Holy Place, its length corresponding to the width of the temple – twenty cubits long and twenty cubits wide. He overlaid the inside with six hundred talents of fine gold. The gold nails weighed fifty shekels. He also overlaid the upper parts with gold. For the Most Holy Place he made a pair of sculptured cherubim and overlaid them with gold. The total wingspan of the cherubim was twenty cubits. One wing of the first cherub was five cubits long and touched the temple wall, while its other wing, also five cubits long, touched the wing of the other cherub. Similarly one wing of the second cherub was five cubits long and touched the other temple wall, and its other wing, also five cubits long, touched the wing of the first cherub. The wings of these cherubim extended twenty cubits. They stood on their feet, facing the main hall. He made the curtain of blue, purple and crimson yarn and fine linen, with cherubim worked into it.[64]

Before the entrance of the temple, two bronze pillars are erected, which are 8.2 meters high and 1.8 meters thick, and are called *Boaz* ("in him is strength") and Jakin ("he establishes"). Once the construction phase is complete, Solomon summons to Jerusalem the elders of Israel to place the golden sacred objects in the throne hall and the Ark of the Covenant in the Holy of Holies. "When all the work Solomon had done for the temple of the LORD was finished, he brought in the things his father David had dedicated – the silver and gold and all the furnishings – and he placed them in the treasuries of GOD's temple."

According to the description, the Temple of Solomon is architecturally subdivided into three parts: It consists of a fifty cubits-long colonnade, which leads to a square, central main hall

64   2 Chronicles 3:1-17.

113

in which the sacred objects such as the seven-branched Menorah, the table of the bread of the Presence (shewbread) and the altar of incense are kept. In the inner sanctuary is the 20 cubit-long Holy of Holies in which the Ark of the Covenant is kept. Converted to today's dimensions, the temple is thus 10.5 meters wide. The portico is 5.25 meters long, the main hall is 31.5 meters long and the Holy of Holies – as the location of the Ark of the Covenant – is 10.5 meters long.[65]

The main hall is separated from the Holy of Holies by a curtain. Apart from the portico, both rooms are paneled with cedar and the Holy of Holies is even covered in it from floor to ceiling. The wood panels are decorated with flowers and tendrils and stylized trees of life as a metaphor for the fruitful Garden of Paradise. Solomon has windows built into the temple that are secured with metal rods. So whoever wants to break into the temple from outside to steal the golden sacred objects will be disappointed.[66] The Levites who are guarding the temple can only be overcome by a military power.[67] Therefore, the Ark of the Covenant is very securely housed in the Temple of Solomon. Alone the attempt of theft is punished by death.

A structure is built around the portico, the main hall and the Holy of Holies: "Against the walls of the main hall and inner sanctuary he built a structure around the building, in which there were side rooms. The lowest floor was five cubits wide, the middle floor six cubits and the third floor seven. He made offset ledges around the outside of the temple so that nothing would be inserted into the temple walls."

Amazingly, here we discover the description of an apse, a termination to a choir, the likes of which we first find in France's medieval Gothic cathedrals. Here, too, small chapels are inserted like "side rooms." This apse is three meters high. From bottom to top, the individual rooms of the structure are each 2.5 meters, 3 meters and 3.5 meters. Here, too, we discover a similarity to the Gothic cathedrals because the force that is exerted outwards by the great height of the

---

65   1 Kings 7:44; cf. Bieberstein, Klaus, Im Zentrum das Leben – den Tod in der Peripherie, Jerusalem kultursemiotisch gelesen, in: "uni.vers," issue 6/2004, Universität Bamberg, p. 28.

66   1 Kings 6:4.

67   1 Chronicles 26:20.

construction is compensated for and redirected by abutments. The walls of the temple are 3 meters thick and made of unhewn stone because the altar law forbids cutting stones for the construction.[68] The roof of the temple is covered with beams and cedar planks.[69] The large Altar of Burnt Offering stands in the courtyard, before the entrance to the actual temple. Next to the Altar of Burnt Offering stands a bronze basin (laver) in the shape of a lotus basin that is standing on 12 bulls for the high priests to wash themselves.[70]

If we take a look at the portico, we notice that – with a height of 120 cubits (54 meters) – it is higher than the remaining temple and strikingly stretches into the sky like the bell tower of a cathedral. Viewed from the front, the temple has the architecture of an abstract basilica, which is defined by the characteristics of the elevated central aisle and lower side aisles. As a result, the Temple of Solomon can be viewed as the Biblical blueprint for the Gothic cathedrals of the Middle Ages.

It is 956 B.C.

The Fate of the Ark of the Covenant

King Solomon dies circa 926 B.C. His legacy in the form of the Temple of Solomon must have seemed very impressive to the inhabitants of Jerusalem because this was the first thing to be built on the plateau of the Temple Mount. Now a dwelling for the Ark of the Covenant rises up into the city's sky and the people of Jerusalem can only dream of what wonderful treasures are hidden inside it. The archaeologists Israel Finkelstein and Neil Silberman note that the Temple of Solomon must originally have been a smaller site than described in the Bible. But over the course of the city of Jerusalem's economic growth, the Temple got bigger and bigger.[71] Stories about the legendary treasure of the Temple of Solomon seem to have also spread to the kingdoms of Assyria and Egypt. The Bible reports that in 926 B.C. the Egyptian King Shishak in-

---

68   Zwickel, Wolfgang, Der Salomonische Tempel, Mainz: Verlag Philipp von Zabern, 1999, p. 49ff.
69   1 Kings 6:5-10.
70   Ibid., p. 29.
71   Finkelstein, Israel and Neal A. Silberman, David und Salomo, Archäologen entschlüsseln einen Mythos, Munich: C.H. Beck, p. 157f.

vades Jerusalem during the reign of Solomon's son Rehoboam as King of Jerusalem und Judah.[72] The attack of the Egyptian Pharaoh Shoshenq I on a relief in the Temple of Amun at Karnak has been archaeologically confirmed. The archaeologists Finkelstein and Silberman agree that the Biblical King Shishak and the Egyptian Pharaoh Shoshenq I were one and the same person.[73] The Bible tells how Shishak, a pharaoh of the 22nd dynasty with Libyan heritage, destroyed the city of Jerusalem and plundered the Temple of Solomon. He stole the treasures from the main hall: "Shishak king of Egypt came up against Jerusalem, and took away the treasures of the house of the LORD, and the treasures of the king's house; he took all: he carried away also the shields of gold which Solomon had made."[74]

The Jewish historian Flavius Josephus describes this event a little more drastically because Shoshenq I "spoiled the temple, and emptied the treasures of God, and those of the king, and carried off innumerable ten thousands of gold and silver, and left nothing at all behind him."[75] It becomes obvious here that Shoshenq I plundered the treasures, i.e the main hall, but not the Holy of Holies with the Ark of the Covenant.

There are two reasons why it is impossible for the Ark of the Covenant to have been stolen by Shoshenq I's troops. Firstly, the Ark of the Covenant is mentioned again in subsequent Biblical reports. Secondly, Jerusalem is no longer mentioned in writings on the relief in the Great Hypostyle Hall in Karnak. Finkelstein and Silberman conclude that during the reign of Shoshenq I as a place Jerusalem was simply too insignificant to be worth being plundered by Egyptian troops. According to Finkelstein and Silberman, circa 926 B.C. Judah was mostly an isolated tribe. As a result, it is difficult to imagine that a culture so lacking in material objects would have produced treasures that were of interest to Shoshenq I. In other words: The invasion of Jerusalem by Pharaoh's troops, as described in the Bible, didn't take place at all because the mountains

72   1 Kings 14:24f.
73   Finkelstein, Israel and Neal A. Silberman, David und Salomo, Archäologen entschlüsseln einen Mythos, Munich: C.H. Beck, p. 67.
74   2 Chronicles 12:9.
75   Flavius Josephus, Antiquities of the Jews, Book 8, Chapter 10:3.

of Judah would have been completely uninteresting to Shoshenq I. Consequently, the treasures of the main hall remained unscathed in the Temple of Solomon and the Ark of the Covenant remained unscathed in the Holy of Holies.[76] Whether the archaeological argumentation or the Biblical statement is correct, the Ark of the Covenant remained in Jerusalem.

In 597 B.C. the Babylonians attack Jerusalem. The attack on Jerusalem is archaeologically confirmed by the discovery of two clay tablets with cuneiform script that was deciphered. They report: "In the seventh month (of Nebuchadnezzar) in the month Chislev the king of Babylon assembled his army, and after he had invaded the land of Hatti [Syria/Palestine] he laid siege to the city of Judah. On the second day of the month of Adara [March 16th 597] he conquered the city.[77]" The Babylonians capture King Jehoiakim and install a ruler that looks kindly on them: Zedekiah. For almost 400 years, Jerusalem's Temple of Solomon remained untouched on Mount Zion. Even the Babylonian attack of 597 B.C. was rather mild.

However, in 587 B.C. the armies of the Babylonian King Nebuchadnezzar II invade Jerusalem again and pillage and burn the temple. At first, it seems as if the Ark of the Covenant and all other temple treasures have been destroyed or transported away to Babylon to be melted down. However, the Bible reports that King Jehoiakim, who swore an oath of fealty to the Babylonian King, rises up against Nebuchadnezzar II. The King of Babylon refuses to put up with this aggression and mobilizes his armies against Jerusalem. Due to its fortifications and elevated geographic location, the city is unable to be taken in a surprise attack. As a result, the Babylonians besiege Jerusalem for 18 whole months.[78] Flavius Josephus describes the invasion of the Babylonians rather graphically:

> And now it was that the king of Babylon sent Nebuzaradan, the general of his army, to Jerusalem, to pillage the temple, who had it also in command to burn it and the royal palace,

---

76   Finkelstein, Israel and Neal A. Silberman, David und Salomo, Archäologen entschlüsseln einen Mythos, Munich: C.H. Beck, p. 72f.
77   Keller, Werner, Und die Bibel hat doch recht, Forscher beweisen die Wahrheit des alten Testaments, Düsseldorf: Econ-Verlag, 1955, p. 267.
78   2 Kings 25:1-21; Jeremiah 39:1-18.

and to lay the city even with the ground, and to transplant the people into Babylon. Accordingly, he came to Jerusalem in the eleventh year of king Zedekiah, and pillaged the temple, and carried out the vessels of God, both gold and silver, and particularly that large laver which Solomon dedicated, as also the pillars of brass, and their chapiters, with the golden tables and the candlesticks; and when he had carried these off, he set fire to the temple [...][79]

The troops of the Babylonian King Nebuchadnezzar II steal the table of the bread of the Presence and the seven-branched Menorah. However, the theft of the Ark of the Covenant by the Babylonians is mentioned neither in the Bible nor by Flavius Josephus. Even the records of the treasures of Nebuchadnezzar II found during excavations in Babylon that were held as part of an expedition of the German Oriental Society (DOG) in 1898 do not list a golden shrine that might be remotely connected to the Ark of the Covenant.[80]

The Ark of the Covenant also remained unscathed during this attack because it was first hidden. Let's not forget that Jerusalem had been besieged 18 months prior to this by the Babylonian army. The high priests and the Levites thus had sufficient time to bring God's shrine to a safe place, but the siege forced them to hide the Ark within Jerusalem's city walls. In the Second Book of Chronicles, we read that King Josiah circa 620 B.C., almost 30 years before the Babylonian invasion, instructs the Levites to carry the Ark of the Covenant back to the Holy of Holies. Obviously, it was first hidden in an unknown location to prevent the golden shrine from being melted down and used to pay annual tributes.[81] As the situation in Jerusalem escalated, it is very probable that the Levites decided to leave the Ark in its hiding place.

In this context, Chapter 52 of the Book of Jeremiah is very interesting as it describes how Nebuzaradan, the captain of the guard, takes the chief priest of the temple, Seraiah, the second priest Zephaniah and the three Levite keepers of the door to the king of Babylon to

79   Flavius Josephus, Antiquities of the Jews, Book 10, Chapter 8:1-7.
80   Andrews, Richard, Tempel der Verheißung, Das Geheimnis des heiligen Berges von Jerusalem, Bergisch-Gladbach: Lübbe-Verlag, 1999, p. 42.
81   2 Chronicles 35:3.

Riblah. There they are interrogated and put to death. It is very obvious why: King Nebuchadnezzar II's torturers were not capable of getting the chief priest and Levites to confess where they hid the Ark.[82]

But where was this hiding place? The Babylonian Talmud provides information on this. It was composed circa 70 A.D. after the destruction of Jerusalem by the Roman armies of Emperor Titus and its main contributors were the rabbis Abba Arikha, Samuel Jarchinai and Rab Ashi. The Jerusalem Talmud and the Babylonian Talmud provide a commentary on the Biblical events of the Old Testament. In the Tract *Shekalim* of the Talmud Yerushalmi we find the following passage:

> The family of R. Gamaliel and of R. Hananiah, chief of the priests, made fourteen prostrations; this extra prostration was made towards the wood-chamber, because, according to an ancestral tradition, the ark was hidden there. Once a priest was engaged there, and he noticed that one of the paving-stones on one place appeared different from the others. He went out to tell others of it; but he had not yet finished speaking, when he gave up the ghost; thereby it was known to a certainty that the ark of the covenant was hidden there.[83]

The Babylonian Talmud, on the other hand, reports that "R. Jehudah, however, says: The ark was concealed in its place (Temple), as it is written [1 Kings viii. 8]: 'And they had made the staves so long, that the ends of the staves were seen out in the holy place in the front of the Debir, but they were not seen without; and they have remained there until this day.'"[84]

Within the rabbi community, at the time of the creation of the Talmud, there was a heated debate on where the Ark had ended up after the invasion by the army of King Nebuchadnezzar II. Thus, in the Babylonian Talmud, a few passages later we read a less ambiguous statement of the rabbis on where the Ark was hidden:

> Said R. Na'hman b. Itz'hak: We have also learned it in a Mishna in Shekalim [VI., b]: "Once a priest was engaged there, and

---

82   Jeremiah 52:24-27.
83   Talmud Yerushalmi, Shekalim, Pereq, 6,1-2.
84   Babylonian Talmud, Yomah V, 53b.

he noticed that one of the paving stones on one place appeared different from the others. He went out to tell others of it; but he had not yet finished speaking, when he gave up the ghost. Thereby it was known to a certainty that the ark of the covenant was hidden there."[85]

In the Mishneh Torah, on the other hand, the interpretation of the Talmud scholar Moses Maimonides from the 12th century, we read the following about the whereabouts of the Ark:

> The Ark was placed on a stone in the western portion of the Holy of Holies. The vial of manna and Aharon's staff were placed before it. When Solomon built the Temple, he was aware that it would ultimately be destroyed. [Therefore,] he constructed a chamber, in which the ark could be entombed below [the Temple building] in deep, maze-like vaults. King Josiah commanded that [the Ark] be entombed in the chamber built by Solomon [...] When it was entombed, Aharon's staff, the vial of manna, and the oil used for anointing were entombed with it. All these [sacred articles] did not return in the Second Temple.[86]

When the Levites were commanded by King Josiah circa 620 B.C. to remove the Ark from the Holy of Holies, they brought God's shrine to an underground hiding place beneath the wooden chamber. A stone marked the entrance to the underground storage place of the Ark of the Covenant. As there were also other buildings next to the Temple of Solomon, including the King's Palace and storage rooms, it is certain that the Ark of the Covenant was hidden beneath the Temple Mount in one of the innumerable chambers that were discovered by the English Charles Warren Expedition in the 1860s.[87]

---

85   Babylonian Talmud, Yomah V, 54a.
86   Mishneh Torah, Moses Maimonides, Book 8:4,1.
87   The Second Book of the Maccabees, which was written in the 2nd century B.C., mentions that the Prophet Jeremiah, who prophesied the destruction of the temple and Jerusalem by the Babylonians, hid the Ark of the Covenant together with the tent of meeting and the altar of incense in a cave on Mount Nebo (cf. 2 Maccabees 2:4-7). Nebo is the mountain in present-day Jordan from which Moses saw the Promised Land before he died and was buried there. However, it is extremely improbable that Jeremiah was able to smuggle the Ark of the Covenant through the Babylonian enemy lines. The Ark would have been carried off by the Babylonians. The Babylonian inventories prove that this was not the case.

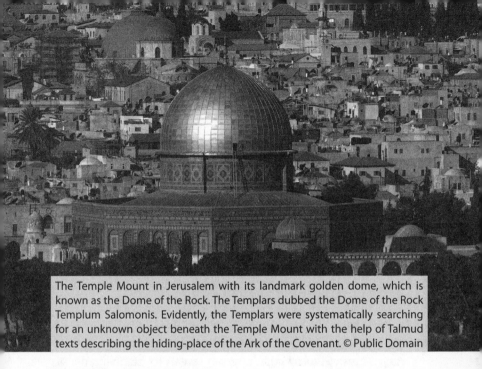

The Temple Mount in Jerusalem with its landmark golden dome, which is known as the Dome of the Rock. The Templars dubbed the Dome of the Rock Templum Salomonis. Evidently, the Templars were systematically searching for an unknown object beneath the Temple Mount with the help of Talmud texts describing the hiding-place of the Ark of the Covenant. © Public Domain

The Glory of the Kings

Since the Babylonian invasion of Jerusalem in 587 B.C., the Ark of the Covenant has been missing. Various theories have been proposed about the fate of this Biblical treasure. A highly debated theory is the possibility that the Ark of the Covenant is located in Ethiopia. The *Kebra Negast* is the main reason for this speculation. This manuscript was composed in Coptic between 1314 and 1321 A.D. in Ethiopia and consists of 117 chapters. *The Glory of the Kings* resembles the minutes of a discussion of a synod of 317 bishops who are debating fundamental questions of belief. The question "What is the Glory of the Kings?" is answered with the claim that the glory of the Roman empire pales in comparison to the Empire of Ethiopia because Ethiopia owns the Ark of the Covenant that Moses had made to store the tablets of God's covenant law. But how could the Ark of the Covenant have reached Ethiopia?

The Kebra Negast reports that the Queen of Sheba, Makeda, learns from a merchant based in her kingdom, Tamrin, of the wisdom and the riches of Solomon and decides to travel from Ethiopia to Israel. She gives King Solomon great treasures and his wisdom causes her to believe in the one God Yahweh. Solomon, who is known from Babel to Ashkelon as a womanizer, is said in the Bible to have impregnated several hundred women. He sleeps with Makeda and gives her a ring as a symbol of recognition for his future child. On the journey home, the Queen gives birth to a son: Menelik I.[88]

As a young man, Menelik I travels with some companions to Jerusalem, seeking Solomon's blessing, and identifies himself to his father with the ring that his mother Makeda was given by Solomon. Solomon shows his appreciation to Menelik by giving him the cloth that covers the Ark of the Covenant. He tries to convince Menelik to succeed him as King of Judah.[89] But Menelik I wants to return to his mother. When he returns to Ethiopia, his companions reveal to him that they took the Ark of the Covenant out of the Holy of Holies without his knowledge and replaced it with a copy because they were upset that they had to leave Jerusalem.[90] The Ethiopian Zacharias pressures Azarias, the son of the High Priest Zadok, to use the keys of the High Priest and the secret windows of King Solomon to enter the Holy of Holies.

Azarias proves to be corrupt as he reveals to Menelik's people how they can enter the Holy of Holies: "Come now, let us take [with us] our Lady ZION; but how are we to take her? I will show you."

We discover that they produce an imitation that they swap for the real Ark of the Covenant in the Holy of Holies. Azarias answers:

> Give ye to me each of you ten didrachmas, and I will give them to a carpenter so that he will make haste to prepare for me good planks of wood – now because of his love of money he will fasten them together very quickly – of the height, and breadth, and length and size of our Lady [ZION]. [...] And I will take the framework without the pieces of wood thereof being fixed together, and I will have them put together in ETHIOPIA. And I will set them down in the habitation of ZION, and will drape them with the draperies of ZION, and I will take ZION [ed: the Ark of the Covenant], and will dig a hole in the ground, and will set ZION there, until we journey and take it away with us thither. And I will not tell the matter to the king until we have travelled far.[91]

88   Kebra Negast, Munich: Verlag der K.B. Akademie, 1909 (Abhandlungen der philosophisch-philologischen Klasse der königlich-bayerischen Akademie der Wissenschaften 23), Chapter 32.
89   Ibid., Chapter 33.
90   Ibid., Chapter 45.
91   Ibid., Chapter 45.

We read about the theft of the Ark in a hush-hush operation. The Angel of the LORD opens the gates of the temple and the Holy of Holies to the intruders. "Now they found all the doors open, both those that were outside and those that were inside – to the actual place where AZÂRYÂS found ZION, the Tabernacle of the Law of God; and it was taken away by them forthwith, in the twinkling of an eye, the Angel of the Lord being present and directing. And had it not been that God willed it ZION could not have been taken away forthwith."[92]

They steal the Ark and store it in Azarias' house. Then Azarias' brothers return to the temple and make a new Ark on site with the boards. When the Ethiopians leave Jerusalem, the city is in turmoil. Solomon is surprised about the noise. He notices the disappearance of the Ark and sends out soldiers to catch up with Menelik and bring back the Ark of the Covenant.[93] However, Menelik is carried by an angel with the Ark to Ethiopia before Solomon can put a stop to his escape. Menelik has the Ark carried ahead of him in battles. Since this time, the Empire of Ethiopia has been unconquerable. Makeda abdicates the throne in favor of her son.

Henceforth, the local tradition has been that the Ark of the Covenant remains in Ethiopia. The Kebra Negast ends with the Jews being depicted as the enemy of God who do not deserve to own the Ark of the Covenant.[94] The Jews are destroyed when Christ arrives. Strange that such a people who longed for the downfall of the Jews would be chosen by God to protect the Israelites' Ark of the Covenant.

This report about the transportation of the Ark to Ethiopia becomes problematic when we realize that no High Priest would ever have allowed the golden chest with its cherubims to be taken out of the Holy of Holies and replaced with a copy. The Kebra Negast mentions secret windows that were supposedly only known to King Solomon and through which the robbers entered to steal the Ark. It is not mentioned how they knew about the secret windows. King Solomon did not have his temple built to have the Ark of the

---

92   Ibid., Chapter 48.
93   Ibid., Chapter 60.
94   Ibid., Chapter 117.

Covenant stolen. The Ark was the manifestation of God in Israel. It was placed under maximum security. Therefore, the fact that Menelik I was flown with the Ark to Egypt by an angel is not very believable. If we assume that his companions would have been capable of stealing the Ark from the temple and replacing it with an imitation, at least the Levites should have sounded the alarm and had the intruders arrested before this trick could have been carried out.

It becomes even more problematic if we take a look at the Bible and notice that the Ark of the Covenant was mentioned and described again after the visit of the Queen of Sheba and that it remained in the Jerusalem temple. This Ark is definitely not the imitation of Menelik's entourage. Furthermore, the theft of the Ark and its transportation by Menelik's companions would have been mentioned in the Bible. However, neither a theft of the Ark nor an imitation nor a Menelik are mentioned in a single word. This obvious problem of the claim about the supposed Ethiopian possession of the Ark of the Covenant due to the theft of Menelik's companions is something that British journalist Graham Hancock attempts to explain away in his book *The Sign and the Seal* by the behavior of the Jewish despotic king Manasseh.

Manasseh ruled the Southern Kingdom of Judah between 696 and 641 B.C. He was feared for his brutal tyranny, for his currying favor with the Assyrian kings Sennacherib and Esarhaddon and notorious for reintroducing heathen idols.[95] The Bible tells how Manasseh had the God Baal installed in the Temple of Solomon so that he could be worshiped instead of Yahweh.[96] Hancock concludes from this that the High Priests brought the Ark of the Covenant to safety from Manasseh before the King could melt it down together with the Jewish temple treasures. Hancock believes that the High Priests initially brought the Ark to the 3/4 mile wide Egyptian island Elephantine in Upper Egypt on the Nile River where it was kept in a temple dedicated to Yahweh and the goddess Anath-Bethel.[97] The Elephantine Papyri confirm that a garrison of Jewish soldiers lived on the

---

95   1 Chronicles 33:1-18.
96   2 Kings 21: 1-18.
97   Hancock, Graham, Die Wächter des heiligen Siegels, Bergisch-Gladbach: Lübbe-Verlag, 1999, p. 391.

island circa 650 B.C. The temple was destroyed circa 410 B.C. and subsequently rebuilt.[98]

Hancock suspects that the Ark was brought from there up the Nile in the direction of Ethiopia, where the island of Tana Kirkos in Lake Tana subsequently became its resting place for several centuries.[99] On the island, Ethiopian Jews, the Falasha, guarded the Ark. Even today, old legends are circulating among the priesthood of the island that lead one to suspect the supposed presence of the Ark of the Covenant there. According to Hancock, the Ark of the Covenant was then taken from the island of Tana Kirkos to Lalibela, the capital of the old Empire of Ethiopia. Lalibela with its 13 monolithic red basalt rock-cut churches, which were hewn out of a piece of the cliffs in the 12th century, is a UNESCO World Heritage Site. Hancock claims to have discovered traces of the Templars inside these churches. He concludes from this that the Templars searched for the Ark here. In one church there is a Templar red cross in a Star of David, as well as the depiction of the Dome of the Rock with a crucifix at the top – a symbol for the Templar occupation of the Temple Mount.

Hancock believes that during their stay in Jerusalem the Templars talked to the Ethiopian King Lalibela, who was staying in Jerusalem from 1160 to 1185 and who told them that the Ark of the Covenant was in Ethiopia. Subsequently, the Templars traveled to Ethiopia and made a deal with the King. Graham Hancock goes so far as to claim that the rock-cut churches of the town of Lalibela – formerly Roha, which changed its name to Lalibela in honor of its king and was erected as a new Jerusalem – were built with the help of the Templars. Ultimately, he claims, the Ark of the Covenant was brought to Aksum where it is today still located in the Church of Our Lady Mary of Zion and watched over by a chosen guard.

However, Hancock's theory falls short due to its logical flaws in reasoning: If we are to assume that a delegation of Templars traveled to Ethiopia and found the Ark there, then they would have violently taken the shrine and transported it to France. The Templars were warrior monks who, to put it mildly, were not afraid to use

98   Parfitt, Tudor, Die Jagd nach der verschollenen Bundeslade, Munich: DTV, 2009, p. 165f.
99   Hancock, Graham, Die Wächter des heiligen Siegels, Bergisch-Gladbach: Lübbe-Verlag, 1999, p. 209ff.

their swords. They were in search of the holiest object in human history. As we already know from Bernard of Clairvaux's treatise "In Praise of the New Knighthood," the Templars identified themselves as *the true Israelites*. The true Israelites could only discover the reason for their existence by possessing the Ark of the Covenant. There is proof that the rock-cut churches of Lalibela were not built by the Templars, but by Ethiopian master builders. The supposed Templar crosses are religious Christian-Coptic symbols that suggest an Aksumite origin.[100] The Jewish temple on the island of Elephantine also paid tribute to heathen gods. Undoubtedly, such a blasphemous place would have been just as unsuitable for the Ark as the Temple of Solomon, which was briefly desecrated by Manasseh by the installation of heathen idols. Furthermore, the Jewish reports about Elephantine don't mention a single word about the Ark of the Covenant.

However, the greatest weakness about Hancock's theory is the fact that the Ark of the Covenant is mentioned again in the Bible *after* the reign of King Manasseh. As we have already seen, King Josiah instructed the Levites circa 620 B.C. to put the Ark back in the Holy of Holies in the Temple of Solomon. This occurred twenty-two years *after the death* of Manasseh. It is obvious that, for fear of Manasseh's worship of idols, the Levites removed the Ark from the Holy of Holies and hid it. After Manasseh's death, King Josiah instructed them to bring the Ark back to its intended resting place. Whether or not they followed Josiah's command is unclear. It is also possible that they left the Ark in its hiding place until the conflict had died down, or that they hid it again after they returned to the temple. The hiding place for the Ark of the Covenant, which King Solomon (according to the description in Book 8, Chapter 4:1 of the Mishneh Torah) had installed under the temple was undoubtedly easy to access, but still effective and not easy to find. The Ark remained in the many labyrinthine passageways of the Temple Mount.

As the Talmud confirms, the Ark remained in this hiding place until the Babylonian troops of Nebuchadnezzar II besieged and ultimately plundered Jerusalem circa 587 B.C. Subsequently, as we have seen, the Bible remains silent about the fate of the Ark.

---

100   Buxton, David, The Abyssinians, New York: Praeger, 1970, p. 103f.

Tudor Parfitt, Professor of Modern Jewish Studies at the School of Oriental and African Studies of the University of London, checked Hancock's theory and the claim of the Ethiopian-Coptic church that the Ark of the Covenant is located in Aksum.[101] After extensive research in Aksum and the vicinity, he came to the conclusion that all Ethiopian records that were composed before and after the Kebra Negast did not mention a single word about the Jewish Ark of the Covenant. In addition, the Kebra Negast lacks the temporal proximity to the events described as it wasn't composed until the beginning of the 14th century and partially put together from the Old and New Testament. Parfitt's research proves that the Ark of the Covenant is neither in Aksum nor in Ethiopia. The myth was spurred from the desire of the Ethiopians to enhance their self-worth from the claim that they possessed the Ark. As a result, every Ethiopian church contains copies of the tablets of the covenant law that are known as *tabot* and allegedly document the supposed claim of the Ethiopians to the Ark of the Covenant.[102]

To date, the Christian Coptic church of Ethiopia claims that they own the Ark of the Covenant. Thus, in June 2009, during a stay at the Vatican for a press conference, the Patriarch Abuna Paulos announced that the Ark of the Covenant with the Mosaic tablets of the covenant law is located in the Church of Our Lady Mary of Zion in Aksum. The leader of the Ethiopian Orthodox Church said: "The Ark of the Covenant is in Ethiopia for many centuries. I repeat (the Ark of the Covenant) is in Ethiopia and nobody … knows for how much time. Only God knows." However, after this surprising statement, he added a slight reservation: "I have seen it with my own eyes and only few highly qualified persons could do the same, until now."[103]

---

101   That said, Tudor Parfitt's own hypothesis about the whereabouts of the Ark of the Covenant is even more adventurous. Parfitt believes that "the drum of the ancestors" – the Ngoma Lungundu – of the Lemba people of Zimbabwe is the Ark of the Covenant. According to DNA analyses, the Lemba are direct descendants of the Kohanim, a subgroup of the tribe of Levi. Moses allegedly had the drum crafted as a container for the Ten Commandments. This bizarre Ark ended up in Zimbabwe. In his enthusiasm for the Lemba people, Parfitt forgets that the Bible doesn't mention a single word about the Ark of the Covenant as a drum. It was always a box.

102   Parfitt, Tudor, Die Jagd nach der verschollenen Bundeslade, Munich: DTV, 2009, p. 174f.

103   Badde, Paul, Hat die äthiopische Kirche die heilige Bundeslade, in: Die Welt, June 22 2009, http://www.welt.de/kultur/article3974007/Hat-die-aethiopische-Kirche-die-heilige-Bundeslade.html.

The Ark could not be shown to anyone, just a priest who had dedicated his whole life to guarding the divine shrine. The *Adnkronos* news agency must have misinterpreted this information because on November 23, 2009, it reported that the Ark of the Covenant, a few days after the Patriarch's press conference, was presented to the global public – and a few days later it retracted this statement. To the disappointment of many supporters of the Ethiopian theory, nothing of the kind was shown to the world.

In actual fact, there is not the slightest proof for the former existence of a Queen of Sheba or her son Menelik. After researching ancient oral folk tales about the palace of the Queen of Sheba, in 2007 the archaeologist Helmut Ziegert from the University of Hamburg and his excavation team claim to have discovered what Ziegert believes to be part of the Queen's palace from the 10th century B.C.[104] Ziegert concludes that the Ark of the Covenant rested on a particular stone altar. He believes that the Ark was brought to Ethiopia because Jerusalem, as a constantly fought over location, had become too dangerous for the Ark. In an interview that he gave to the *National Geographic* magazine in 2008, Ziegert described the Ark of the Covenant that was located in Aksum in the Church of Our Lady Mary of Zion in Aksum: "It is a 50 by 50 box made of cedar wood. It contains two one centimeter-thick square stone tablets engraved in Ancient Hebrew with the Ten Commandments."[105]

Professor Ziegert was able to indirectly entice this information out of the guardian of the Ark of the Covenant. Thus, the archaeologist ultimately proves the absurdity of the theory: the Bible tells how the Ark was crafted by Bezalel from *acacia wood*, not from cedar wood. Moreover, the dimensions do not match the Biblical dimensions. The fact that the supposed Ark of Aksum was crafted from cedar wood and is thus not authentic matches the description of the Armenian pilgrim Dimotheos. He saw the Ark in Aksum in 1868 and described it as Indian in origin with ancient Ethiopian characters, and he estimated that it was made in the 14th century,

104   Ziegert, Helmut, press release, Archaeological Institute of the University of Hamburg, 5/7/2008.
105   Schüle, Christian, Die Hüter der Bundeslade, in: Die Bundeslade, article in the National Geographic, November 2008, p. 90.

that era in which the Kebra Negast also came into being.[106] Whatever the Patriarch of the Ethiopian church saw or Professor Ziegert heard from the guardian of the Ark, it was definitely not the real Ark of the Covenant. Instead, it was merely a Christian imitation.[107]

The Ark Under the Temple Mount

We now know that following the Babylonian invasion of Jerusalem in 587 B.C. the Ark of the Covenant remained in its hiding place under the Temple Mount. After that it is no longer mentioned in the Bible. In the Book of Jeremiah, we read how the Prophet foretells of a time in which the Ark of the Covenant will no longer play a role because it will disappear: "'In those days, when your numbers have increased greatly in the land,' declares the LORD, 'people will no longer say, 'The ark of the covenant of the LORD.' It will never enter their minds or be remembered; it will not be missed, nor will another one be made.'"[108]

In other words: It won't be destroyed, but it will be hidden. After the destruction of Jerusalem by the Babylonians, the Bible is silent about the Ark of the Covenant and only mentions it again in the New Testament Books of Hebrews and Revelation. The Holy of Holies of the second temple, which Zerubbabel, the governor of Judah and grandson of King Jehoiakim, had built some time before 516 B.C., and also the Holy of Holies of the second temple of Herod, the regent of Judah, which commenced construction circa 19 A.D. and was completed in 63 A.D., remained empty. Today, the remains of the Temple of Solomon can be found beneath the ruins of the temples of Zerubbabel and Herod. The remains of the Wailing Wall that we see today originate from the time of the Herodian temple.[109] It is even more difficult for archaeologists to provide proof of the Temple of Solomon.

---

106   Sapritchian Dimotheos, Deux Ans de Séjours en Abyssinie, Jerusalem, 1871, p. 135ff.; cf. Grierson, Roderick and Munro-Hay, Stuart, Der Pakt mit Gott, Auf der Suche nach der verschollenen Bundeslade, Bergisch-Gladbach: Lübbe-Verlag, 2001, p. 400ff.
107   In the 13th century, the Armenian writer Abu Salih told of a supposed Ethiopian ark, but this one had Christian crosses. Cf. Grierson, Roderick and Munro-Hay, Stuart, Der Pakt mit Gott, Auf der Suche nach der verschollenen Bundeslade, Bergisch-Gladbach: Lübbe-Verlag, 2001, p. 467.
108   Jeremiah 3:16-17.
109   Hamblin, William J. and Seely, David R., Salomos Tempel, Mythos und Geschichte des Tempelberges in Jerusalem, Stuttgart: Belser Verlag, 2007, p. 41ff.

So did the Temple of Solomon ever exist? In 2007, unapproved excavations at Jerusalem's Temple Mount by the Islamic trust *Waqf* brought to light animal bones, shards of ceramic bowls and jugs. The pottery fragments have lines on them that are typical for the time of the first temple and date back to the 8th to 6th century B.C. This rather chance finding, which was examined and published by the archaeologists Yuval Baruch, Ronny Reich, Israel Finkelstein and Sy Gitin, is a sensation.[110] The artifacts prove that there is a layer of earth in existence from the time of the Temple of Solomon that is waiting to be exposed.

However, archaeological excavations prove to be problematic for the Israel Antiquities Authorities, IAA, as the area of the Temple Mount is under the administration of the Islamic trust *Waqf* and excavations are even strictly forbidden. Excavations would be a sacrilege that would result in war-like reactions. In the last few years, there has been an increase in accusations by the Israel Antiquities Authorities that Islamic construction work on the Temple Mount has destroyed relics from the eras of Solomon and Herod due to the bulldozers and caterpillars. For instance, in October 2006, the Israeli newspaper *Haaretz* reported that it came to the first dispute between the Israeli and Islamic authorities when illegal construction work of the *Waqf* on the underground El-Marwani Mosque on the Temple Mount resulted in three hundred truckloads of earth and rubble being disposed of in the Kidron Valley. However, the subsequent finds proved to be very revealing. Under the direction of Gabriel Barkay, Israeli archaeologists not only found numerous relics from the era of Herod's Temple, but also a fragment of a jug from the era of the Temple of Solomon inscribed with the Ancient Hebrew characters "Heh," "Ayin" and "Kof." Furthermore, an arrowhead was discovered like one used by the Babylonian army of King Nebuchadnezzar II, who invaded Jerusalem in 587 B.C. and destroyed the temple.[111] The Islamic trust thus unintentionally

110   Press release of the Israel Antiquity Authorities, IAA, 21.10.2007, Rockefeller Museum Building, Jerusalem, 91004.
http://www.antiquities.org.il/article_Item_eng.asp?sec_id=25&subj_id=240&id=1282&-module_id=#as.
111   Shragai, Nagav, First Temple artifacts found in dirt removed from Temple Mount, Haaretz, 10/19/2006, cf. Hendel, Fillel, Finds on Temple Mount from First Temple, Israel National News, 10/21/2007.

made sure that the existence of the Temple of Solomon was archaeologically proven, and so the discovery even strengthened the Jewish claim to Jerusalem.

If the Temple of Solomon really existed, as these findings suggest, it should be possible to pinpoint the location of the Temple of Solomon and even that of the Holy of Holies. The archaeological architect Leen Ritmeyer managed to do just that. Ritmeyer reconstructed the original area of the Temple Mount at the time of King Solomon based on the records of the Mishneh Torah and, in particular, based on the statements in the Book of Middot from the year 200 A.D., which concerns Jewish measurements. It states that the original Temple Mount was comprised of an area of 500-cubit square, where a cubit equals 2 feet, i.e. 57 centimeters, so 285 by 285 meters. Further on, we read that the largest area was in the south of the Temple Mount, the second largest in the east, the third largest (viewed from the temple) in the north and the smallest area in the west. Ritmeyer began to take precise measurements on the Temple Mount and noticed that the old temple's Holy of Holies was in the exact location of today's *es-Sakhra*, the stone within the Dome of the Rock that is fissured and protrudes about 1.80 meters from the surface of the Temple Mount. A few meters adjacent to the rock, there is a rectangular hollow in the ground that is located precisely in the center of the suspected Holy of Holies. Ritmeyer identified this hollow as the place in which the Ark of the Covenant stood in the Temple of Solomon because the rectangular indentation measures 80 by 130 centimeters. To recap: the Ark of the Covenant measured approx. ±131.25 cm in length, ±78.75 cm in height and ±78.75 cm in width.[112] Ritmeyer's discovery is thus a further sensation and no coincidence. Now we not only know the location of the Temple of Solomon, but also that a Holy of Holies existed in which the Ark of the Covenant was kept.

At the time of the occupation of the Temple Mount by the Templars, the Dome of the Rock was called "Templum Salomonis" and turned into a church. Hugues de Payns and his followers knew the exact location of the Holy of Holies due to their Biblical and

112   Ritmeyer, Leen and Kathleen, The Secrets of Jerusalem's Temple Mount, Biblical Archeology Society, Washington D.C., 1998, p. 91ff.

Talmudic studies of the Mishneh Torah. Thus, it was possible for them to search for the secret underground hiding place that King Solomon had created to hide the Ark in times of crisis. This breathtaking story seems to have come to the attention of the chroniclers of the First Crusade, Fulcher of Chartres and Albert of Aachen, through the Templars and Talmudic manuscripts. In the first half of the 12th century, Albert of Aachen writes the following in his *Historia Hierosolymitanae expeditionis*:

> [...] Moreover, in the middle of this modern tabernacle a stone mountain of natural rock sticks up, comprising almost the third part of an acre in area, two cubits in height, on one side of which there are positioned steps leading down to cavernous places; on another side, indeed, there is something which in truth those who observed it call a little door of stone, but always sealed. And in that place certain holies of holies are said still to be kept in the opinion of some people.[113]

The manuscript *Qualiter sita* from an anonymous author, which was written circa 1103, reports that the seven-branched Menorah, the Ark of the Covenant, the Tabernacle and other temple treasures are hidden beneath the Dome of the Rock.[114] This is where the aforementioned chronicler of the First Crusade, Fulcher of Chartres (1059-1127), chimes in as he also reports that the Ark of the Covenant and the temple treasure were hidden under the rock.[115] Even though the report of Albert of Aachen mentions a door to a cavern in the Dome of the Rock, his text corresponds to the Mishneh Torah and also to the Syriac Apocalypse of Baruch, which was written circa 100 A.D. and reports that five angels hid the temple treasures in the ground of the Temple Mount during the Babylonian invasion.[116] Undoubtedly, the High Priests and the four Levites were given angelic attributes because they rescued the Holy of Holies from the heathen Babylonians: Four bearers of the

113   Albert of Aachen, Book 6, Chapter 24.
114   Anonymus, Qualiter sita est civitas Hierosolymitana, 1103, in: Tobler, T. and Molinier, A., Itinera Hierosolymitana, Geneva, Volume I, 1879, p. 347ff.
115   Fulcher of Chartres, Book I, Chapter XXVI,7.
116   Syriac Apocalypse of Baruch, 6,4-8.

Ark and the consecrated High Priest brought the golden chest with the tablets of the covenant law to safety in an underground cavern.

Another record is attributed to the Jewish historian Eupolemus who described the Babylonian invasion of Jerusalem in Greek in 157 B.C.[117] Eupolemus writes that the Babylonians robbed the temple accoutrements. But he explicitly says they didn't steal the Ark of the Covenant. According to Eupolemus, the divine chest with the tablets of the covenant law was hidden by the Prophet Jeremiah in the rock of the Temple Mount. In the Talmud, however, we read that the Ark of the Covenant was brought to safety from the attack by Josiah.[118]

Thus, there is evidence that, after the Babylonian invasion and at the time of the Templars of Hugues de Payns, the Ark was still hidden under the Temple Mount.

Raiders of the Lost Ark

An article in the *New York Times* from spring of 1911 wrote about the illegal excavation of the English nobleman Montagu Brownlow Parker under the Temple Mount. "Have Englishmen found the Ark of the Covenant?" is the newspaper headline emblazoned in bold black letters.[119]

Parker, the second son of the 3rd Earl of Morley, was a gentleman and adventurer who previously gained the rank of Captain during various stints in the military and enjoyed all privileges of the British peerage. In 1908, he met the self-appointed Swedish Bible researcher Valter Juvelius, who claimed to have read the Book of Ezekiel and located the secret hiding place of the Ark of the Covenant under the Temple Mount. Parker seemed captivated by the prospect of discovering the greatest archaeological treasure in human history. Paying no heed to the warnings, he decided to perform excavations under the Temple Mount and use the results of the research of Charles Wilson and Charles Warren from the *Palestine Exploration Fund*, who uncovered a wide network of tunnels, cisterns and caverns in the 1860s,[120]

117   Eupolemus' text fragments have been preserved in the manuscripts of the Church Father Eusebius of Caesarea.
118   Grierson, Roderick and Munro-Hay, Stuart, Der Pakt mit Gott, Auf der Suche nach dem verschollenen Bundeslade, Bergisch-Gladbach: Lübbe-Verlag, 2001, p. 167ff.
119   New York Times, 5/7/1911
120   Cf. Gibson, Shimon and Jacobsen, David M., Below the Temple Mount in Jerusalem, Oxford: Tempus Reparatum, 1996 (BAR International Series 637).

as a starting point for his own search for the Ark of the Covenant. Since those days in which Wilson and Warren explored the underground terrain of the Temple Mount under partially hair-raising and life-threatening conditions, no more archaeological excursions had been carried out. The Turks still reigned the city. Now the excavations under the Temple Mount resembled a suicide squad more than ever. However, the mistrustful hostility of the Turkish administration failed to scare Parker off. He embarked on a trip to find sponsors and collected the incredible sum of 125,000 dollars.[121]

In summer of 1908, accompanied by Valter Juvelius, Clarence Wilson, Captain R.G. Duff and Major Foley, he set sail for Palestine on board a yacht – a bunch of naive British snobs who couldn't even master the simplest archaeological excavation methods and were more interested in boozy parties than researching Biblical history.[122] When they arrived in Palestine, Parker and his colleagues spent some months exposing the tunnel systems, which were blocked off at the time of the 1867 Warren Expedition by boulders, preventing Warren from entering further into the inside of the Temple Mount. However, Parker's excavations failed and, disappointed, he returned to England.

Nevertheless, in 1911, Parker and a troop of tunnel construction engineers set off for Jerusalem. He bribed the Turkish governor Ahmed Bey with 25,000 dollars and had himself and his companions locked inside the Dome of the Rock during the Islamic festival of Nabi Musa, the festival of Moses.[123] Parker was familiar with the research reports of Charles Warren. That was how he knew that directly under the *es-Sakhra* stone of the Dome of the Rock there was a cavern that Charles Warren had discovered and mapped, which is located under the Holy of Holies of the Temple of Solomon.

Parker and his colleagues used crowbars to lift the stone slabs off the ground and climbed down into the cave system of the Temple Mount. These caverns lead to a canal that empties into the Kidron Valley, as Charles Warren proved by his measurements. However, be-

121   Silberman, Neil, In Search of Solomon's Treasures, London, 1980, BAR International Series 07/08, p. 33.
122   Vester, Bertha Spafford, Our Jerusalem, London: Evans Brothers, 1951, p. 227f.
123   *New York Times*, 5/4/1911.

fore Parker and his companions could enter deeper into the caverns, a guard on the Dome of the Rock was alerted by the noise. He was so terrified that he mistook Parker and his companions for ghosts and ran away in panic. Only later did he report the Englishmen breaking into the holy mount – by which time the English treasure hunters were far away. The subsequent escape of Parker and his colleagues is worthy of a Hollywood movie because they rushed through the streets of Jerusalem and then sought the refuge of the yacht of Clarence Wilson as they set sail. However, this adventure had dramatic consequences. The bribed official was soon killed by a raving mob of Islamic believers. The subsequent riots on the streets of Jerusalem were not dissimilar to the intifada of 2000 when Prime Minister Ariel Sharon provocatively marched on to the Temple Mount to emphasize the Israeli claim to Jerusalem.

The article in the *New York Times* ended with an astonishing statement of Rabbi Solomon Schechter, the founder of the United Synagogue of America and President of the Jewish Theological Seminary of America. Schechter confirmed that the Jewish Talmud scholars assume that the Ark of the Covenant is hidden under the former location of the Holy of Holies of the Temple of Solomon. At the time of King Solomon, a hiding place was created for the event that the Ark of the Covenant was endangered by attacking warriors or fire. According to Schechter, there are many unexplored chambers and passageways under the Temple Mount.

Regardless of whoever brought the Ark of the Covenant to safety from the Babylonians in that secret hiding place under the Temple Mount in 587 B.C., we can now list the following amazing facts:

- Both the Ark of the Covenant and the Temple of Solomon actually existed.

- The Ark of the Covenant was hidden under the Temple Mount before or during the 18-month Babylonian siege of Jerusalem.

- The Ark of the Covenant was never in Ethiopia.

- The Queen of Sheba and her alleged son Menelik I are inventions of the Ethiopian Jews.

- During the founding of the Knights Templar, the Ark of the Covenant was still under the Temple Mount in a hiding place that was already created at behest of King Solomon.

- The Temple Mount is filled with a labyrinth of passageways that are mostly unexplored.

- As we have already seen, the Templars exposed tunnel systems under the Temple Mount and explored caverns and passageways under the Dome of the Rock and the Al-Aqsa Mosque.

- The Templars of Hugues de Payns found the Ark of the Covenant under the Temple Mount.

But what happened to the Ark of the Covenant after the Templars found it?

Chapter Four

God's Temple

Archaeology is the search for fact, not truth.

— Dr. Henry Jones Jr.

In the direct vicinity of the "La reine de Saba" café, there is a bookshop opposite Chartres Cathedral. The store front display features the books *Les mystères de la cathédrale de Chartres* and *Les mystères des templiers*[1] by the French author Louis Charpentier, which are arranged next to cathedral guides and art prints. It was in 1994 that I first came across these books. Back then, I wasn't that interested in Gothic cathedrals, and the visit to Chartres was just a stop on the way to my vacation in Britanny. However, I hoped that Charpentier's books would at least be a good read on the beach, and so I bought them.

When I first stuck my nose into these books on the beach of Plouescat, I was gripped by a strange fascination. I was amazed that Charpentier, a writer and lateral thinker, who was born 1905 and died 1979, was obviously not afraid of stating hypotheses that not only brazenly contradicted conventional historiography, but above all the beliefs of art history.

For instance, Charpentier suggested that the Templars were responsible for the development and introduction of Gothic architecture in France. He claimed that Chartres, together with other Notre Dame cathedrals, formed the constellation Virgo, that the Templars of Hugues de Payns found the Ark of the Covenant under the Temple Mount in Jerusalem and ultimately brought it to

---

1   Engl: The Mysteries of Chartres Cathedral, Cologne: Gaia Verlag, 1996 and Macht und Geheimnis der Templer (Power and Secrets of the Templars), Olten: Walter Verlag, 1986.

France. Outrageous hypotheses that were just begging for someone to check them by performing incredibly intensive research.

To get right to the point: Charpentier was wrong. Some of his
hypotheses are untenable and don't pertain to the matter at hand,
but instead detract from the really fascinating aspects. The Ark of
the Covenant is not in Chartres and the Cathedral does not make
up part of the constellation Virgo. The truth is even more unusual.

But let's not get ahead of ourselves.

As we have seen in the past chapters, the Templars were searching for the Ark of the Covenant under the Temple Mount, which
was hidden in 587 B.C. before or during the Babylonian siege of
Jerusalem.

But did they bring the shrine to France? Charpentier's proposed answer to this question is conceivably simple and completely logical. When the Templars found the Ark of the Covenant
and brought it to France, there must have been written accounts
or monuments that survived the centuries to tell the tale of this
remarkable event. As we have also seen, the poetic novels of Chrétien de Troyes and Wolfram von Eschenbach documented the
Templars' possession of a "grail" that has incredibly similar properties to the Jewish Ark of the Covenant with the two tablets of the
covenant law. We also know that Bernard of Clairvaux in his treatise "In Praise of the New Knighthood" made strange references to
the Templars as "the true Israelites." We know that an important
treasury of relics was kept in Clairvaux. The Cistercians and – very
probably also the Templars – thus possessed important relics. An
even more precise question would be: Would the Templars leave
behind information about this in an encrypted form stating *where*
they hid the Ark? Would archaeologists and researchers be capable
of deciphering their encoded messages?

We have to admit that to date no written sources have been
discovered that contain unambiguous statements of Hugues de
Payns or other brothers of the Templar Order such as: "We found
the Ark of the Covenant"! Whatever is waiting to be discovered by
future researchers in the corridors of the Vatican Secret Archives is
at present pure speculation. And so we can now search for archaeo-

logical and art history clues. Charpentier suggested examining the Gothic cathedrals of France for these clues. And that is precisely what we are going to do now.

In his book *The Mysteries of Chartres Cathedral*, Louis Charpentier claimed that the Templars played a significant role in the development of Gothic architecture. Charpentier: "Gothic appeared after the first Crusade and more particularly after the return in 1128 of the first nine Knights Templar." As we know, 12 years later, Suger, the Abbot of St.-Denis, erected a Gothic vault on top of the Romanesque foundation walls of his abbey.[2]

To understand Gothic architecture and its possible relationship to the Templar treasure, we must take a closer look at the character of Abbot Suger.

Abbot Suger of St.-Denis

Suger was born 1081 in St.-Denis to a family that owned lands 11 miles north of his native town and that belonged to the *minores milites*, a social class that was lower than the knighthood, but higher than the farmers of that time. The accounts of Suger's life, which were recorded by the monk and Suger's close friend William of St. Denis, mention that the young Suger had two brothers – Radulphus and Petrus – and was given in 1091 by his father Helinandus as an oblate to the Benedictine Abbey of St. Denis.[3] Suger was educated at the priory of St. Denis de l'Elstrée. In 1104, Suger met Louis VI, son of the French King Philip I. A deep friendship blossomed between the two of them. In 1107, Abbot Adam of St.-Denis sent the promising young monk Suger to Normandy, where he was instructed to bring order to the economically suffering Abbey of Berneval-le-Grand, not far from the coastal town of Dieppe. Furthermore, this excursion was a welcome opportunity for Suger to acquire the administrative skills for which he later became so famous. On March 9, 1107, together with Pope Paschal II, he consecrated the Benedictine priory La-Charité-sur-Loire. In 1109, Suger became the head of the pro-

2   Charpentier, Louis, Die Geheimnisse der Kathedrale von Chartres, Köln: Gaia Verlag, 1996, p. 34.
3   Annas, Gabriele, Abt Suger von St. Denis, eine historisch-biographische Skizze, in: Speer, Andreas und Binding, Günther, Abt Suger von St. Denis, Ausgewählte Schriften, Darmstadt: Wissenschaftliche Buchgesellschaft, 2005, p. 80.

vostship of Toury-en-Beauce near Chartres. He was assigned an increasing amount of responsibility and earned the growing trust of the Pope, as well as the King. He was appreciated for his diplomacy. For example, Suger succeeded in settling the decades-long dispute between St.-Denis and the Bishop of Paris by Pope Paschal II issuing a protective privilege, with the result that the claim of the Bishop of Paris to the Abbey was revoked.

In April 1107, there was a meeting between Suger, Pope Paschal, King Philip I and his son Louis VI, called "the Fat." We are uncertain what they were debating, but according to Suger's accounts they were discussing church matters that were not more clearly defined. At this time, Suger had not yet been ordained a priest. Nevertheless, even in his younger years, an immense diplomatic pressure weighed on his shoulders. In many ways, his career was similar to that of the ambitious Cistercian monk Bernard of Clairvaux who was appointed an Abbot earlier than the Cistercian Rule usually allowed. Suger and Bernard became close friends – a special circumstance that we will encounter again later on in a dramatic manner. After 1107, there is documentation of regular contacts between Suger and the papacy.

On January 28, 1122, Suger met Pope Calixtus II, who received him in Bitonto, Italy, together with Abbot Hugh IV of the Parisian Abbey of Saint-Germain-des-Prés. In 1122, a concordat was reached between Henry V and Pope Calixtus II in which the Pope permitted the King to be present at the election of the bishops. The elected bishop had to swear an oath of fealty to the King. In turn, the King had to hold the investiture and grant the Pope the sole right to appoint bishops. In Italy, Suger attempted to – more or less successfully – mediate an investiture dispute between the German Emperor and the Pope. The Emperor had forfeited his clerical power. Thanks to his friendship to King Louis VI, Suger made sure that the Church and the King worked hand in hand.

On March 11, 1122, Suger was ordained a priest, and one day later he was ordained Abbot of St.-Denis. Suger managed to settle the Abbey's debts within a few years and ushered in an era of economic prosperity for St.-Denis.

In 1124, King Louis VI rushed into the Abbey of St.-Denis and asked the Abbot for clerical assistance because the troops of German Emperor Henry V having been marched to the borders of the kingdom.[4] Louis VI called for support in the battle against Henry V. In the shadow of the relics of the patron saint and first Bishop of Paris, Saint Dionysius (Saint Denis), he took up the flag of the county of Vexin for which he was the governor – he also owned the town of Gisors – and swore his oath to the Abbey. Undoubtedly, this story was an attempt by Suger to link the French kings to St.-Denis – a form of propaganda.[5] Although it is dubious whether this Oscar-worthy scene actually took place, the flag of St.-Denis was henceforth carried to war as a banner and will go down in history as the "Oriflamme" of the French kings. Among others, the following people heeded the call of the King: our old friend Templar founder Count Hugues I of Champagne, as well as Theobald V of Blois, Count Hugues II of Burgundy, William II of Nevers, Rudolph of Vermandois and Charles of Flanders.[6] The counts drummed up their troops. Emperor Henry V was so intimidated by the military power that he ordered his army to retreat.

On October 25, 1131, the King's second son, Louis VII, was crowned heir to the throne after his first son, Philip, died in a riding accident. Suger intervened here also. At the behest of Pope Innocent II, he anointed Louis VII king. On June 17, 1137, Suger accompanied his childhood friend Louis VII together with Bishop Godfrey of Chartres to Bordeaux in Aquitaine, where he attended the marriage of the future king with Eleanor of Aquitaine, daughter of William X of Aquitaine, who had passed away in 1137. In August 1137, King Louis VI died and by so doing involuntarily gave up the throne. The diplomatic services of Suger were now an integral part of the King's court.

However, Suger seemed to be pursuing an ambitious goal because since 1125 he had been collecting impressive sums of money to renovate the Abbey Church.[7] As he wrote in his work *De consecratione*, Suger intended to convert the Abbey Church of St.-Denis.[8]

---

4   Abt Suger von St. Denis, Vita Ludovici Grossi Regis, c. XXVIII, p. 218.
5   Grosse, Rolf, St. Denis zwischen Adel und König, Stuttgart: Thorbecke Verlag, 2002, p. 32ff.
6   Ibid., p. 222ff.
7   Kimpel, D. and Suckale, R., Die gotische Architektur in Frankreich 1130-1270, Munich: Hirmer Verlag, 1985, p. 83 with comment 42 (p. 480).
8   Abt Suger von St. Denis, De consecratione, 14,104sq.

Since 625, the building had been used by the Merovingian dynasty under Dagobert I as a tomb for the French kings – starting with Hugh Capet, the Carolingian and Capetian dynasties would make use of this prestige. However, the church was simply too small for the church services. Women, children, old people were crushed and trampled to death by crowds of people. Suger writes:

> At times you could see, a marvel to behold, that the crowded multitude offered so much resistance to those who strove to flock in to worship and kiss the holy relics, the Nail and Crown of the Lord, that no one among the countless thousands of people because of their density could move a foot; that no one, because of their very congestion, could [do] anything but stand like a marble statue, stay benumbed or, as a last resort, scream.[9]

King Louis VI died on August 1, 1137. A few months later, an event occurred that was to change the history of Europe: In the presence of the heir to the throne Louis VI and the most important archbishops and bishops, the builders began laying the foundation stone for the west portal of the Abbey Church. However, art historians assume that work on the west portal had already begun back in 1135.[10]

On June 9, 1140, exactly three years later, the west façade was inaugurated. The work progressed rapidly: Already by July 14, 1140, the foundation stone had been laid for the construction of the eastern part of the church. This was rather unusual. Usually, when building cathedrals, the eastern part was begun first so that the first masses could already be held in the sanctuary during the construction phase. It is probable that the rotten condition of the west portal led to the decision to begin renovations there first. Suger wrote: "For three years we pressed the completion of the work at great expense, with a numerous crowd of workmen, summer and winter, lest God have just cause to complain of us: *Thine eyes did see my substance yet being unperfect.*"[11]

---

9   De Consecratione II, 30-35, in *Abbot Suger on the Abbey Church of St.-Denis and its Art Treasures*, edited, translated and annotated by Erwin Panofsky, 2nd edition, Princeton University Press, Princeton, 1979, p. 87-88.

10   Crosby, Sumner McKnight, *The Royal Abbey of St. Denis from its Beginnings to the Death of Suger*, New Haven: Yale University Press, 1987 (Yale Publications in the History of Art, 37), p. 32.

11   De Consecratione V, 1-5, in Abbot Suger on the Abbey Church of St.-Denis and its Art Treasures, edited, translated and annotated by Erwin Panofsky, 2nd edition, Princeton University Press, Princeton, 1979, p. 105.

In the Abbey Church of St.-Denis circa 1136 the first ribbed vaults were built. From 1137 – 1140 the western façade was created based on the plan of Abbot Suger. St.-Denis is dedicated to the martyr and patron saint of Paris, Saint Denis, and is regarded as the prototype of all Gothic cathedrals. © Tobias D. Wabbel

The conversion of the eastern part of St.-Denis took exactly three years and eleven months and ended on June 11, 1144. For the festive inauguration, King Louis VII, his wife Eleanor of Aquitaine and the entire clergy were present. Generous donations were collected and the bishops even gave their rings. Count Theobald II of Champagne donated jacinths and rubies.[12] Strangely, Suger didn't mention any other noble donors except Count Theobald II of Champagne – and King Louis VII, who presented them with radiant emeralds.

Henceforth, the Abbey of St.-Denis, the first Gothic-style building, was an architectural status symbol for the French monarchy. Whereas in the German empire under Henry V architecture was still Romanesque and horizontal – case in point Worms Cathedral, which commenced construction in 1130 – France's church construction was transforming into a vertical architecture of light that was rising towards the heavens. The Capetian dynasty, which provided the kings of France from 987 to 1328, now had a church construction that particularly expressed its power and proximity to the clergy. Suger elevated Saint Dionysius (Denis) in his manuscript *De administratione* to the patron saint of King Louis VI and the entire monarchy.[13] He described him as an extremely diligent and pious man and the famous guardian of churches.[14]

Suger asked King Louis VII to keep the public away from the inauguration celebrations to thus ensure a dignified procession.[15] "Then, when we had humbly asked the glorious and most humble Louis, King of France, to keep away, through his peers and nobles, the impeding crowd from the procession itself, he answered, more humbly by far, that he would gladly do this in person as well as through his retinue."[16]

Here it becomes clear the influence that Suger had on the King. Louis VII obeyed his instructions – during this era, in addition to Suger, Bernard of Clairvaux was the only other person to acquire

---

12   De Consecratione V, 25-35.
13   Abt Suger von St. Denis, De administratione, 33,155ss.
14   Ibid., 81,371s.
15   Abt Suger von St. Denis, De consecratione, 82,509ss.
16   De consecratione VI, 45-49, in Abbot Suger on the Abbey Church of St.-Denis and its Art Treasures, edited, translated and annotated by Erwin Panofsky, 2nd edition, Princeton University Press, Princeton, 1979, p. 115.

this authority. Keeping the people away from the inauguration of a church was definitely not a usual or standard procedure. After all, abbey churches such as St. Remi in Reims were openly accessible to the people during their inaugurations. Behind closed doors, the reaction of the King and the nobility to the inauguration of the Abbey Church with its huge stained glass windows and church treasures must have seemed overwhelming.[17] The church treasures of St. Denis gave rise to Bernard of Clairvaux expressing his displeasure at the exhibited riches. At the same time, Bernard loudly denounced the Cluny Romanesque architecture.[18]

Abbot Suger was not unimpressed by Bernard's political and religious interventions because the Abbot of Clairvaux was regarded as the greatest and most influential thinker of his era. Artistically, Bernard also provided fundamental stimuli, which inspired Suger in the construction of St. Denis.[19] As a result, Suger was unable to free himself from the Cistercian concepts of the Reformist Benedictine interpretation. The strictly ascetic lifestyle, which was also reflected by the sparse yet large buildings such as Pontigny Abbey, definitely didn't stand in contradiction to the lavishly appointed Church of St.-Denis.[20] Bernard was just as submissive to the King as Suger, but in his wisdom was regarded even more the spiritual embodiment of France. The correspondence between Suger and Bernard of Clairvaux proves that there was an active exchange of ideas that was reflected in the architecture.

It was also Bernard of Clairvaux who, at the peak of his fame on March 31, 1146, at the behest of Pope Eugenius III, in the Burgundian town of Vézelay, called upon men to join the Second Crusade to reconquer the Principality of Edessa – in present-day Turkey and parts of Syria – which had been captured by Imad ad-Din Zengi on December 24, 1144. Pope Eugenius III appointed Louis VII the sole commander of the army.[21] On February 16, 1147, Louis VII sum-

---

17   Ibid., 85,530ss.

18   Simson, Otto von, Die gotische Kathedrale, Darmstadt: Wissenschaftliche Buchgesellschaft, 1968, p. 142.

19   Porter, Arthur Kingsley, Romanesque Sculptures of the Pilgrimage Roads, Boston: Marshall Jones Company, 1923, p. 222f.

20   Simson, Otto von, Die gotische Kathedrale, Darmstadt: Wissenschaftliche Buchgesellschaft, 1968, p. 159.

21   Runciman, Steven, Die Geschichte der Kreuzzüge, Munich: DTV, 1995, p. 556

moned a ceremonious assembly in Étampes to name representatives to continue with his official duties during his absence. Suger was not pleased at all. He let the King know in a protest note that he had a deep mistrust of his venture to go to the Middle East.[22] However, the French nobility, whom Louis VII asked for military assistance, completely let him down. Other matters were suddenly supposedly more pressing: After Louis VII named both Abbot Suger and Count William II of Nevers as his regents, William II declined with the words that he was – suddenly – considering joining the Carthusian Order and was therefore unable to participate in state politics.

The town of Vézelay in Burgundy. In the Basilica of St. Madeleine, which was built circa 1120, Bernard of Clairvaux preached about the Second Crusade in 1146. © Tobias D. Wabbel

On February 18, 1147, in a letter to Pope Eugenius III, Bernard of Clairvaux began a hymnic treatise to Abbot Suger who, during Louis' absence, ruled the land with a calm hand scarcely like any other regent before him:

> I know profoundly this man, and I know that he is faithful and prudent in temporal things, that he is fervent and humble in

---

22   Ibid., p. 556.

things spiritual. If there is any precious vase adorning the palace of the King of Kings, it is the soul of the venerable Suger.[23]

So Suger was the right man for Bernard in France. But it did not look auspicious for Crusade number two. However, Louis VII didn't care about that because he saw the words of Pope Eugenius III and Bernard of Clairvaux as his orders. Consequently, in addition to Abbot Suger, Louis VI promptly appointed two other representatives: Archbishop Samson of Reims and Count Rudolph of Vermandois. According to historical accounts, however, it was only actually Abbot Suger who ruled the country during Louis' absence.[24]

Bernard of Clairvaux was highly impressed by Abbot Suger. Henceforth, a deep friendship was ignited between the two men. Both had things in common: their admiration of the French King – and the history of the Israelites.

On June 8, 1147, the 26-year-old King Louis VII set out from St.-Denis to the East. He was joined by the regiment of the Templar Preceptor Everard des Barres.[25]

As the King's regent, Suger ensured that the clergy, in particular Pope Eugenius III, was on friendly terms with the Capetian royal dynasty of King Louis VII. The intense spirituality that Louis VII was feeling, just like his father before him, deeply moved him. Not a single one of Suger's decisions as a regent was influenced by Pope Eugenius III. The Abbot of St.-Denis was completely trusted by both clergy and royalty.[26] When the King left the country for Jerusalem, a few counts and barons revolted with armed force to take the King's possessions and lands. Suger successfully enlisted vassals such as Geoffrey of Anjou, Theobald of Blois, William III of Nevers and Thierry of Flanders to take up their swords for him and King Louis VII to stop the looters and robber barons. During this

23   Bernhard von Clairvaux, Sämtliche Werke, Volume 2, Innsbruck: Tyrolia Verlag, 1995, Letter 309.
24   Annas, Gabriele, Abt Suger von St. Denis, eine historisch-biographische Skizze, in: Speer, Andreas und Binding, Günther, Abt Suger von St. Denis, Ausgewählte Schriften, Darmstadt: Wissenschaftliche Buchgesellschaft, 2005, p. 107.
25   Runciman, Steven, Die Geschichte der Kreuzzüge, Munich: DTV, 1995, p. 565.
26   Cartellieri, Otto, Abt Suger von Saint Denis, 1081-1151, Berlin: Ebering, 1898 (Historische Studien 11), p. 52.

time of crisis, he also regularly consulted bishops for advice.[27] Consequently, he was able to continue his regency with a resolute rule.

Suger also seemed to have the financial side of the administration under control, when King Louis VII's Crusade devoured vast amounts from the royal coffers and Suger was forced to borrow money from the Templar Order, the Knights of St. John and other sponsors.[28]

When Bernard of Clairvaux preached about the Crusade in the German town of Speyer, King Conrad III and his competitor Welf VI from the House of Welf (Guelph) decided to enlist. Bernard vehemently defended the German Jews when the Cistercian monk Radulph incited pogroms that ended in bloody massacres. This is something we will come back to later. The armies of King Roger II of Sicily, Emperor Manuel I Komnenos of Byzantium and King Géza II of Hungary also joined the Crusade.

Pope Eugenius III, who was hoping for a purely French crusade, didn't like this at all. Eugenius III feared that the large number of participating kings could destroy the campaign by their conflicting intentions.[29] And that was precisely what happened. The Crusade ended in disaster. On July 25, 1147, after a two-day siege of Damascus, the armies were wiped out by the army of Turkish commander Anar.

Once again, Louis VII sought the help of Everard des Barres, who had been appointed Templar Grand Master in 1149, and whose troops met up with the army of King Louis VII in the mountains of Asia Minor near Chones and thus enabled them a safe return home to France.[30] When the King arrived in France, thanks to Abbot Suger's rigorous budgetary policy, all debts had been paid which the Crusade had caused by devouring money from the royal coffers.[31]

Nevertheless, Suger intended to achieve one final political coup in 1150: a third crusade to the Holy Land. However, in view of the past disaster, Eugenius III was highly skeptical about this plan. In autumn 1150, Suger was infected with a grievous fever. On death's doorstep, Bernard of Clairvaux and Suger exchanged their final

---

27   Ibid., p. 53.
28   Ibid., p. 55.
29   Runciman, Steven, Die Geschichte der Kreuzzüge, Munich: DTV, 1995, p. 561.
30   Wilcke, Ferdinand, Die Geschichte des Ordens der Tempelherren, Wiesbaden: Marix Verlag, 2005, p. 65ff.
31   Cartellieri, Otto, Abt Suger von Saint Denis, 1081-1151, Berlin: Ebering, 1898 (Historische Studien 11), p. 55.

letters. Bernard wrote: "To his dear and intimate friend Suger, by the grace of God Abbot of S. Denys, Brother Bernard wishes the glory which is within and the grace which cometh down from above."

Bernard encouraged Suger to meet death bravely. Bernard responded to Suger's request to see the Abbot of Clairvaux once more before his death by stating that he didn't yet know whether he could come, but he will try. The reason was obvious: Bernard was also very old and very sickly. "But whichever it is," continued Bernard of Clairvaux, "I have loved you from the first, I will love you without end. I say with all confidence that I cannot lose one so loved to the end. He is not lost to me, but he goes before."[32]

Suger died on January 13, 1151. Bernard of Clairvaux and King Louis VII lost their best friend. At this time, Abbot Suger's brilliant architectural heritage had become the model for the cathedrals of Sens, in Burgundy, and Senlis, to the north-east of Paris.

God's Temple

Abbot Suger saw King Solomon as a role model. The Abbey Church of St.-Denis was his Gothic interpretation of the Temple of Solomon in Jerusalem, in which the Ark of the Covenant was kept in the Holy of Holies. Just as King Solomon had the Temple built to honor God's promise to his father David, Abbot Suger saw himself as a new Solomon.[33] "I used to compare the least to the greatest: Solomon's riches could not have sufficed for his Temple any more than did ours for this work had not the same Author of the same work abundantly supplied for His attendants," wrote Suger in *De consecratione*.[34] Suger even regarded his friend Louis VII as King David.[35] But Suger went even further. In his discussion about the Ark of the Covenant, Suger not only saw the Capetian royal dynasty, but also the clergy of St.-Denis, as the descendants of King David.[36]

32   Bernhard von Clairvaux, Sämtliche Werke, Volume III, Innsbruck: Tyrolia Verlag, 1992, Letter 266.
33   1 Kings 6,1-37; 2 Chronicles 3,1-17.
34   De Consecratione II, 84-88, in Abbot Suger on the Abbey Church of St.-Denis and its Art Treasures, edited, translated and annotated by Erwin Panofsky, 2nd edition, Princeton University Press, Princeton, 1979, p. 91.
35   DelPlato, Joan, On Jews and the Old Testament Precedent for Sacred Art Production: The Views of some Twelfth-Century Abbots, in: Comitatus: A Journal of Medieval and Renaissance Studies, Volume 18, Article 3, p. 35f.
36   Panofsky, Erwin, Abbot Suger on the Abbey Church of St. Denis and its Art

Moreover, Suger stressed that he must provide for his monks as for the cattle that pulled the cart with the Ark of the Covenant.[37]

St.-Denis was thus more than just an ordinary abbey church and in no way a depiction of the Heavenly Jerusalem. The interpretation of the Gothic cathedrals as an embodiment of the Heavenly Jerusalem goes back to the book *Die Entstehung der Kathedrale* (The Origins of the Cathedral) by Austrian art historian and Nazi party member Hans Sedlmayr, which was published in 1950. Sedlmayr's premise was developed back in the 1930s when he was a Professor of Art History at the University of Vienna. Henceforth, the Gothic cathedral as a depiction of the Heavenly Jerusalem has been featured repeatedly in books on art history and was uncritically accepted by the majority of scholars.[38]

The fact that this interpretation makes no sense from an art history perspective is proven alone by the description of the Heavenly Jerusalem in the Book of Revelation. In Revelation the Heavenly Jerusalem is described as being "12,000 stadia in length, and as wide and high as it is long.," and the buildings are just as high.[39] One stadium is equivalent to 185 meters.[40] According to this, then Heavenly Jerusalem is in the shape of a cube. However, not a single Gothic cathedral is in the shape of a cube. In contrast, this quadratic shape is more similar to the Holy of Holies in the Temple of Solomon, which was 20 cubits in height, width and length.

As the renowned Professor of Art History Wilhelm Schlink from the University of Freiburg notes, the Heavenly Jerusalem is *exclusively* described as a city in medieval texts such as the *Bible Moralisée* from 1179, but not as a cathedral. In contrast, the sole depiction of a Gothic construction inside the walls of Jerusalem in the *Bible Moralisée* indicates the divine salvation of the Temple of Solomon.[41]

Treasures, Princeton: Princeton University Press, 1979, p. 123.

37   Büchsel, Martin, Die Entstehung der Gotik, Freiburg i.Br.: Rombach Verlag, 1997, p. 79.

38   Schlink, Wilhelm, The Gothic Cathedral as Heavenly Jerusalem: A Fiction in German Art History, in: Kühnel, Bianca (ed.), The Real and Ideal Jerusalem in Jewish, Christian and Islamic Art, Jerusalem: Hebrew University, 1998 (Jewish Art 23/24.1997/1998), p. 275.

39   Revelation, 21:11-15.

40   The dimensions are from the 2 Maccabees 11:15, which states the distance between the Jewish fortress of Beth-Zur and Jerusalem as 150 stadia (1 stadium = 185 meters).

41   Haussherr, Reiner, Templum Salomonis und Ecclesia Christi, in: Zeitschrift für Kunstgeschichte 31 1968, p. 101-121.

Since Emperor Justinian I, who had the Hagia Sophia built in Constantinople, up to the present day, Christian builders have been referring to King Solomon and regarding themselves as his successor.[42] They were building according to God's orders. Just as God created the universe, they erected a new house for God, as did King Solomon once upon a time. A higher mission was unconceivable at that time. In his definitive book *The Gothic Cathedral,* Otto von Simson emphasizes the fact that the Temple of Solomon played a huge role in the medieval texts of the stonemasons' guilds. According to von Simson, due to its divine dimensions, the Temple of Solomon was regarded as a prototype of Christian ceremonial buildings and the appearance of the Christian Church in the liturgy was observed by mentioning the Temple.[43] Consequently, the first three readings of the Roman Breviary are dedicated to the report on Solomon's consecration of the Temple and God's blessing of the Temple.[44] So, in the liturgy, the divine promise of the Church – ecclesia – is fulfilled by the Temple of Solomon.

The Augustinian choirmaster Richard of St. Victor (1110-1173) – one of the most famous theologists of the Middle Ages and a close friend of Bernard of Clairvaux – interpreted the Church as the Temple of Solomon in *De Salomone et templo*, his commentary on the book of Ezekiel. For Richard of St. Victor the winding staircase in the Temple of Solomon connected the bottom to the middle and top floor and, in his opinion, was identical to the spiral staircases in the bell towers of churches which – like the western façade of St.-Denis – were constructed over three floors.[45]

Thus, in view of this Temple interpretation and the medieval understanding of the Bible, it is not surprising that many features of the Temple of Solomon were borrowed in the Middle Ages by the Christian Church: the seven-branched lampstand or Menorah and the cherubims from the Holy of Holies, as well as the cast bronze

42   Scheja, Georg, Hagia Sophia und Templum Salomonis, in: Istanbuler Mitteilungen 12, 1962, p. 47f.
43   Simson, Otto von, Die gotische Kathedrale, Darmstadt: Wissenschaftliche Buchgesellschaft, 1968, p. 60.
44   2 Paral 7:1-16; 7:12-16.
45   Richard von St. Viktor, Liber exceptionum, Texte critique avec introduction, notes et tables, Châtillon, Jean (ed.), Paris: Vrin, 1958, (Textes philosophiques du moyen âge 5), p. II, lib. 777, Cap. 1f.: 'De Salomone et templo', p. 313ff.

basin (laver) in the courtyard of the Temple of Solomon that was standing on 12 bulls and is still found today in the form of the font. The draperies under the base of the clerestories – i.e. the window façades above the aisles of the cathedrals – correspond to the fence of curtains in front of the Tabernacle, which were hung on posts, in which the Israelites stored the Ark of the Covenant while wandering through the Sinai Desert. The bronze pillars Jakin and Boaz in the portico of the Temple of Solomon are represented by the double tower façade of Gothic cathedrals.[46]

In a study from 2002, the American art historians Jacqueline Frank and William Clark showed that early Biblical descriptions of the Temple of Solomon mention double towers and battlements like those of a Gothic cathedral.[47] In his book *The Jewish War*, Jewish historian Flavius Josephus described that the Temple had a golden door[48] – the door of the main portal of the western façade of the Abbey Church of St.-Denis was made of gilded bronze. Furthermore, Frank and Clark showed evidence that the geometry of St.-Denis clearly matches the dimensions of the Temple of Solomon. Consequently, with the extended conversion of the Abbey Church of St.-Denis, Abbot Suger carried out a tripartition, which was adopted by most cathedral architects and was based on the dimensions of the Temple of Solomon: The Temple was divided into a portico, the Holy Place for the treasures and the Holy of Holies for the Ark of the Covenant. The Abbey Church of St.-Denis is also divided into portico, nave and chancel with its chapels arranged in a circle. Like St.-Denis, the Temple of Solomon had two altars.[49] In both constructions, the altars are only accessible via steps as the altar in the Holy of Holies was elevated.[50] Frank and Clark concluded that Abbot Suger erected the altar of the martyrs in the Abbey Church of St.-Denis in exactly the same place as the location of the

---

46   Ohly, Friedrich, Die Säulen des Salomonischen Tempels und die Doppelturmfassade, in: Frühmittelalterliche Studien 32, 1998, p. 7ff.

47   I Henoch 89:73; cf. the depiction of the Temple of Solomon in: Grabar, A., Early Christian Art AD 200-395, New York, 1968, p. 74, Fig. 66.

48   Flavius Josephus, Der Jüdische Krieg, Book V., p. 212ff.

49   Frank, Jacqueline and Clark, William, Abbot Suger and the Temple in Jerusalem: a New Interpretation of the Sacred Environment in the Royal Abbey of St. Denis, in: Anderson, Christy (ed.), The Built Surface, Aldershot: Ashgate, Publishing Company, Burlington, 2002, p. 116.

50   Ezekiel 41:8

Ark of the Covenant in the Temple of Solomon.[51] So it is obvious that Abbot Suger used the Temple of Solomon as a prototype.[52]

This leads us to justifiably ask: might we find clues in the Abbey Church of St.-Denis that lead us to deduce that Abbot Suger knew the secret of the Templar treasure if he acted in the tradition of King Solomon? Is it possible to find clues in St.-Denis that indicate that the Templars were in possession of the Ark of the Convenant? Let's take a closer look at Abbot Suger's architectural legacy.

The Ark of the Covenant of St.-Denis

The Abbey Church of St.-Denis[53] is about 10 miles north of the center of Paris, surrounded by a mall and office buildings. It's Tuesday. On this unusually hot, cloudless spring morning, young couples are lounging on the lawn that surrounds the cathedral.

I approach the western façade, which is divided into three semicircular entrance portals and three construction zones. The round arches of the portals have Romanesque characteristics. The blind arcades of the second zone under the entrance portals, which serve as decorations, have been turned into pointed arches by the stonemasons. My observation confirms the written account of Abbot Suger, who reports that the construction work on the renovation of the Abbey Church of St.-Denis began at the west portal which, apart from its three portals, looks incredibly simple.

In the top zone, I catch sight of a rose window above the center portal, and to the left and right on each side are four round-arched blind arcades with figures of saints. Under each one are two windows in the shape of a pointed arch. The top edge of the western façade is completely lined by a crenelation – just like the Temple of Solomon in the Biblical descriptions of the Old Testament.

It is not our purpose here to explain the history of Gothic architecture, but please note that even aesthetically attractive archi-

51   Frank, Jacqueline and Clark, William, Abbot Suger and the Temple in Jerusalem: a New Interpretation of the Sacred Environment in the Royal Abbey of St. Denis, in: Anderson, Christy (ed.), The Built Surface, Aldershot: Ashgate, Publishing Company, Burlington, 2002, p. 117.
52   Simson, Otto von, Die gotische Kathedrale, Darmstadt: Wissenschaftliche Buchgesellschaft, 1968, p. 139.
53   Since 1966, St.-Denis has been classed as a cathedral. However, I will continue to use the term abbey church.

tectural details fulfilled tasks relating to static equilibrium. Nothing was left up to chance and every part of the cathedral fulfilled a function. For instance, the history of the pointed arch: In actual fact, the first pointed arch appeared in the Islamic buildings of Palestine, even before Abbot Suger ordered construction to begin on St.-Denis.[54] The most striking examples are the Dome of the Rock and the Al-Aqsa Mosque on the Temple Mount in Jerusalem, which were built 691 and 705 A.D. respectively.[55] Gothic elements appeared as early as the end of the 11th century in Burgundy in the Benedictine Cluny Abbey, which was founded circa 910. Otto von Simson remarks that Cluny, as the largest abbey of the Middle Ages, was built vertically, so stretching up into the heavens, an architectural attribute that wasn't applied to France's Gothic cathedrals until later on.[56] The third expansion of Cluny Abbey – known as Cluny III – was carried out in 1089 under the Benedictine Abbot Hugh, and this was the first time the pointed arch appeared on European soil. The building complex became increasingly spacious and stretched into the heavens so that the abbey surpassed the dimensions of Old St. Peter's Basilica in Rome, one reason why Bernard of Clairvaux criticized Cluny's obsession with everything gigantic, which made a mockery of every architectural simplicity of the Cistercians.

Gothic architecture mainly has Benedictine origins, but Islamic and Cistercian influences undoubtedly also play a significant role. Thus, it makes sense that monks, who participated in the construction of Cluny and accompanied the Crusaders on their journey to conquer Jerusalem, profited from the expertise of Islamic architecture. However, as in the case of St.-Denis, after the arrival of the pointed arch there was no clear architectural progression: initially, Gothic and Romanesque architecture were competing with each other. Numerous churches with Romanesque attributes, which had to be renovated for construction reasons, were continued in the Gothic style of architecture. This was initially the case in St.-Denis. Until the introduction of Gothic architecture, Romanesque basilica

---

54   Warren, John, Creswell's Use of the Theory of Dating by the Acuteness of the Pointed Arches in Early Muslim Architecture, in: Muqarnas 8, 1991, p. 59ff.

55   Ben-Dov, Meir, In the Shadow of the Temple, New York: Harpercollins, 1985, p. 280.

56   Simson, Otto von, Die gotische Kathedrale, Darmstadt: Wissenschaftliche Buchgesellschaft, 1968, p. 13.

were characterized by barrel vaults with rectangular ground plans, thickset walls and small windows. It was dark in these churches. Cluny and the Abbey of la Madelaine in the Burgundian town of Vézelay, where Bernard of Clairvaux was preaching about the Second Crusade in 1146, was one the few exceptions.

Abbot Suger decided to use the existing foundations from the 7th century construction of King Dagobert to incite an architectural revolution. The massive walls of the Romanesque churches were replaced by filigree walls that stretched upwards and were divided into bays. Bays marked the wall sections which ended in the ribbed vaults. Now sunlight flooded the Abbey Church through the large window façades. Art historian Hans Jantzen referred to a diaphanous structure[57]: a shaped wall becomes translucent.

The high walls were supported by ribbed vaults. The thrust of the walls was neutralized at the outer façades by abutments and pinnacles. Pinnacles are pointed turrets that place weight on the abutments of the building and thus enable a balanced static equilibrium. Only the static equilibrium of high walls and abutments that hold the weight enables the barrel vaults to be replaced by pointed-arch ribbed vaults. In other words: the construction of a cathedral is dependent on higher geometry and in-depth knowledge of static equilibrium.

The western façade of the Abbey Church now only has a right tower. The left, northern belltower was badly damaged in 1837 when it was struck by a bolt of lightning. However, architect François Debret used heavier stones for the reconstruction than the sandstone from which the Abbey Church was originally built. As a result, there was a risk of the weight of the north tower leading to the western façade's collapse, and so the tower was taken down again.[58]

I approach the entrance portals of the western façade and inspect the archivolt arches that are embellished with figures and the stair-shaped frame surrounding the portals, also known as the jamb, which is decorated with Biblical scenes. At first glance, the three

57   Jantzen, Hans, Über den gotischen Innenraum und andere Aufsätze, Berlin: Gebr. Mann Verlag, 1951, p. 7-20.
58   Blum, Pamela Z., The Lateral Portals of the West Facade of the Abbey Church of Saint-Denis, in: Abbot Suger and Saint-Denis: a symposium, Gerson, Paula Lieber (ed.), New York: Abrams, 1987, p. 200.

portals don't seem to feature a consistent design because there are some jambs without figures. The sculptures that were once admired there were smashed and destroyed during the French Revolution of 1789 by raving mobs with hammers and crowbars.[59] Some of France's most beautiful Gothic cathedrals experienced a similar destiny during the Revolution, including the cathedrals of Châlons-sur-Marne in Champagne or Noyon in Picardy. Drawings from 1729, which were published by Bernard de Montfaucon, depict royal figures of the Merovingian dynasty.[60] The portal was pretty much restored to its original state in the 19th century by François Debret.[61]

The current iconographic depictions that I can now admire on the portals are still the subject of art history and archaeological debates. It is not immediately apparent which part is from the era of Abbot Suger and which was only added during the restoration work. For instance, art historian Martin Büchsel solely ascribes the left portal to sculptor Joseph-Sylvestre Brun, who did some restoration work on the Abbey Church in the 19th century. However, American art historian Pamela Z. Blum did some meticulous detective work to successfully determine the parts of the portal which restoration was based on the original work from the time of Abbot Suger. As a result, we now know that the iconography was completely the work of Abbot Suger's architects and, if it was changed at all over the centuries, these changes were only minor.[62]

The center portal shows the Last Judgment with Jesus Christ on a throne in the middle, stretching out his arms. With the right hand he is giving a blessing and with the left hand he is giving a dismissive gesture. Behind him is a cross held by two angels. This image painfully reminds me that the cross was an instrument of torture and tool of suffering. Two other angels are holding a nail and the crown of thorns, known as the Arma Christi (Weapons of Christ) or the Instruments of the Passion. The 12 apostles, shown

59   Büchsel, Martin, Die Geburt der Gotik, Freiburg i.Br.: Rombach Druck und Verlagshaus, 1997, p. 109.
60   Blum, Pamela Z., The Lateral Portals of the West Facade of the Abbey Church of Staint-Denis, in: Abbot Suger and Saint-Denis: a symposium, Gerson, Paula Lieber (ed.), New York: Abrams, 1987, p. 212.
61   Ibid., p. 111.
62   Blum, Pamela Z., The Saint Benedict Cycle on the Capitals of the Crypt at Saint-Denis, in: Gesta, Vol. 20, No. 1, 1981, p. 82.

in ecstatic poses, are by the side of Jesus Christ. In the direct vicinity, I recognize the Virgin Mary and the disciple John interceding. To the left and right, at Jesus' feet, the dead are rising from their sarcophagi. Beneath the tympanum, on the inside jamb, arranged vertically to the portal door, there are eight wise and foolish virgins who are visible on both the left and right. The door to paradise is opened to the wise virgins. Beneath the left foot of the Lord is a monk who is looking up to Jesus Christ with an imploring gesture. His head is shaved in a tonsure. He is Abbot Suger.[63]

Now I take a look at the right, south portal. The tympanum depicts the last communion of Saint Dionysius (Denis) and his companions prior to martyrdom. Denis was sent by Pope Fabian in Rome circa 250 A.D. to Gaul to announce Christianity and, according to the accounts of Gregory of Tours circa 251 A.D., to act as the Bishop of Paris. The Roman governor was furious about the missionary visits of Saint Denis and had him and his two companions Rusticus and Eleutherius beheaded. Legend has it that Denis picked up his head and carried it for six miles to die where the Frankish King Dagobert I erected the Romanesque abbey church in 625 A.D., which Abbot Suger had restored and expanded in the Gothic style.

In this depiction, Christ is passing Saint Denis the host. Larcia, who denounced Saint Denis to the Roman prefect and became a Christian during the trial, is depicted to the left of the Saint – on his right, on the other hand, is the governor Fescinius (or Sisinnius) who is pronouncing his merciless sentence over Denis. At the very top, in the apex of the archivolt, we see Saint Denis holding a bishop's miter in his hand and receiving a martyr's crown from an angel. His executors are carved in stone at his feet.

I am surrounded by a bus load of Japanese tourists who are lining up in front of the right portal for photos. I have a hard time continuing my study of the depictions. So I decide to take a look at the left, north portal. In the outer archivolt, I recognize Jesus Christ who appears in an aureole of heavenly light, surrounded by two angels. He is handing Moses, to his right, the two tablets of the covenant law. To the left of Jesus, I recognize Aaron. He is holding

63   Gimpel, Jean, Die Kathedralenbauer, Hamburg: Deukalion Verlag, 1996, p. 11.

the sprouting stave that identifies him as the chosen High Priest from the tribe of Levi. These depictions are based on the original plan of Abbot Suger.[64]

I find that very interesting. The congruence between the words *Virgo* for virgin and *Virga* for the sprouting stave of Aaron, which was kept in front of and in the Ark of the Covenant, seems to reflect the entire theme of the portal. The sprouting stave of Aaron from the Old Testament represents the seed of the plant of Jesus, symbolically known as *flos*, which Mary carries in her. These *typological* correspondences between the Old and the New Testament are found everywhere in St.-Denis. The typology compares events and people of the Old Testament with the New Testament. Thus, Moses corresponds to Jesus Christ; the Ark of the Covenant as a symbol for God's covenant with the Israelites corresponds to the Virgin Mary, who carries Jesus Christ in her as the new divine law.

Beneath Jesus Christ I recognize the Ark of the Covenant with its poles and an angel praying over it. To the left of the Ark of the Covenant appears King David with his lyre; to the right, next to the Ark, his son Solomon who is carrying the Temple. At the foot of the tympanum, above the portal door, the Temple of Solomon is visible. To his right appears the Babylonian King Nebuchadnezzar II who is pillaging and burning Jerusalem. To the left, next to the Temple, the Israelites are being led away in chains and deported through the Babylonian troops into exile. The jambs to the left and right of the portal door are adorned with reliefs of the signs of the zodiac. To the top left, I see the Virgin Mary, followed by Taurus, Aries, Pisces, etc. The Virgin appears to play an important role in St.-Denis. I write this down in my notebook.

Pamela Blum used medieval accounts of the writer *Pseudo-Dionysius, the Areopagite* to prove that for the left portal Abbot Suger planned an unambiguous typological statement about the role of the Christian Church with regard to the Temple of Solomon and the Mosaic Law.[65] This unknown author, who gave himself the pseudonym *Dionysius the Areopagite*, had an immense influence

64   Blum, Pamela Z., The Laterial Portals of the West Facade of the Abbey Church of Saint-Denis, in: Abbot Suger and Saint-Denis: a symposium, Gerson, Paula Lieber (ed.), New York: Abrams, 1987, p. 213.
65   Ibid., p. 217f.

On the left, north portal of the western façade of St.-Denis, you can see the Ark of the Covenant beneath Jesus Christ who is being given the tablets of the covenant law by an angel. The Ark as a sign of God's covenant with the Israelites typologically refers to the Virgin Mary who is making a new covenant with God through the birth of Jesus. Consequently, the Ark of the Covenant corresponds to the Virgin and vice versa. © Tobias D. Wabbel

on medieval theology, and from the 9th century was considered to be the same person as the patron saint of the Abbey Church of St.-Denis and first Bishop of Paris, Saint Denis.

The Temple of Solomon becomes the church, to be precise the Abbey Church of St.-Denis. The Mosaic Law of the Old Testament is expressed in Christ's New Testament law. Aaron's sprouting stave represents the seed of the flower of Christ which his mother, the Virgin Mary, carries in her. Accordingly, the Ark of the Covenant between David and Solomon that I can see in the archivolt of the left portal is just as much a typological representation of the Virgin Mary. The Ark contains the Old Law. The Virgin Mary carries the New Law in her in the form of Jesus Christ. Consequently, the left portal is definitely not a figment of the imagination of the restorer, but is based on a strict Mariological concept of Abbot Suger. In other words: Suger wanted to venerate the Virgin Mary.[66]

---

66   Ibid., p. 213

Here in St.-Denis we see the first architectural starting point for Mariolatry, with which Bernard of Clairvaux was obsessed and which the Knights Templar adopted from him. To recap: the Templar Order dedicated itself to the veneration of the Virgin Mary. However, above all you have to see Suger's plan for the portals in reverse: The virgin signs in St.-Denis refer to the Ark of the Covenant.

The Japanese tourists are now joined by a French school class with approximately thirty kids in their late puberty who are busy trying to drive their teacher mad with their loud chatter and laughter.

As I flee to the portico – the narthex – of the Abbey Church, I am received by a pleasant coolness. A strange mood overcomes me as I enter the central aisle through the portico. In this part of the church circa 775 there were two – at the time badly dilapidated – ambulatories, which were completed under the direction of Abbot Fulrad. Suger had the eastern apse ripped down and replaced by the current apse.[67]

I look through the Abbey Church. The nave of the central aisle of the kings' basilica is flanked by aisles with arcade walkways to the left and right that are each divided by six pillars: 12 pillars for the 12 Apostles, but also for the 12 tribes of Israel. Above the arcade arches there is a triforium, which is decorated by rows of stained glass windows with depictions of saints. In Gothic cathedrals, the triforium is generally found beneath the window façade of the clerestory. In St.-Denis an accessible triforium was added circa 1231 under the clerestory and has since provided even more intense light in the nave, the room for the believers attending church services.

As I approach the right side aisle, I notice that a bay of the central aisle forms two side aisle bays and thus a ratio of 1:2. Art historians call this *square schematism*.[68] Suger used the crossing square, which forms at the junction of the central aisle and transept aisle, as the basic principle of the overall construction, at a ratio of 1:1. According to this, each bay corresponds to a southern (right) and northern (left) bay.

---

67   Crosby, Sumner McKnight, Excavations in the Abbey Church of St.-Denis 1948 the Façade of Fulrad's Church, in: Proceedings of the American Philosophical Society Vol. 93, No. 5 (30. November 1949), p. 347ff.

68   Square schematism appeared for the first time in St. Michael's Church between 1010 and 1033 in Hildesheim.

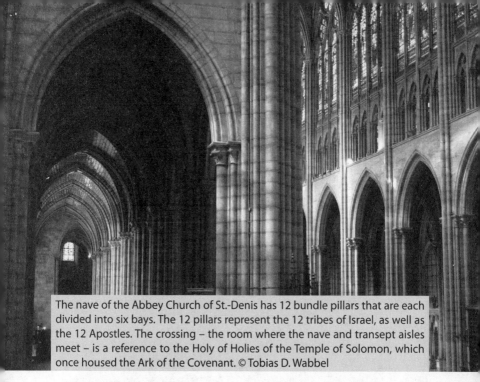

The nave of the Abbey Church of St.-Denis has 12 bundle pillars that are each divided into six bays. The 12 pillars represent the 12 tribes of Israel, as well as the 12 Apostles. The crossing – the room where the nave and transept aisles meet – is a reference to the Holy of Holies of the Temple of Solomon, which once housed the Ark of the Covenant. © Tobias D. Wabbel

The light of the midday sun whose rays are refracting through the colorful stained glass windows on to the stone slabs on the floor is magical. The choir in the east shines in a magnificent firework of colors: ruby red, emerald green, sapphire blue and, between all these, ethereal shades of mystical beauty. The Church looks unusually light through the windows and clerestory that are close to the floor. St.-Denis is a temple of light. I take photographs in a rush of intoxication. Abbot Suger must have planned these light effects right down to the last detail. So it's no wonder that the nobility, bishops and King Louis VII who attended the inauguration of the Abbey Church were overcome with awe as it is known that even Abbot Suger's Holy Chalice was studded with precious stones that refracted the light streaming through the windows into all colors of the spectrum. In my mind's eye, I can see men standing with tears in their eyes in an incense-filled abbey church, genuflecting and reverently praying to God, ecstatically singing liturgical chorales.

I approach the southern transept. This is where the tombs of France's kings begin. I discover the tombstone of King Philip the Fair, who ordered the arrest of all Knights Templar in France on October 13, 1307.

With its portico, nave and apse, the Abbey Church of St.-Denis is divided into three areas, just like the Temple of Jerusalem: portico, Holy Place and Holy of Holies. According to art historians William Clark and Jacqueline Frank, the location of the altar of the martyrs in the apse is identical to that of the plinth on which the Ark of the Covenant once stood in the Temple of Solomon. Abbot Suger uses his architecture to make a precise reference to this room in the Temple of Solomon. © Tobias D. Wabbel

To my surprise, I notice that I can only enter the semicircular chancel to which nine chapels are connected if I buy a ticket for the crypt. So I buy an admission ticket outside for seven euros, reenter the church through the south portal and climb the steps to take a look at the windows of the chevet chapels.

At the top there are a few tombs of the Merovingian kings. I sit on one of the chairs and look around the chancel. Once again, the area is surrounded by 12 pillars. Tripartite dosserets rise to the vertex of the vault. On the altar is a gold-plated reliquary with the bones of Saint Denis. Whether or not the bones are authentic is uncertain. I look around to check whether anyone is watching me. Then I climb over the barrier and inspect the altar. I stand in front of the altar and, with my back to the apse, look into the nave of the central aisle of the basilica and then to the left and to the chapels. The colorful sunlight, which penetrates the chapel windows, falls from the left side to the floor of the chancel.

Suger described this natural marvel as *lux mirabilis et continua clarissimarum vitrearum,* as a miraculous, continuous light that streams through the whole church in divine brightness and illuminates the beauty of the interior.[69] This unique spectacle is only possible because the stained glass windows in the apse chapels take up more space than the Gothic walls.[70] Suger considered the windows to be particularly important. This was also reflected in the costs for the craftsmen and the materials used, which were much higher than other construction measures in the Abbey Church.[71] Just to take care of the windows Suger employed a master and had workers come from foreign countries to manufacture the windows.[72] Suger regarded the windows not only as a mystical element for the liturgy, but above all as a treasure of the inside of the church which was very complicated and costly to manufacture, both due to the pigmented dye applications to the glass, as well as due to the dye added during the glass melting process. This process was described by Roger of Helmarshausen, a Benedictine monk who was born

---

69   Abt Suger von St. Denis, De consecratione, 49,300ss.
70   Westermann-Angerhausen, Hiltrud: Glasmalerei und Himmelslicht – Metapher, Farbe, Stoff, in: Westermann-Angerhausen, Hiltrud (ed.): Himmelslicht – Europäische Glasmalerei im Jahrhundert des Kölner Dombaus (1248-1349), Ausstellungskatalog, Cologne: Schnütgen-Museum, 1998, p. 95ff.
71   Abt Suger von St. Denis, De administratione, 188,849ff.
72   Ibid., 263,1172f.

circa 1070, died 1125 and was a monk at Helmarshausen Abbey between 1100 and 1107.[73] We recognize the purpose of Suger's painted glass iconography not just through the appearance of the window, but also in the titles the Abbot gave the windows.

Out of the corner of my eye, I catch sight of a medallion in a window of the chapel of Saint Peregrine, which is shining in a bright blue light. Before the tourists catch me and tell on me, I slip across the barrier to the altar area and approach the window.

I consult my art history guide book. Suger considered this window in the chapel of Saint Peregrine to be particularly important. It occurs to me how interesting this is. The striking image at the top is part of the "anagogic window," which is split into five round medallions. The bottom medallion shows Jesus between the depiction of the Christian Church, *ecclesia*, and the Jewish Synagogue, *sinagoga*, the temple, in the form of two women. But I notice something else: Spread above Jesus' body are seven dots that are connected into a braid. As I take a closer look at the image, I recognize that it is a depiction of the Jewish Kabbalah. Jesus is touching *ecclesia* and *sinagoga* by placing his hands on the heads of the women. Kabbalah is the synonym for the Revelation of God and the Ten Commandments on Mount Horeb (Sinai). I glance at my notebook.

The Kabbalistic tree of life of the Hebrews reflects the divine conditions of the ten Sefirot. The image features Binah (Understanding), Gevurah (Power), Hod (Majesty), Chokhmah (Wisdom), Chesed (Kindness), Netzach (Eternity) and Tiferet (Beauty). Seven out of 10 Kabbalistic symbols appear in St.-Denis in the anagogic window. But then I recognize that it's eight symbols: Kether, the Crown, is worn by Jesus on his head. Malkuth (Kingdom) and Yesod (Foundation) are missing. According to Suger, Jesus Christ embodies all these attributes. Jesus Christ is the son of God. He turns the Synagogue of Judaism into the Church. However, as the two most important attributes of Kabbalah are missing, I interpret that as meaning that Jesus is definitely not the foundation for the Christian kingdom.

The image seems to combine an obvious and a subtle message: Christ originates from Judaism, the Church originates from

---

73   Brepohl, Erhard, Theophilus Presbyter und das mittelalterliche Kunsthandwerk, Gesamtausgabe der Schrift De diversis artibus in zwei Bänden, Volume 1: Malerei und Glas, Cologne: Böhlau-Verlag, 1999, p. 196.

the Synagogue, the Temple of Solomon. However, Christ is unable to found his kingdom because the two most important aspects of Kabbalah are missing. I note down the strange aspect that there is only one Jewish-Kabbalistic symbol in a Christian church and focus on studying the other iconographies. Further up the window I recognize Moses, holding the divine tablets of the covenant law.

But then I catch my breath because in the top medallion of the anagogic window I see a depiction of the Ark of the Covenant with its poles. To the left and right of the Ark of the Covenant appears a tiny quotation:

FEDERIS:EX.ARCA.CRUCE./XRI.SISTITUR.ARA.
FEDERE. MAIORI. VULT. IBI. VITA./MORI.

I attempt to translate it: "On the Ark of the Covenant is established the altar with the Cross of Christ; Here Life wishes to die under a greater covenant."

The "anagogic window" in the chapel of Saint Peregrine in the Abbey Church of St.-Denis consists of five round medallions. One of them shows Jesus Christ above the Ark of the Covenant with four wheels, the Quadrigae Aminadab. The inscription Quadrigae Aminadab is referring to the house of Aminadab in Kiriath Jearim. In Aminadab's house the Ark of the Covenant was guarded by him and his son Eleazar for 20 years. The Quadrigae is Aminadab's cart on which the Ark was brought by King David to Jerusalem. Abbot Suger regarded himself as a guardian of the Ark of the Covenant. © Tobias D. Wabbel

Obviously, Suger meant that the temple becomes the Church, Judaism becomes Christianity. This window was particularly important to Suger because he mentions it in his manuscript *De administratione*.[74] Wheels are mounted at the four ends of the Ark of the Covenant. The Four Evangelists appear in the corners as man, eagle, lion and bull. On the Ark of the Covenant is a sprouting cross that is held by Jesus Christ. Between the cross and Christ is a yellow curtain. Beneath the Ark of the Covenant I recognize two inscriptions in green and yellow. I read: *Quadrigae Aminadab*.

My heart beats faster. The yellow curtain is none other than the curtain that separated the Holy Place from the Holy of Holies of the Temple of Solomon. Applied to St.-Denis, this refers to the separation of the nave from the choir.[75] The apse, the area of St.-Denis in which the altar of the martyrs is situated, is the Holy of Holies of the Temple of Solomon.

The inscription *Quadrigae Aminadab* refers to the house of Aminadab in Kiriath Jearim. In Aminadab's house the Ark of the Covenant was guarded by him and his son Eleazar for 20 years. The *Quadriga*e is Aminadab's cart on which the Ark was brought by King David to Jerusalem. I have a vague suspicion that St.-Denis is an architectural homage to the Temple of Solomon. But Aminadab's house was only a temporary place to keep the Ark of the Covenant. Perhaps St.-Denis was too. Suger, who emphasized the importance of this window with the depiction of the Ark of the Covenant, *is* both Aminadab and Solomon. He regarded himself as a guardian of the Ark, the protection of which he particularly emphasized as the builder of the Abbey Church of St.-Denis.[76]

I consult my notebook again. I remember that Suger made an unambiguous reference to the Ark of the Covenant. I leaf through a few pages and then find the passage. In *De ordinatio* Suger reveals his particular focus on the Israelites' Ark of the Covenant when he writes:

We, Suger, the undistinguished Abbot of the Blessed Denis, believe it proper and useful in God's sight for all the faithful,

---

74   Abt Suger von St. Denis, De administratione, 267,1186f.

75   Büchsel, Martin, Die Geburt der Gotik, Freiburg i.Br.: Rombach Verlag, 1997, p. 81.

76   Hoffmann, Konrad, Sugers "Anagogisches Fenster" in St. Denis, in: Wallraf-Richartz-Jahrbuch 30, 1968, p. 55ff.

especially for the prelates of the Church, to provide for those committed to the service of the Almighty God; to alleviate their labors and the toil of their struggles by all means, spiritual or temporal, and to sustain them with the necessities of life lest they break down on the road. For to these [prelates] it has been betokened, under the command of God, how it behooved them to take care of and protect the Ark of the Covenant of the Lord with the skins of oxen and cows in order to ward off violent rainstorms and all kinds of damage [...].[77]

There is no doubt that Suger did not mean this allegorically because he indicated that his typological images are only accessible to the *literati* (educated class), the observers who can understand them literally.[78] Isn't Suger instead referring to the transport of the Ark of the Covenant from Jerusalem to Paris at night during fog, wind and rain by the Templars when he wrote that the Ark was protected "with the skins of oxen and cows in order to ward off violent rainstorms and all kinds of damage?" I remember that rainstorms are rather rare in Israel.

If this is the case, there must be more references here in St.-Denis to the transport of the Ark to the kings' basilica of St.-Denis. References that are clear enough to eradicate any doubt that the Templars found the Ark of the Covenant in Jerusalem and transported it to France.

I close my notebook and examine all chapel windows of the ambulatory. However, to my disappointment, I don't find anything else. The anagogic window with the depiction of the Ark of the Covenant remains the one exception up here. I photograph the window and, disappointed, turn to the stairs of the nave. I see a few visitors climb up the steps to the crypt. I promptly decide to take a look under the Abbey Church of St.-Denis. I don't have any high hopes.

Meanwhile, the Abbey Church is filled with groups of visitors from every possible country. I hear bits of Spanish, Italian and German. A group of giggling French school girls stumbles up the stairs

77   Ordinatio, 2-12, in Abbot Suger on the Abbey Church of St.-Denis and its Art Treasures, edited, translated and annotated by Erwin Panofsky, 2nd edition, Princeton University Press, Princeton, 1979, p. 123.
78   Büchsel, Martin, Die Geburt der Gotik, Freiburg i.Br.: Rombach Verlag, 1997, p. 73.

to the choir and almost knocks me over. Once I have reached the south portal again, I climb down the steps to the crypt. The temperature drops by a few degrees and I shiver.

As I walk through the dimly lit corridors of the crypt, I consult my notebook again. Just like the upper choir, the crypt has ambulatory chapels. The American archaeologist and probably the most famous expert on the Abbey Church of St.-Denis, Sumner McKnight Crosby, used calculations and measurements of the choir and crypt to prove that Abbot Suger is referring to the cosmological system of the Roman astronomer Claudius Ptolemy. The seven semicircles that I am inspecting and that form the chapels of the crypt represent the medieval interpretation of the solar system: Moon, Mercury, Venus, Sun and then the three planets Mars, Jupiter and Saturn.[79] So the ambulatory was constructed with the help of cosmological dimensions. The earth is the center, which corresponds with the altar of the martyrs in the upper choir. The Ptolemaic system is based on the assumption that the sun orbits the earth. McKnight Crosby concluded that Abbot Suger must have acquired the knowledge about the Ptolemaic system from Abbot Thierry of Chartres, whose manuscript *The Heptateuch* regards the teaching of Ptolemy as the basis of all astronomical research. The original Arabic manuscript about Ptolemaic science was not officially translated into Latin until 1175. However, Suger must have already acquired Ptolemaic knowledge from Abbot Thierry of Chartres circa 1140.[80]

Now I can clearly see that Abbot Suger used astronomical and geodetic knowledge in the construction and expansion of his abbey church – an extremely important aspect that we will encounter again in the construction of France's cathedrals.

I study the chapters of the pillars. According to the research of Pamela Z. Blum, they show three different rows of motifs that together make up an iconographic scheme: Scenes from the Old Testament, scenes from the life of Saint Benedict of Nursia and scenes from the life of Suger with reference to Saint Denis.[81] The total of

---

79   Crosby, Sumner McKnight, Crypt and Choir Plans at St. Denis, in: Gesta, Vol. 5, January 1966, p. 6.
80   Ibid., p. 8
81   Blum, Pamela Z., The Saint Benedict Cycle on the Capitals of the Crypt at Saint-Denis, in: Gesta, Vol. 20, No. 1, 1981, p. 73ff.

seven Benedict scenes are not accessible because a barrier prevents visitors from entering the room in which the royal tombs are kept.

However, I can exclude the Benedict scenes. As I reach the north-east section of the crypt's termination to the choir, on a chapter I discover the depiction of monks in a procession. The front monk is holding a staff with a cross. It is shaped like a Templar cross pattée. He is followed by two more monks. They are carrying a shrine with the help of two poles. Beneath the box, which has a saddle roof and thus resembles a reliquary, an incense holder is hanging. I deduce that this probably represents the inauguration of the Abbey Church. The shrine might be referring to Saint Denis. On the other hand, it lacks the typical depiction of a pilgrim who is reverently crawling under the shrine and worshiping the saint's relics. Therefore, it is very probably not a reliquary. The light is so dim that I use my gasoline lighter so that I can photograph the scene from all sides. I write in my notebook: "Ark-like object, Templar cross depicted on chapter."

Monks are carrying an Ark-like object with an incense holder under it. This scene is carved into the chapter in the crypt of St.-Denis. You can see the Templar cross at the head of the procession. Perhaps it is the shrine of Saint Denis. However, it closely resembles the Ark of the Covenant as it was depicted in the Middle Ages. As Abbot Suger regarded himself as the guardian of the Ark of the Covenant, we can assume that Suger had the Abbey Church dedicated to the Ark of the Covenant. © Tobias D. Wabbel

I move on. An American family is reverently admiring the tombstones of the Capetian royal dynasty, which are made of polished black granite. A sign off to the side announces that archaeological excavations are taking place here. Sarcophagi from the 7th century cast eery shadows in the twilight. I wonder what else could be hidden behind the walls of the Abbey Church.

I examine every angle, every pillar, every chapter. Apart from the depiction of the strange shrine and the Templar cross, I don't notice anything else. I have already come to terms with my rather meager findings. As I stop next to the plaque with all royal descendants of the Merovingian, Carolingian, Capetian and Valois dynasties and glance to the right, my breath catches in my throat. I rub my eyes.

I spy a box in the shape of a house, on the roof there are two elevations to the left and right: the Ark of the Covenant, depicted as a house, as was typical in the Middle Ages. It reminds me of the depiction of the monks on the chapter who are carrying a strange box. The cart is being drawn by a horse or oxen. I can't tell exactly which. But to the left side I see a few heads carved into the sandstone. They are looking at the Ark of the Covenant. They have pageboy haircuts. I count them.

There are exactly nine heads. No doubt about it. Nine heads of monks or knights. As I glance at my notebook, I find that this is believed to be a depiction of the transport of the relics of St. Edmund (841-869), King of East Anglia. I recall that the Abbey Church of St.-Denis owned feuds and abbeys in England. But no feud was connected to St. Edmund who was buried in the Benedictine Abbey of Bury St. Edmunds in the county of Suffolk. The Abbey Church of St.-Denis had no connection to an unimportant East Anglian martyr. Therefore, this scene cannot show the transport of the relics of St. Edmund. It would be too obvious for this chapter to show the nine Knights Templar accompanying the Ark of the Covenant.

I have found the iconographical evidence that the nine Knights Templar were in possession of the Ark of the Covenant. The image shows none other than the transport of the Ark to France, as described by Abbot Suger. I write in my notebook: "Chapter in front of the northern exit to the crypt. Nine Templars, Ark of the Covenant. Bingo! Charpentier! The old boy was right."

In the crypt of St.-Denis, we also find the amazing depiction of the nine Templars of Hugues de Payns who are looking at the Ark of the Covenant. They can be recognized by their pageboy haircuts, which were typical for the 12th century. The Ark is being transported to France. © Tobias D. Wabbel

Only then do I realize that it is not possible to do more in-depth research without visiting Chartres again. I wonder what I might have missed during my last visits there.

"Off to Chartres," I write in my notebook.

The Victory of Gothic Architecture

The route to Chartres takes me via the Paris ring road to the A10 freeway. My brain is pumping out stress hormones as a semi cuts me off and squeezes by just inches from my car's hood. Annoyingly, Chartres is not yet signposted in St. Denis. Before Versailles I start to loudly cuss. My GPS is going crazy in the bottleneck of the Parisian freeway tunnel and I am forced to follow the wrong signs. At some point, I brake with screeching tires just in time to take the turnoff to Orléans so that a Frenchman behind me almost crashes into me and, blowing his horn, flashes me an obscene gesture.

I ignore the "Merde! Idiot!" he is screeching at me from out of his car window and try to concentrate. To my annoyance, it is only once I have passed Versailles and left behind the mad hectic of the Parisian traffic that my GPS finally gets back its reception. My suspicion to travel via Orléans to Chartres is confirmed by the cold indifference of the navigation system. As I gradually see the suburbs disappear in my rear-view mirror with their prefab buildings, industry areas, car dealers and supermarkets, the route increasingly takes me through the rolling hills of Île-de-France. Here and there, seemingly endless fields lined by little woods and villages appear along the freeway.

I take a deep breath and try to relax. The findings of the past few days are repeatedly going through my head. The search for the Templar treasure is more than just a fantasy. That much is certain. The facts are clear. The Templar treasure consisted of the Ark of the Covenant with the Mosaic Law. A more impressive treasure is inconceivable, both financially and religiously. The possession of the Ark of the Covenant by the Templars meant that they had established a direct connection to Yahweh, God. If someone were to stumble upon this Biblical artifact, this sensation would completely overshadow the tomb of the Pharaoh Tutankhamen and all layers of Troy. A look at the Biblical chest and in particular at the tablets of the covenant law, which Moses chiseled in stone again after descending from Mount Horeb (Sinai) and after smashing the divine originals out of fury over the wicked worshiping of the Golden Calf by the Israelites, would reveal – well what would it reveal exactly? That the God of the world's three most popular religions was simply a product of the imagination of the Hebrews, a people in need who allegedly wandered through the Sinai Desert for forty years? Or would the discovery of the Ark reveal that God really did *choose* the people of Israel? That we can't accept mythology without criticism, but should take it more literally than science tells us to? What would happen after the discovery of the Ark of the Covenant?

I focus on the traffic – and the facts.

Louis Charpentier, a hobby historian and journalist, posed a few interesting questions. And that was all he wanted to do. Charpentier suggested in his book *The Mysteries of Chartres Cathedral* that the Templars of Hugues de Payns might have found the Ark of the Covenant in Jerusalem. Furthermore, he believed that they might have come across secret documents in Jerusalem that explained the mysteries of the antique architecture which, in his opinion, was the basis for the construction of the Temple of Solomon and thus the principle of Gothic architecture. That the Ark was found is now a fact, but the documents are speculation.

Charpentier writes that Gothic architecture first emerged after the return of Hugues de Payns and his followers circa 1128. Medieval architecture was full of pointed arches even earlier, as we have already seen. However, the breakthrough didn't happen until Abbot Suger's plan to build a temple based on the completely new architectural attributes of *pointed arches, ribbed vaults* and *flying buttresses and abutments*. It was only these ingredients that enabled the large window façades close to the floor, the clerestory and interrupted triforia which were responsible for the ethereal light streaming into the choir and nave of the Abbey Church.

Charpentier points out in his book that France's biggest cathedrals were built after 1140 when the Templar Order was granted its most important privileges by the papacy and thus formed a type of state bank. Accordingly, only the Templar Order had the financial possibilities to realize such gigantic projects as the construction of cathedrals which swallowed up decades of construction time and unbelievable sums of money.

Regrettably, there are no written documents from the Templar era that might prove this suspicion. Charpentier speculates that this emergence of cathedrals was *intentional.* It was intended by an organization who had the necessary knowledge and expert master builders at their disposal, as well as the means to finance them. Finally, and this is obvious, it must have been of a religious order. But the secular clergy, the bishops, canons and priests, had neither the knowledge nor, apart from the great metropolitan sees, the means. Only the monastic Orders, in particular the Benedictine and Cistercian Orders, had both the knowledge the money and the master builders, but they kept everything for their own abbeys. Neither the monks of Cluny nor Cîteaux built Chartres. We move from one puzzle to the next.[82]

82   Charpentier, Louis, Die Geheimnisse der Kathedrale von Chartres, Cologne:

In 1145, Pope Eugenius III permitted the Templars to build their own churches. The word *church* is a wide definition and includes chapels and cathedrals. The principal builder of a cathedral was the bishop of the respective town. The first Gothic cathedrals were built in Burgundy, in Île-de-France, in Champagne and in Picardy, precisely that north-east region of France that the poets Chrétien de Troyes and Wolfram von Eschenbach described in their Grail epics. It was the region of the Templars because it is noteworthy that not a single founder of the Order came from the south or west regions of France, but only from Picardy, Burgundy and Champagne.

St.-Denis was an abbey church and thus not a bishop's see. The first cathedral where the bishop preached *ex cathedra*, with the authority of the office, was in Sens, not far from Troyes, built circa 1140. It was dedicated to Stephen the Martyr.

The story of Stephen is at first glance just another Biblical legend. But let's take a closer look at this story to draw our attention to a very curious aspect: Saint Stephen was the first martyr to be put to death for his belief in Jesus Christ. His tale of woe is connected to the Ark of the Covenant, even though he remarks that God does not dwell in a house. The *Legenda aurea* of Jacobus de Voragine tells of his defense speech in which he respectfully talks of the laws of Moses and the Ark of God:

> And after, he purged him of the blame of the tabernacle, and of the temple, in praising the tabernacle in four manners, one was because he was commanded of God to make it, and was showed in vision it was accomplished by Moses, and that the ark of witness was therein, and he said that the temple succeeded tabernacle.[83]

St. Stephen – French: Étienne – was one of the first seven deacons appointed by Jesus' Apostles and thus a second generation apostle. In the New Testament, the character of *Stephen* is only mentioned in connection with the Ark of the Covenant. Thus, Ste-

Gaia Verlag, 1996, p. 13f.
83   The Legenda aurea of Jacobus de Voragine, translated by Richard Benz, Gütersloh: Gütersloher Verlagshaus, 2004, p. 47.

phen is the patron saint of the Ark of the Covenant. When he noted in his defense speech that God doesn't dwell in a house, but also praised the law of Moses and the Ark, this makes him the eponym for the first western cathedral – an extremely remarkable contradiction. Saint Stephen was depicted in the southern transept of Chartres Cathedral, the martyrs portal. This depiction is regarded by art historians as practically identical to the preceding depiction of Stephen in Sens Cathedral. So why was Saint Stephen, the martyr and patron saint of the Ark of the Covenant, that apostle who stated that God does not dwell in a house, chosen to be the eponym for the first cathedral – the house of God?

Why was the first Gothic cathedral erected in Sens, in Burgundy, the region where the Templar founders Hugues de Payns, Count Hugues I of Champagne and André de Montbard, the uncle of Bernard of Clairvaux, came from?

Sens seems to be followed by a veritable explosion of cathedral constructions: In 1150 there was Notre-Dame de Noyon in Picardy, that same year Langres Cathedral in Burgundy, followed by Notre Dame de Senlis, to the north-east of Paris, in 1153, Notre Dame de Laon in 1157, Notre Dame de Paris in 1163, Notre Dame de Chartres and Notre Dame d'Évreux in 1194, St. Étienne de Bourges in 1195, Notre Dame de Coutances in 1218, Notre Dame de Sées and St. Étienne de Metz in 1220 and St. Étienne de Châlons-sur-Marne in Champagne in 1230. Circa 1220, the largest cathedral in France was finally inaugurated: Notre-Dame d'Amiens, in Picardy. Suger's Gothic abbey church subsequently triggered a flood tide of construction activity and it is noteworthy that, apart from a few exceptions, the cathedrals were either dedicated to the Virgin Mary or Stephen the Martyr. To recap: The Virgin Mary as the mother of Jesus, the symbol for the new covenant with God, is regarded as the typological representation of the Ark of the Covenant, the symbol for the old covenant of the Hebrews with Yahweh. As we have also seen, Stephen is the quintessential patron saint of the Ark of the Covenant. So why do we encounter the Virgin who was devoutly venerated by Bernard of Clairvaux and the Templars and who became the Templars' patron saint in addition to Saint

Stephen? Chartres seems to be a key for a deeper understanding of the answers to these questions.

I pay the toll and turn on to Route nationale 10 in the direction of Chartres. As I pass the crest of a hill, I spy the majestic silhouette of Chartres Cathedral on the horizon and across the rape-seed fields of Beauce. The monumental construction was erected on a hill that is situated in a valley and is a pilgrimage stop en route to Santiago de Compostela. The sight must have been overwhelming for the medieval believers. I stop at the side of the road to take a photograph. After 20 minutes, I turn on to Rue Jean Mermoz, approach the town center in the midst of the most severe after-work traffic and decide to look for a room in the next best hotel.

Chartres Cathedral

In view of the Easter holidays all hotels are fully booked. After Santiago de Compostela in Spain and the Basilica of St. Madeleine in Vézelay, Chartres is still one of the most popular pilgrimage destinations in Europe. I had completely overlooked this aspect in my planning. Only after a few hours of searching does a nice old lady in Rue du Muret take pity on me and rent me a room for two days.

Early the next morning, I set off for the Cathedral. Bells ring through the air and announce the end of the early mass this Friday morning. There's not a cloud in the sky and the temperature is unusually warm for this time of day and year. "On Friday, there aren't any chairs covering the labyrinth," my landlady told me before I set off.

I approach the north portal of the Cathedral. Apart from a few exceptions, the apse of a cathedral faces Jerusalem – i.e. the east. But that's not the case in Chartres. The cathedral deviates from this by 43 degrees, 5 degrees further north than the point where the sun rises during the summer solstice of June 21.[84] This deviation is generally explained by the fact that Chartres was built on a Druid meeting place of the tribe of the Carnutes – the name Chartres is derived from the Roman name for the settlement, Carnutum. This meeting place was supposedly naturally aligned this way. Consequently, from the fourth century, all subsequent churches were built with this deviation. Right from the outset, the churches and

---

84   Ladwein, Michael, Chartres, Stuttgart: Verlag Urachhaus, 1998, p. 19

cathedrals of Chartres seem to be born under a bad sign: In 594, this church built out of wood burned down. In 743, the troops of Hunald, Duke of Aquitaine, pillaged and burnt the small city of Chartres. During this, the church burst into flame.[85] In 858, the newly built church was set alight by Danish seafarers and burnt down right to the last wooden plank. In 876, the Bishop of Chartres inaugurated the Cathedral, which for the first time ever had been built out of stone. To honor this occasion, a grandson of Charles the Great (Charlemagne), Charles the Bald, gave the Cathedral the tunic of the Virgin Mary, which was 0.45 meters by 5.35 meters in length and which she was said to have worn during the birth of her son Jesus. Charles the Great allegedly received the ball of fabric as a gift during his crusade against Jerusalem. Legend has it that the Bishop of Chartres held up the Veil of the Virgin to the Norman attackers led by Rollo in 911 and that they, filled with divine reverence on seeing the tunic, fled in panic. In 962, the Cathedral was once again set fire to. These are eventful times: Pillaging, burning and plundering were daily occurrences.

However, under Fulbert of Chartres the town enjoyed an intellectual heyday that lasted right up to the mid-13th century. As the Bishop's chancellor, Fulbert founded the cathedral school of Chartres. He was ordained bishop in 1006. Fulbert expanded the library and introduced the philosophical concept of Scholasticism, which went back to the Greek philosopher Aristotle and involved scientific proof based on previous consideration of logical argumentation – deduction – and was basically the accumulation of theoretical knowledge that was severely criticized centuries later by such great humanists as Erasmus of Rotterdam. Under Fulbert, the cathedral school of Chartres became the most influential philosophical center north of the Alps. The associated cathedral lodge set benchmarks throughout Europe.

However, all philosophical wisdom was powerless against pure violence: In 1020, the Cathedral burnt down again and was promptly reconstructed in the Romanesque style of architecture.[86]

---

85   Ibid., p. 19ff.
86   Simson, Otto von, Die gotische Kathedrale, Darmstadt: Wissenschaftliche Buchgesellschaft, 1965, p. 259. Von Simson was wrong here. The fire occurred in 1020.

On April 10, 1028, Fulbert of Chartres died.[87] Decades passed without the Cathedral suffering any damage. On September 5, 1134, the city blazed again and the Cathedral wasn't spared either. Arson cannot be ruled out as the cause. However, the building had a relatively lucky escape. Immediately afterwards the two towers of the western façade were erected.

Circa 1140, Thierry became the new chancellor of the cathedral school of Chartres. As we have already seen, he provided Abbot Suger with the knowledge of the Ptolemaic world view for the construction of the chevet and the crypt of St.-Denis. Henceforth, the astronomical knowledge of the East was incorporated in the secrets of architecture of the West. The west portal of Chartres was taking shape. In 1146, Bernard of Clairvaux preached about the Second Crusade in Chartres. Initially, it seemed as if Fulbert's construction was to enjoy a luckier destiny. However, on June 10, 1194, the unthinkable happened. A fire raging in the small city of Chartres spread to the Cathedral. A few windows and the western façade with its towers survived the catastrophe.[88] However, the crypt of Fulbert's Cathedral remained completely intact. The tunic of the Blessed Virgin was miraculously saved. For the people of this era this "miracle" was reason enough to believe in divine providence, which they felt was commanding them to build a new and much more beautiful building for God.

Like an act of defiance, shortly afterwards they began building the new cathedral in Gothic-style architecture, based on the remains left over from the disastrous fire of 1194. The builder, whose identity is still unknown today, wanted to adjust the new Gothic building to the proportions of the crypt of Fulbert's cathedral.[89]

As I reach the north portal, I get my military compass and a map of France out of my canvas bag. I sit on the steps of the portal, unfold the map on the cold stones and orient the map with the compass. The last visitors of the early mass are leaving the north portal and disappearing into the old town. My compass measures a deviation of the Cathedral by 43 degrees.

---

87   Ibid., p. 258.
88   Ibid., p. 261.
89   Ibid., p. 263.

The western façade of Chartres Cathedral. The different heights of the bell towers prove that in 1194 the building was rebuilt in Gothic style on top of the burnt down remains of the Romanesque Fulbert's Cathedral. It is not known who built Chartres Cathedral. © Tobias D. Wabbel

But that's not all. On the map I discover that the apse of Chartres Cathedral is precisely pointing to St.-Denis. A coincidence that can be explained away by the fact that the deviation occurred due to the old building foundations on the stones of which they built the current cathedral? I don't think so.

Before I can get up to go into the Cathedral, I make a fascinating discovery. I take my tape measure out of my pocket and extend the line of Chartres across St.- Denis. To my surprise, it ends in Laon, which is known to be one of the oldest cathedrals in France. So the apse of Chartres not only points to St.-Denis, but also to Laon. Just for the hell of it, I place the tape measure on Sens and across Chartres. I shake my head in disbelief because it ends in Sées in Normandy. Sées is a small town with just shy of 4,500 inhabitants. At the time Sées cathedral was built in the 12th century, Sées would have only had a few hundred people and just a few houses. The current cathedral was built in 1210 after its predecessor construction was burnt down in 1174 by the troops of the English King and Count of Anjou, Henry II. Notre Dame de Sées is practically unknown and a jewel of Norman Gothic.

I place the tape measure on Amiens and extend it across St.-Denis. It ends exactly in Notre Dame de Paris. But there's more. Chartres, St.-Denis and Laon form an axis like Amiens, St.-Denis and Notre Dame. The intersection of this cross is always St.-Denis. Except for Chartres, these four cathedrals have one thing in common: a depiction of the Ark of the Covenant on the west portal. In Chartres the Ark of the Covenant adorns the north portal. According to the 43-degree deviation, the north portal of Chartres points exactly in the direction of St.-Denis. I realize that there is a geodetic correlation here and St.-Denis forms the center.

I suddenly remember Louis Charpentier's thesis that the Notre Dame cathedrals form the constellation Virgo. Irrespective of Charpentier, this possibility was also confirmed by E. Ann Matter, Professor of Religious Studies at the University of Pennsylvania.[90]

90 Matter, E. Ann, The Virgin Mary – a Goddess?, in: Olson, Carl, The Book of the Goddess – Past and Present, New York: Crossroad, 1983, p. 86; cf. Green, Arthur, Shekhinah, the Virgin Mary and the Song of Songs: Reflections of a Kabbalistic Symbol in its Historical Context, in: AJS Review, Vol. 26, No. 1 (April 2002), p. 27

But how is this exact arrangement even possible without modern geodetic measurements by theodolites or rather GPS satellite navigation? Why did the cathedral builders build their houses of God in those towns that projected a depiction of the constellation Virgo in the sky?

In the hot and barren wasteland of Castile, the Church of San Bartolomé is situated in a craggy canyon. It was built in 1170, but redesigned in 1230. Beneath the sandstones of the gable, you can still see crosses pattées that were left behind by this region's Templars, and in a round window you notice an inverted pentagram. For Spanish archaeologists this was sufficient reason to undertake a more in-depth investigation. Geodetic measurements in the 1990s showed that the Chapel is exactly 327.54 miles away from Cape Finisterre in the west and 327.54 miles away from Cap de Creus in the east.[91] This can be illustrated by a simple geometric reconstruction: If you connect Cape Finisterre in the west and Cap de Creus in the east with a line and draw a vertical straight line from the midpoint into the south of Spain and exactly through the town of Jaén, amazingly the result will be exactly the same distance. From San Bartolomé it's also exactly 118 miles to the Bay of Biscay in the north, as well as 190 kilometers to the River Tagus, near Madrid. The Templars erected this church in 1170 as a Christian center of their land that had been liberated from the Moors. So San Bartolomé was positioned via extremely precise land surveying of the Templars using an astrolabe where it can today still be admired in the Castilian wilderness. The astrolabe goes back to Hipparchus (190-120 B.C.). Arabian astronomers who were far ahead of their time, compared to Europe's science, refined the measurement using the stars. In Spain astrolabes probably became well-known by the Moors. However, it wasn't until the Templars acquired the knowledge about this measuring technique that they brought it back to the West after the First Crusade. Thus, the exact distance of the Church of San Bartolomé is definitely not a coincidence. The same applies to the Gothic cathedrals in the north of France. Due

91   Kirchner, Gottfried, Terra-X: Schatzsucher, Ritter und Vampire, Munich: Wilhelm Heyne Verlag, 1995, p. 35f.

to the precise arrangement of the cathedrals, we can deduce that the Templars were responsible for these measurements.

I consult Charpentier's book *The Mysteries of Chartres Cathedral*. Both Charpentier and Ann Matter postulate that the cathedrals of Bayeux, Rouen, Abbeville, Amiens, Reims, Paris, Chartres and Évreux depict the constellation Virgo. In this case, Chartres would correspond to the star Gamma Virginis, better known as *Porrima*. I consult my star chart of the northern sky. However, as much as I would like to, I am simply unable to reconstruct the constellation Virgo from Charpentier's depiction.

At lunchtime, I am still sitting on the steps and wondering what the decisive error is that I'm making. At least Charpentier was right that the cathedrals of the north of France depict a constellation. However, it's not as easy as Charpentier would have the reader believe. In accordance with the depiction of Virgo on my star chart, I gradually reconstruct something completely different than Charpentier. If at all, the cathedrals of Metz, Toul, Châlons-sur-Marne, Meaux, Sens and Bourges depict *a part* of the constellation Virgo. These cathedrals were all dedicated to Stephen the Martyr.

Then I take a look at the Notre Dame cathedrals. I move my finger over the map to every single town with a cathedral dedicated to the Virgin Mary. I use a pen to draw the cathedrals on the star chart. I am not expecting much and, for the hell of it, I begin in Bayeux and Coutances in Normandy, move my finger on to Sées, Chartres, Paris, Senlis. I tell myself that up to now, this could all be a coincidence. But then I am able to find Amiens, St. Omer on the coast of the English Channel, even Tournai in Belgium, Cambrai, Noyon, Laon and Reims and draw them on to the star chart. In Meaux the Notre Dame and St. Stephen's cathedrals intersect. I am speechless.

This is an uncanny finding: The Notre Dame cathedrals that I have drawn on to the star chart form precisely the constellation Draco – and not that of Virgo. And, on the contrary, a large part of the constellation Virgo is made up of St. Stephen's cathedrals. The virgin is standing on the dragon. This motif is a reference to the Revelation of the New Testament. The seventh angel sounds the

raco Constellation

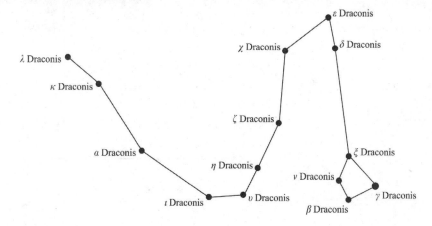

otre Dame Cathedrals

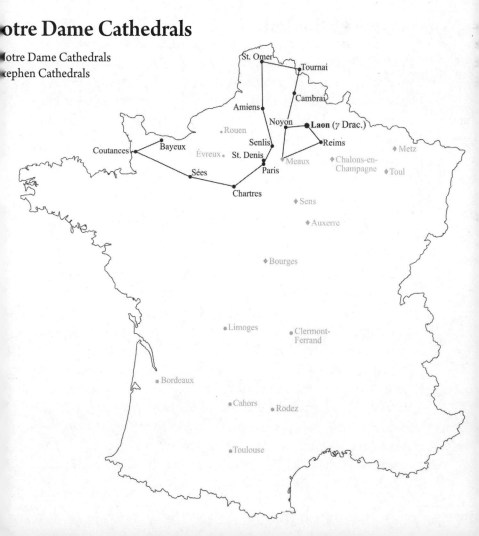

otre Dame Cathedrals
:ephen Cathedrals

Virgo Constellation

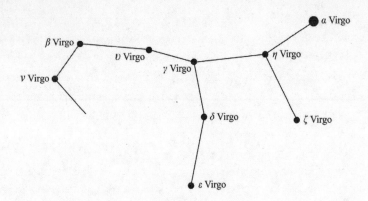

Notre Dame Cathedrals

- Notre Dame Cathedrals
- Stephen Cathedrals

seventh trumpet and announces the kingdom of Jesus Christ. After Christ's kingdom has been announced, the temple of God opens in heaven. "And there was seen in his temple the ark of his testament: and there were lightning, and voices, and thunder, and an earthquake, and great hail."[92] Then we read that the Virgin, the mother of God, conquers Satan in the form of a dragon. In Revelation we read in the chapter *The Woman and the Dragon*:

> And there appeared a great wonder in heaven; a woman clothed with the sun, and the moon under her feet, and on her head a crown of twelve stars: And she being with child cried, travailing in birth, and pained to be delivered. And there appeared another wonder in heaven; and behold a great red dragon, having seven heads and ten horns, and seven crowns on his heads. And his tail drew the third part of the stars of heaven, and did cast them to the earth: and the dragon stood before the woman which was ready to be delivered, for to devour her child as soon as it was born.[93]

The Ark of the Covenant, the Virgin and the Dragon are thus inseparably connected. However, these Bible passages remind me of something completely different, and when I think about it I shudder: The last Templar Grand Master Jacques de Molay carved the graffiti of the virgin and dragon into the stone walls of the tower of Gisors Castle where he was imprisoned. Obviously, Jacques de Molay wanted to leave behind a clue for future generations about the hiding place of the Ark of the Covenant.

Thus, we can deduce that the cathedrals of the north of France were arranged in the constellations of Draco and Virgo for a particular reason. The land surveying and astronomical skills of the Templars and builders were responsible for this. The cathedral designers who arranged their constructions so precisely left behind an encrypted message for future generations about the hiding place of the Ark of the Covenant. In the New Testament Book of Revelation, the divine chest appears in the temple of the Lord when the Virgin conquers the Dragon.

---

92   Revelation 11:19
93   Revelation 12:1-4

Now I realize that I have to search for this symbolism. It's clearly no coincidence. This precise, conceptual arrangement of the cathedrals is definitely not a product of the Roman town planning or heathen meeting places, but part of the master plan of the cathedral builders of the 12th and 13th century. But which plan is meant here? Why were towns chosen in which the Virgin Mary's cathedrals were built in the constellation Draco and St. Stephen's cathedrals built in the constellation Virgo?

To my astonishment, Laon Cathedral forms the head of the constellation Draco: Gamma Draconis is the brightest star in this constellation. On the star chart, Chartres corresponds to the star Alpha Draconis. Gamma Draconis traditionally bears the Arabic name *Etamin*: the head of the dragon. Alpha Draconis, on the other hand, is called *Thuban*, in Arabic which translates to *basilisk*. A basilisk is a hybrid of a winged dragon and dog or another animal.

Now I suddenly realize that the Templars, the medieval bankers, not only exerted great influence on the construction plans of the cathedrals. The financing of such gigantic construction projects would also have been impossible without their monetary aid. The clergy and the Bishop of Chartres provided modest funding for the reconstruction after the fire of 1194, and the highly devout population gave what they could. However, all this was only a fraction of what the construction of Chartres Cathedral devoured over many decades. The amazing architecture of the stonemasons of Chartres and other cathedrals demanded generous payments.

The north portal, the steps of which I am sitting on, was begun in 1204 and completed circa 1215, at a time in which Guillaume de Chartres was the 15th Grand Master of the Templar Order. If the Templars financed the construction of the cathedrals, which were a depiction of the Temple of Solomon, and exerted their influence on the stonemasons' lodges, they must have left clues that reveal where the Ark of the Covenant was hidden. Maybe here in Chartres.

So Charpentier was wrong with his claim that the Virgin Mary's cathedrals depict the constellation Virgo. But was he also wrong with his thesis that the Templars left their signature on the Gothic cathedrals, above all in Chartres? I stuff my things into my shoulder bag, get up and set off in search of answers.

The West Portal

The west façade of Chartres has three pointed-arch portals. In the tympanum of the center portal I recognize the Savior Jesus Christ, the Judge of the World. His right hand is lifted in blessing; his left hand is held on the Book of Life. Beneath the Savior the Apostles are arranged in geometric perfection. Like in St.-Denis, there is apparently a whole lot of typology here too. The events of the Old Testament are manifested in the events of the New Testament. Moses corresponds to Jesus. I find him on the right jamb of the left portal, on the very outside, by the tablets of the covenant law he is holding in his hand. Beneath the Apostles, on the left jamb of the center portal, I spy the Queen of Sheba, King David and King Solomon.

In the archivolts of the right portal of the west façade, I recognize the depiction of the Geometry of Euclid, to the right adjacent to this the Arithmetic of Boethius and under this the Astronomy of Ptolemy. Here we have a reference to the Ptolemaic system. However, it seems as if the stonemasons wanted to carve a deeper message into the portals: namely the message of the seven liberal arts. The builder of Chartres Cathedral knew the secrets of the school of Chartres because on the right portal I find the Dialectic of Aristotle and the Rhetoric of Cicero. Under this I recognize Grammar and Donatus, as well as Music and Pythagoras. I suspect that the Cathedral builder is encouraging the observer to interpret the iconography not only typologically, but also literally and historically. These depictions go back to Bishop Geoffroy de Lèves, a friend of Bernard of Clairvaux.[94]

Like St.-Denis, the west façade of Chartres Cathedral is split into three zones. Above the three portals are three windows and above these a rose. The left, northern bell tower is higher than the southern, right tower. Without towers the bottom construction resembles a solid block that reminds me of the Biblical description of the Temple of Solomon.

94   Schäfke, Werner, Frankreichs gotische Kathedralen, Cologne: DuMont Verlag, 1979, p. 145

The Interior

As I enter the portico of the Cathedral, I am met by a cool darkness. Not a trace of the ethereal light that so enchanted me in St.-Denis. Once my eyes have become accustomed to the dim light, I notice that the floor of the Cathedral slopes down from the choir. The explanation that after every onslaught of pilgrims the floor had to be cleaned so that the water could drain more easily is today no longer accepted. However, other explanations are even less plausible.

The light of Chartres sparsely seeps through the clerestory like clear mountain water running up from black basalt. It is difficult to distinguish between light and darkness here because the stained glass windows, which are often designed in dark colors anyway, are greatly soiled by centuries of dirt. As a result, it takes a few minutes for the mystical eeriness of the Cathedral to manifest before my eyes. Here too, the ratio of 1:1 was used and the proportions of the crossing square applied to the remaining construction areas of the Cathedral, the absolute measure. I jot down: "The nave is divided into six bays, on both sides there are a total of 12 bays just like St.-Denis." One bay of the side aisle corresponds to a quarter of the crossing. Above the arcades I see closed triforia above the clerestory.

The chairs have been removed from the nave so that I am surprised by the sight of the labyrinth. I walk along the labyrinth and make notes. It has 113 points, 11 concentrated bends and 28 reversal points. Black marble that is set in white limestone. Then I measure it with my tape measure. The labyrinth has a diameter of 12.885 meters. I roughly estimate the distance I have walked. The path length is approximately 261.5 meters. There are 273 white slabs. The design of the labyrinth can probably be attributed to the builder Villard de Honnecourt who wrote a stonemasons' lodge book of 33 pages and worked in Chartres between 1200 and 1210. Apart from a few modifications, one of his drawings matches the labyrinth of Chartres.

I stand in the center of the labyrinth, where metal bolts are hooked into the ground, which up until the French Revolution were attached to a round copper plate that was probably adorned by a depiction of Theseus and the Minotaur (a reference to the battle of the

King of Athens with the Minotaur in the labyrinth). The name of the builder used to be engraved on the copper plate. However, we have no idea who was responsible for the construction of Chartres.

Then I turn around and take a look at the West rose window. I jot down: "Depictions of the Last Judgment with delicate tracery, in the window below the tree of Jesse, Moses, King David, King Solomon and Jesus right at the top. The Jewish roots of the Savior." I estimate the dimensions of the West rose. Its size matches that of the labyrinth. As I refer to my notebook, I see that this also has a diameter of 12.885 meters. The walk through the bends and points indicates a search. The labyrinth thus refers to the Apocalypse. I remember the Bible passage in which the virgin is standing on the dragon and then the Ark of the Covenant appears. Perhaps the labyrinth refers to the realization that the cathedrals are the key to the Ark. It is very probably also an allegory for the search for what is or was hidden here in Chartres: the presence of God in the form of the Ark of the Covenant, the Jewish roots of Jesus in the form of King David and his son Solomon, as depicted on the west portal.

The first visitors and tourists enter the cathedral. A lady from Cologne whispers to her husband: "Is this bigger than Cologne?" The little gray-haired man with a Kaiser Wilhelm beard and metal-rimmed glasses replies: "I'm not sure, darling, but it's really cool!" Children rush to the labyrinth and begin to walk through it. Their parents firmly tell them not to make such a noise and then hesitantly enter the labyrinth themselves. A tour group from Italy takes a seat on the benches that are standing in front of the labyrinth and listens to their guide who, in a hushed voice, explains the four-part ribbed vault to them.

I rapidly try to get away from them, mount the camera on the tripod and study the windows for iconographical features. The entire south façade of the nave is covered with depictions of donations of the craftsmen's guilds who built Chartres. Sometimes a window was donated and sometimes it was stones, wood or other materials. One window shows the entire construction activity of the Cathedral, from the design with engineer's square and compasses to the roof gable and keystone. In this window, I discover the depiction of a box that is held on two poles by two men. I photograph it.

In the south-east part of the southern transept, I identify the depiction of Saint Denis who is passing the Oriflamme to the Knight Jean III Clément du Mez who donated the window.[95] The skin of the Knight Clément is brownish and his tunic that he wears over the armor is blue. On his chest is a white cross pattée. The symbol of the Templars. From 1225, Jean III Clément du Mez was the Marshal of France, the representative of the commander of the royal army of Philip II, the son of King Louis VII. Knight Jean III Clément died circa 1260. Beneath Saint Denis and Knight Jean III Clément, I photograph a blue crest that also has a white cross pattée. The cross pattée on the surcoat identifies a knight as a Templar. This depiction refers to the closeness of the Capetian royal dynasty to the Templar Order. And to the close relationship between Chartres and St.-Denis.

The choir, which was created between 1519 and 1714, is an impressive example of stonemasonry and shows the life of Jesus Christ in 40 reliefs: from his birth to the Crucifixion and Resurrection. I move on and reach the ambulatory with its chapels. Here I discover a window high up on which two men are holding a golden reliquary under which I can see a white cloth. The official art history explanation is that this cloth is Mary's tunic. However, the shrine is incredibly similar to the Ark of the Covenant. This suspicion is supported by the astonishing fact that the window is dedicated to the patron saint of the Ark of the Covenant, Stephen the Martyr. The fact that it is probably not a reliquary is made clear by the missing pilgrim crouching underneath it and worshiping the relic with his hands together in prayer. Mary's Veil would also be draped over the reliquary and not underneath it. I write in my notebook: "St. Stephen's window has a strange correspondence with the Ark," and then I take detailed photographs.

The five windows under the tracery rose of the north portal are equally revealing. Here I find the depiction of the high priest Melchizedek, who in the First Book of Moses (Genesis) 14:17-

---

95   Kurmann-Schwarz, Brigitte und Kurmann, Peter, Chartres – Die Kathedrale, Regensburg: Verlag Schnell & Steiner, 2001, p. 160.

In the south-east part of the southern transept, there is a depiction of Saint Denis who is passing the Oriflamme to the Knight Jean III Clément du Mez who donated the window. On the chest of the Knight Clément is a white cross pattée, the sign of the Templars. From 1225, Jean III Clément du Mez was the Marshal of France, the representative of the commander of the royal army of Philip II, the son of King Louis VII. The royal family was very close to the Templars. © Tobias D. Wabbel

One window of an ambulatory chapel shows two priests who are carrying a golden box. The official art history interpretation is that Mary's tunic is stored inside the box. However, the window is dedicated to Saint Stephen, a clear reference to the Ark of the Covenant. © Tobias D. Wabbel

19 blesses the Biblical patriarch Abraham and brings him wine and bread. To the right of him are David, Mary's mother Anne, Solomon and Moses' brother Aaron, who is recognizable by his sprouting stave and the 12 precious stones on the breastplate of his high priest's garment. Through my telephoto lens I recognize Nebuchadnezzar II beneath Melchizedek. The Babylonian king is standing in front of a statue of a heathen idol. Beneath King Solomon, I can decipher the name Jeroboam, the King of the northern Israelite kingdom who reigned after Solomon's death and had golden calves worshiped in Bethel and Dan.

The tracery of the rose is framed to the left and right by four tiered lancet windows that show depictions of the golden fleur-de-lis against a dark blue background. Next to it is a yellow castle against a red background as the crest of the donor of the window, Blanche of Castile, wife of French King Louis VIII. In addition, 12 of the fleur-de-lis appear in the rose, a reference to the 12 tribes of the Israelites and the 12 prophets of the Old Testament. In another ring 12 kings of the Israelites are depicted – Manasseh, Ahaz, Osias, Abijah, Solomon, David and others. In the outer ring I can also make out the 12 prophets of the Israelites in 12 semicircles around the rose. The Capetian royal dynasty is using the rose window in the northern transept to emphasize that they are part of the Israelite line. As a result, they are hardly any different from the Templars whom Bernard regarded as "the true Israelites." Since the Templar Grand Master Everard des Barres saved King Louis VII's life and safely escorted him with his troops to France, the Order of warrior monks had been close friends with the Capetian dynasty. This continued under the reign of Louis VIII and Louis IX.

The South Portal

After spending a few more hours in the Cathedral and taking dozens of photos, I leave the Cathedral through the exit of the southern transept. Here I am amazed by the iconography of the portal which focuses on the depiction of the Last Judgment. After searching through and analyzing all the sculptures for an hour, on the right jamb of the left portal of the southern transept I come across the depiction of Saint George, the Dragon Slayer. He has curly hair, a full beard, is wearing a chain mail shirt and over that a monk's habit. In his right hand, George is holding the lance with which he, according to the legend, killed the dragon. His left hand is resting on a shield; when I move a little to the side I see that it is adorned with a Templar cross. The Templars had to wear a beard because it was part of their uniform. So George is depicted as a Templar.[96] And this on the martyrs portal where on the left jamb of the lintel Saint Stephen is featured, a man to whom some of the most important Gothic cathedrals in the north of France were dedicated. I note these fascinating new facts.

I associate some amazing facts with Saint George: He was born in the third century, probably died around 303 in Lydda, Palestine, and rapidly became one of the greatest martyrs in Christendom because he was executed under the reign of the Roman emperor Diocletian as a result of the brutal persecution of the Christians.

96   Ladwein, Michael, Chartres, Stuttgart: Verlag Urachhaus, 1998, p. 108

However, the legend of the dragon slayer didn't crop up until the 12th century after which the Cistercians incorporated Saint George in the Order's legends.[97] Accordingly, the iconography of George as the dragon slayer didn't appear until 1112 to 1129 when it was first featured on an Antiochian coin.[98] During an era in which Bernard founded Clairvaux Abbey, the armies of the First Crusade conquered Jerusalem and the Templar Order was founded in Jerusalem. The *Legenda aurea*, which was composed circa 1298 by Jacobus de Voragine, reports that Saint George appeared to the Crusaders during the storming of Jerusalem.[99] Here we read:

> [...] when the Christian hosts were about to lay siege to Jerusalem, a passing fair young man appeared to a priest. He told him that he was Saint George, the captain of the Christian armies; and that if the crusaders carried his relics to Jerusalem, he would be with them.
>
> And when the crusaders, during the siege of Jerusalem, feared to scale the walls because of the Saracens who were mounted thereon, Saint George appeared to them, accoutred in white armor adorned with the red cross. He signed to them to follow him without fear in the assault of the walls: and they, encouraged by his leadership, repulsed the Saracens and took the city.[100]

However, the legend of Saint George as the dragon slayer didn't appear until Hugues de Payns and his followers settled on the Temple Mount. Afterwards, George very rapidly became the patron saint of the Order of warrior monks. His flag has since been a red cross against a white background. Thus, Saint George is depicted in Templar garb with a red cross on a white shield in a north-west French Bible manuscript and shown fighting Saracens on horseback.[101] Therefore, Saint George is the epitome of the Templar

97   Theologische Realenzyklopädie, Part 1, Volume 12, Berlin: Verlag Walter de Gruyter, 1993, p. 383.
98   Ibid., p. 381.
99   Ibid., p. 383.
100   The Legenda aurea of Jacobus de Voragine, translated by Richard Benz, Gütersloh: Gütersloher Verlagshaus, 2004, p. 232ff.
101   Jerusalemkarte, Königliche Bibliothek Den Haag, Manuscript No. 76F5, folio 1 recto.

Order. Here in Chartres, it is through George that a clear reference is made to the dragon. However, at his feet I don't see a dragon. Another strange thing.

Now I'd like to take one last look at the north portal which was planned circa 1205. I don't have any high hopes. At least, I was able to prove that the Templars were active in Chartres. However, up to now I have been unable to find decisive proof that the Ark of the Covenant was in Chartres. The sun is still unbearably hot. I am tired, my tummy is rumbling and the "La Reine de Saba" brasserie opposite the south portal seems to be calling my name. I feel like a cold beer and a hearty meal. I decide to only take a cursory look at the north portal.

But things don't quite go according to plan.

The North Portal

Wind whistles in my ears as I climb up the steps to the north portal of the Virgin Mary, which depicts scenes from the life of the Virgin Mary and the Old Testament. The portals have roofs and the archivolts are completely covered in Biblical figures. The west portal of Laon Cathedral served as the inspiration for the north portal of Chartres. In actual fact, circa 1205 until 1220 the same planners and stonemasons were working on these portals.[102]

The façade of the northern transept is divided into three portal zones with porticos. Thanks to the stone roofing, the sculptures and delicate stonemasonry were able to withstand the rough weather over the centuries.

I am standing in front of the center portal. In the tympanum, I recognize Mary and Jesus, sitting on a throne beneath a baldachin. They are flanked by two angels. The crowned Mary is being blessed by her son. The archivolts are filled with depictions of angels, the roots of Jesse – the Israelite family tree of Jesus and Mary – the prophets and figures from the Old Testament. References to the Jewish heritage of Jesus. On the left jamb of the portal I identify the high priest Melchizedek, holding the blessing goblet. To the right

102   Toman, Rolf (ed.), Die Kunst der Gotik, Cologne: Verlag Könemann, 1998, p. 54; cf. Adenauer, Hanna, Die Kathedrale von Laon, Düsseldorf: L. Schwann Druckerei und Verlag, 1934, p. 27.

of him, the patriarch Abraham is looking towards the heavens and turned towards Yahweh. I recognize him by the knife he is holding in his left hand which he intends to use to sacrifice his son Isaac on Mount Moriah as a sign of his devotion to Yahweh. The stonemasons positioned Isaac in front of Abraham.

Moses in the middle of the five sculptures clad in billowing robes is holding one of the two divine tablets of the covenant law in his left hand. A thin pole is leaning in the crook of his arm and the top end is decorated with the depiction of an acanthus leaf. On the tip of the pole sits an enthroned basilisk, a hybrid with dragon's wings and an unfriendly looking dog's head. Its teeth are carefully carved. It is a depiction of the *Nehushtan*. During the Exodus from Egypt, the Israelites began railing against their fate and complained about their thirst and the monotonous food. God sent snakes among the Israelites and instructed Moses to make a rod of bronze with a snake wound around it. Whoever was bitten by the snakes and saw the serpent of bronze was not struck down dead by the Lord.[103]

In the Middle Ages, Nehushtan was only rarely depicted as a dragon. I remember seeing a similar depiction in Reims, but the serpent was clearly recognizable as such. No trace of a dragon. As Nehushtan typologically represents the Crucifixion of Christ, in the Middle Ages it was often shown as a snake winding around Jesus' Cross. Moses' face is turned to the north-east and his right hand is paused in front of his thorax. I continue to examine the figure of Moses. However, the decisive clue does not reveal itself to me.

I continue my search. Moses' brother Aaron is not wearing the priest's garment with precious stones, but is instead holding a sheep and a slaughter knife – a symbol for his sacrifice of the lambs in the tent of meeting. David is holding a lance and wearing a crown.

I turn to the left jamb of the right Job-Solomon portal. Here the sculptures of King Solomon and the Queen of Sheba stand out. Beneath the feet of King Solomon, the grinning fool Marcolf is crouching under a baldachin. His character goes back to the northern French manuscript *Dialogus Salomonis et Marcolfi*. In this man-

103   Fourth Book of Mose (Numbers) 21,4-9.

On the left jamb of the center portico of the north portal of Chartres, Moses is pointing with his (broken off) index finger to the head of the serpent of bronze, which is shown as a dragon-like basilisk. Laon Cathedral in Picardy forms the head of the constellation Draco. Therefore, Moses with his tablets of the covenant law is pointing at Laon Cathedral. © Tobias D. Wabbel

On the left jamb of the right portico of the north portal of Chartres Cathedral the figure of Marcolf was carved in stone beneath the jamb sculpture of King Solomon. In the French manuscript Solomon and Marcolf, which was composed circa 1175, the cunning Marcolf is a vassal of King Solomon. Marcolf is Solomon's advisor, but the King mistrusts his suggestions. He has excellent relations with the Templars. From an art history perspective, Marcolf is considered to be the same person as Hiram-Abiff, the builder of the Temple of Solomon. The Templars are thus the same as Hiram-Abiff – they can be regarded as the builders of the new Temple of Solomon in Chartres. © Tobias D. Wabbel

uscript, Marcolf is cunning and extremely ugly and appears with his equally ugly wife at the court of Solomon. King Solomon makes a bet with him: If Marcolf is able to respond to all puzzles, pieces of wisdom and sayings of the King, he will receive a generous reward. Marcolf agrees to the contest, he parries the King's questions by taking the choice of words and tasks of the King *very literally*. Through these literal interpretations, he arrives at the necessary realizations.[104] A request by the builders of the north portal, similar

104   Halfen, Roland, Chartres, Schöpfungsbau und Ideenwelt im Herzen Europas,

to Abbot Suger, to take the Biblical quotations literally and not give them a typological and allegorical interpretation.

In the French manuscript *Solomon and Marcolf*, which was composed circa 1175, the cunning Marcolf is a vassal of King Solomon, or even his brother. Marcolf is Solomon's advisor, but the King mistrusts his suggestions. Verses 488 and 561 describe the excellent relations between the cunning fool Marcolf/Morolf and the Knights Templar.[105] From an art history perspective, Marcolf is considered to be the same person as Hiram-Abiff, the builder of the Temple of Solomon. This aspect justifiably leads me to deduce that the Temple of Solomon has been spectacularly reborn in Chartres.[106] It also leads me to conclude that the Templars are actually the same as Hiram-Abiff. So the Templars are the builders of the new Temple of Solomon in Chartres.

The Queen of Sheba is standing on the shoulders of her servant, a Moor. It is extremely rare to depict the figure of an African on a Gothic building.

I note the new findings and then study the pillars of the north portal. On a relief cylinder on the right side of the entrance to the central portico, I find the depiction of a battle. Soldiers with lances. One of them is wearing a chainmail shirt. Embroiled in a desperate battle. I identify this scene as the theft of the Ark of the Covenant by the Philistines during the Battle of Aphek, as described in the First Book of Samuel.

The scene describes how the sons of Eli, Hophni and Phinehas, are killed. Now the Ark is without guards and is stolen by the Philistines and taken to Ashdod. The next scene shows the headless idol Dagon falling on its face to the earth. The Ark inflicts the Philistines with hemorrhoids so that they decide to give God's shrine back with five golden emerods and five golden mice as atonement gifts. I look at the stonemasonry of a little mouse, the pot of manna, Aaron's rod and the tablets of the covenant law in the Ark. Beneath them is an inscription carved into the stone in the medieval uncial script:

Volume 2: Die Querhausportale, Stuttgart: Mayer Verlag, 2003, p. 188.
105   Ibid., p. 190.
106   Ibid., p. 193.

Relief cylinder on the north portal of Chartres Cathedral. This shows the theft of the Ark of the Covenant by the Philistines during the Battle of Aphek, as well as the Philistine idol Dagon falling to the ground in the city of Ashdod. © Tobias D. Wabbel

Beneath the sculptures the inscription HIC AMITITUR ARCHA CEDERIS is carved into the stone. If, however, you read the "T" in the word "Amititur" in Uncial script as a "C," the inscription means: The Ark that will be hidden here. It clearly refers to Chartres Cathedral as a hiding place for the Ark of the Covenant. What is unusual is that both Uncial script and Antiqua letters are used – this was rare in the Middle Ages. © Tobias D. Wabbel

Hic Amititur Archa Cederis

One pillar on I can see a box on a cart pulled by cows and led by an angel. The Ark looks more like a chest because it has hinges in the shape of fleurs-de-lis and a lock. After the Philistines voluntarily give back the Ark, it is brought back to Beth Shemesh. The following words are carved under this:

On the neighboring relief cylinder the Ark of the Covenant is being transported on an ox-drawn cart back to Beth Shemesh. Underneath this is the following note: ARCHA CEDERIS. However, the Ark of the Covenant was always referred to in the Latin Bible (Vulgate) as "Arca Foederis." As CEDERIS appears here and on the neighboring cylinder, it can't have been a mistake of the stonemasons. The entire arrangement of the inscriptions was thus carefully planned and the work of highly trained clerics. © Tobias D. Wabbel

Archa Cederis

I get the Louis Charpentier book out of my bag. He translated these lines with "Here things take their course; you are to work through the Ark."[107] However, I don't agree with Charpentier's translation at all. Frankly, I think it is utter nonsense.

Instead, I realize that the stonemason responsible for this inscription included two supposed errors in both quotations: Firstly, the Ark of the Covenant is always referred to as "Arca Foederis" in the Latin Bible (Vulgate), so "Ark of the Covenant" and not "Archa Cederis." However, as "Archa Cederis" is mentioned twice, so the stonemason didn't make a mistake. It was his full intention to use the terminology "Archa Cederis." It is definitely not a reference to "cedar" as the Ark was not made of cedar wood, but of acacia wood and cedar in Latin is "cedrus."

Now I am determined to decipher this strange inscription. Secondly, the "T" in the inscription "Hic Amititur Archa Cederis" has been carved into a kind of "C" with a curved tilde. Perhaps this is a kind of ligature for the double letter "TT" because "Amititur" with a "T" does not exist in Latin. However, this is not very probable because there was enough space for the master stonemason to carve a double "T" into the stone. As he did not do this, a "C" is more likely. Accordingly, the inscription would be:

HIC AMICITUR ARCHA CEDERIS

"Amititur" and "Amicitur" are future participles, which make no obvious differentiation between active and passive. If I replace "Amititur" by "Amicitur," this gives the inscription a completely different meaning:

THE ARK OF THE COVENANT THAT WILL BE HIDDEN HERE

Accordingly, "Hic Amititur Archa Cederis" would refer to the loss of the Ark by the theft of the Philistines during the Battle of Aphek. The use of the word "hic" for "here" is extremely unusual in a Biblical description. It should have been "there," i.e. "illic," because that would describe the place of Aphek. However, "Hic Amicitur Arca Foederis" would be referring to the place of Chartres itself: "Hic" for "here" or "local," i.e. Chartres.

107   Charpentier, Louis, Die Geheimnisse der Kathedrale von Chartres, Cologne: Gaia Verlag, 1996, p. 66

Detail from the relief cylinder on the north portal of Chartres Cathedral that shows the Ark of the Covenant causing the fall of the idol Dagon in the temple of Ashdod. It is unusual here that the stonemasons have obviously taken into account every Biblical detail: the pot of manna, Aaron's rod and the tablets of the covenant law in the Ark. © Tobias D. Wabbel

This play on words is so clever that it was undoubtedly the work of a witty cleric who was familiar with all the tricks of medieval Latin and all Bible passages in the Old and New Testament. This was also the view of world-famous British-German art historian Peter Lasko.[108]

My breath catches in my throat and I shake my head in disbelief.

This inscription is the proof that the Ark of the Covenant *was* either in Chartres or *would be* brought to Chartres in the future. It is also possible, however, that the Ark was "ceded" by Chartres – *cedere* – and brought to another place. The fact that the Ark has hinges with the symbols of the Capetian dynasty leads me to conclude that the King of France was involved in this process.

As I turn around, in the center portal I see Moses again holding the dragon-tipped pole. I approach the jamb and take a closer look at the figure of Moses. His right hand is paused in front of his thorax. Then I see that his index finger has broken off. Judging by the direction, he is pointing at the head of the dragon.[109]

Suddenly I understand: Moses is pointing at the *head of the dragon*. This is referring to the constellation Draco. Chartres corresponds to Alpha Draconis. The star was known in Arabia as *Thuban*, which means *basilisk* or dragon-like hybrid. Now I see the basilisk in front of me. So the builders of Chartres were not only familiar with Ptolemaic astronomy, but also knew the Arabian names for the stars. Gamma Draconis corresponds to Laon Cathedral. Now it's finally time for a cold beer.

Once I am sitting in the brasserie opposite the Cathedral, I try to jot down the overwhelming findings about the whereabouts of the Ark of the Covenant in my notebook:

- Abbot Suger, a close friend of Bernard of Clairvaux and King Louis VII, had the Abbey Church of St.-Denis built as a depiction of the Temple of Solomon.

- The Abbey Church of St.-Denis features depictions of the Ark of the Covenant which Abbot Suger advised in his writings should be taken historically and literally.

108   Hancock, Graham, Die Wächter des heiligen Siegels, Bergisch-Gladbach: Lübbe-Verlag, 1998, p. 64.
109   Halfen, Roland, Chartres, Schöpfungsbau und Ideenwelt im Herzen Europas, Volume 2: Die Querhausportale, Stuttgart: Mayer Verlag, 2003, p. 97.

The Ark of the Covenant is being transported away on Aminadab's four-wheel cart. However, the inscription ARCHA CEDERIS could also mean that the Ark is quite literally being "driven" or "brought" to Chartres. © Tobias D. Wabbel

- In his manuscript *De ordinatio* he talks about the transport of the Ark to Europe.

- Hugues de Payns and his eight followers of the Templar Order are depicted together with the Ark of the Covenant in the crypt of St.-Denis.

- The rest of France's Gothic cathedrals were built as a depiction of the Temple of Solomon.

- France's Notre Dame cathedrals form the constellation Draco.

- St. Stephen's cathedrals form the constellation Virgo.

- The Templars were responsible for the financing and planning of Chartres Cathedral.

- The north portal of Chartres was built at the same time as the west portal of Laon. The same planners were involved.

- On the north portal of Chartres the inscription HIC AMICITUR ARCHA CEDERIS confirms that the Ark of the Covenant *was* in Chartres or was *to be* brought to Chartres.

- The star Alpha Draconis corresponds to Chartres. It is called *Thuban* in Arabic, which means *basilisk,* a dragon-like hybrid.

- The statue of Moses on the north portal of Chartres is pointing with its right index finger at the depiction of the serpent of bronze, which is shown as a basilisk.

- The brightest star in the constellation Draco is Gamma Draconis, which is known as *Etamin* in Arabic: "the head of the dragon."

- Projected on to the earth, Gamma Draconis corresponds to the Notre Dame Cathedral of Laon.

"Off to Laon," I write in my notebook.

Chapter Five

The Final Clue

X marks the spot.

— Dr. Henry Jones Jr.

The Secret of Baphomet

I decide to avoid the Paris ring road and instead I take the Route nationale N191 via Étampes, past the old Templar location Savigny-le-Temple, and then switch to the N36 in the direction of Meaux. There, I make a brief stop and take a look at the cathedral from the 13th century. Meaux is the birthplace of the third Templar Grand Master Everard des Barres, who provided King Louis VII with safe passage from the Middle East back to France.[1] Everard des Barres was present at Pope Eugenius III's general chapter in Paris in 1147 when the Templar Order was granted the red cross pattée on the white surcoat. Together with King Louis VII, he devised the military strategy for the Second Crusade. However, after the bloody defeat of Damascus, the King and his troops were forced to return home. Everard saved the life of the King's men in battle and King Louis VII praised this honorable behavior in one of his letters. After Everard des Barres had granted the King safe passage, he returned to the Middle East a second time in 1152. Following his return from the East, he became a Cistercian monk in Clairvaux, where he died in 1176. Meaux Cathedral was begun a year later.

The St. Stephen's Cathedral of Meaux is part of the constellation Virgo. But also part of the constellation Draco. Projected on to the earth, this is the exact place where the stars Gamma Virginis

---

1   Bulst-Thiele, Marie-Luise, Sacrae domus militiae Templi Hierosolymitani magistri: Untersuchungen zur Geschichte des Templerordens 1118/19-1317, Göttingen: Vandenhoeck & Ruprecht, 1974, p. 41ff.

and Beta Draconis intersect. Beta Draconis is *Alwaid* in Arabic. Another name for Alwaid is *Rastaban*: the head of the dragon. This can't be a coincidence because Gamma Draconis – Laon Cathedral – is also known as Rastaban or Etamin. The builders of this amazing cathedral key are hereby confirming through Meaux Cathedral that there must be something extremely significant in Laon. Thus, on the west portal of Meaux I discover the depiction of a bearded knight, wearing a cowl over a chainmail shirt and holding a shield with a Templar cross: Saint George. However, I can't see any dragon around him.

After two hours, I drive on across Route nationale 2 through the villages of the flat Picardy with its attractive landscape and on to Laon. As the cornfields pass me by, previously unknown aspects and unanswered questions come together to form a large mosaic of my findings.

A key role had been played by the highly devout pilgrim and Count Hugues I of Champagne. It was his initiative to search under the Temple Mount for the missing Ark of the Covenant. He was joined by his vasall Hugues de Payns, Saint Bernard of Clairvaux's uncle, André de Montbard, and six other followers. After an at least nine-year search, they found what they were looking for. This must have been by no later than 1128. Accounts show that Clairvaux housed the greatest collection of divine relics. Thus, it seems logical to conclude that the holy Ark of the Covenant, the greatest Biblical artifact, would be the crowning of all this.

The golden box with the inscription "ARCA" from the Cistercian Lichtental Abbey confirms the significance the Ark of the Covenant held for the reform movement. It is very probable that this is an homage to the real Ark of the Covenant which was found by the Templars led by Hugues de Payns beneath the Temple Mount. Are there clues to indicate that the Cistercian Order came into possession of the Ark of the Covenant through the Templars?

Pope Eugenius III was elected Pope on February 15, 1145. Just a few months later, he issued the papal bull *Militia dei*, permitting the Templars to build their own churches. Eugenius III's original name

The Final Clue

was Bernardo Paganelli di Montemagno and he came from Pisa.[2]
He was a pupil of Bernard of Clairvaux who had appointed him
Abbot of Tre Fontane Abbey, outside of Rome. Eugenius III was
neither a bishop nor a cardinal and Paganelli's election to Pope was
thanks to the heavyweight in church politics, Bernard of Clairvaux.
In his manuscript *De consideratione ad Eugenium Papam* – about
the consideration of Pope Eugenius – Bernard of Clairvaux wrote a
veritable catalogue of behavior to his protégé.[3] Bernard emphasized
that the papacy had been characterized by decadence, corruptibil-
ity, disobedience and unchastity. He described Rome as a source
of epidemic, his protégé Eugenius III must have been aware of the
harmful consequences of this decadence that have already driven
so many popes before him to an early grave. For Bernard, Eugenius
III was like a son. Consequently, his tone towards the Pope was
quite demanding. Eugenius III was Bernard's Pope.

Bernard, who was himself regarded as the most powerful man
of the Middle Ages, intended to bring the Cistercian reform concept to Rome. However, nought came of this because the Augustinian monk Arnold of Brescia (1100-1155) – a sworn enemy of
Bernard of Clairvaux – demanded the abolition of the worldly
power of papacy.[4] In Arnold's eyes, the Pope and his comrades-in-
arms were now superfluous. Eugenius III had to flee as a result of
the tense situation in the Roman community. Consequently, the
Pope performed his official duties from his carriage. Eugenius III
was a mild and gentle pope, a Cistercian monk who only reluctant-
ly allowed the papal crown to be placed on his head.

So it's all the more astonishing that Pope Eugenius' closest
confidant, Cistercian monk Nicolaus Maniacutius, mentioned
in his manuscript *Historia Imaginis Salvatoris* circa 1145 that
the treasures from the Temple of Jerusalem and the Ark of the
Covenant were located in the Vatican Chapel of St. Laurentius.[5]

---

2   Merton, Thomas and Hart, Patrick, Blessed Eugenius III, Abbot of Tre Fontane,
Pope, in: Cistercian Studies Quarterly 44, 2009, p. 173ff.
3   Farkasfalvy, D., introduction to De consideratione ad Eugenium Papam, in:
Bernhard von Clairvaux, Sämtliche Werke, Volume 1, Innsbruck: Tyrolia-Verlag, 1990, p. 612.
4   Vacandard, Elphège, Das Leben des Heiligen Bernard von Clairvaux, Mainz:
Verlag Franz von Kirchheim, 1897-1898, Volume 2, p. 506.
5   Maniacutius, Nikolaus, Historia Imaginis Salvatoris, BAV Fondo S. Maria Mag-
giore 2, fols 233-244; cf. Wolf, Gerhard, Salus Populi Romani, Die Geschichte römischer

The personal papal chapel of St. Laurentius is today still called *Sancta Sanctorum* – the "Holy of Holies." Nicolaus Maniacutius first mentioned this name in his manuscript.[6] Maniacutius was an exceptional man: Prior to 1140, Nicolaus was Deacon of St. Damasus in Rome. Then he joined the Cistercian community of St. Anastasius of Tre Fontane, where he lived as a monk under Abbot Bernardo Paganelli, who later became Pope Eugenius III. Just like the later Pope Eugenius III, Nicolaus Maniacutius was a close confidant of Bernard of Clairvaux, the spiritual father of the Templar Order. In *De sacra imagine* Nicolaus Maniacutius expressly emphasized the similarities between the *Sancta Sanctorum* of the Vatican and the Holy of Holies of the Temple of Solomon in Jerusalem. Nicolaus Maniacutius compares Pope Eugenius III to a high priest who was standing in the solitude of the Holy of Holies of the Temple of Solomon and looking at the Ark of the Covenant.[7]

Pope Eugenius III instructed the name of the Chapel of St. Laurentius to be changed to *Sancta Sanctorum*. This fact reflected the political change of direction of the Church under Pope Eugenius III to Judaism – about forty-five years before, the Jews had been massacred in Germany and Hungary during the First Crusade. However, under the Cistercian Pope Eugenius III, a change of course was taken with regard to God's chosen people.

This change of course also corresponded to a belief of the Jewish people in Rome that the Vatican was in possession of the Temple treasure and, above all, the Ark of the Covenant. The Jewish traveler Benjamin of Tudela confirmed that during his stay in Rome he heard from Jewish rabbis that the Pope was in possession of the Temple treasure and the Ark of the Covenant.[8]

Kultbilder im Mittelalter, Weinheim: VCH Verlagsgesellschaft, 1990, p. 64; cf. De Sacra imagine SS. Salvatoris in Palatio Lateranensi, Ex Codice MS Tabularii Sacrosanctae Basilicae Liberaniae, Roma, Camera Apostolica, 1709.

6   Champagne, Marie Thérèse, Treasures of the Temple and Claims to Authority in Twelfth-century Rome, in: Bolton, Brenda and Meek, Christine, Aspects of Power and Authority in the Middle Ages, Turnhout: Brepols, 2007, p. 112.

7   Wolf, Gerhard, Laetare filia Sion, in: Kühnel, Bianca (ed.), The Real and Ideal Jerusalem in Jewish, Christian and Islamic Art, Jerusalem: Hebrew University, 1998 (Jewish Art 23/24.1997/1998), p. 425.

8   Tudela, Benjamin von, The Itinerary of Benjamin of Tudela, Los Angeles: Joseph Simon, 1993, p. 63f.

What is even more interesting is the fact that there was a Templar house in the Lateran Palace of the Vatican.[9] During the papal investigation of the Italian Templars, various brothers of the Order from this house stated to the papal chaplain Pandulf de Sabello that some treasures of the Temple of Jerusalem were stored in the *Sancta Sanctorum* Chapel.[10] However, not a single word was mentioned about the Ark of the Covenant.

Therefore, it had already been removed. The modest Pope Eugenius III, who was intent on keeping the peace, would have had no reason to have Nicolaus Maniacutius record such a monumental fact if it weren't the truth. In fact, the Ark of the Covenant is only mentioned in passing. Maniacutius focuses on emphasizing Judaism as the root of Christianity – for the Pope such a propaganda campaign would have condemned him to death because Jews were still hated throughout the whole of Christendom. Instead, this source gave evidence that the Ark of the Covenant was in the hands of the Catholic Church and the Cistercian Order. The fact that the Ark is no longer mentioned in the Templar house of the Lateran showed that it had long since been removed and hidden elsewhere, even before Pope Eugenius III was forced to leave Rome.

Consequently, Pope Eugenius III must have acquired the Ark of the Covenant through his teacher Bernard of Clairvaux, as well as the Templars of Hugues de Payns and Count Hugues I of Champagne. The story of the Holy Grail, which was recounted to Chrétien de Troyes by Marie of Champagne, the descendant of Templar founder Count Hugues I, and which he documented in his tale *Le Conte del Graal*, showed that the Templars were guardians of a treasure that had clear Jewish attributes. So was there a deal between the Cistercians, the counts of Champagne and Pope Eugenius III?

Wolfram von Eschenbach refined this information in his work *Parzival*, which described the Grail as a thin stone (lapsit exillîs) that was also made of wood (root and branch): the Mosaic tablets of the covenant law in the wooden Ark of the Covenant. The Ark gave the select crowd of Templeisen infinite food as the manna once

---

9   Barber, Malcolm and Bate, Keith, The Templars, Selected Sources, Manchester: Manchester University Press, 2002, p. 306.
10   Ibid., p. 306.

did the Israelites: a Jewish motif of *schechinah*. Bernard of Clairvaux corresponded to Perceval or Parzival. The Grail king Anfortas was André de Montbard, Hugues de Payns was Kyot of Katelangen. The Ark was first in Payns, then in Clairvaux, then in Rome. However, it is not for nought that Bernard of Clairvaux wrote a detailed description of the code of behavior to Pope Eugenius III. He was obviously afraid that the Ark might not be safe enough in Rome.

As a result, without further ado, it was brought to St.-Denis where Abbot Suger, the friend of Bernard of Clairvaux and Pope Eugenius III, was building a new Temple of Solomon. The iconography of the Abbey Church still pays tribute to this event: in the crypt the nine Templars of Hugues de Payns are depicted together with the Ark of the Covenant. Henceforth, Abbot Suger saw himself as the guardian of the Ark in the tradition of King Solomon who had the temple built in Jerusalem. But what happened next with the divine chest?

At that time, it was dangerous to present the Ark of the Covenant in public because this would be evidence that the Israelites were God's chosen people. It would also prove that the Catholic Church under Pope Eugenius III was *being unfaithful* with Yahweh. A public procession with the Ark would have sabotaged the credibility of the Christian belief. After all, in the Middle Ages, since the father of the Church Augustine, it had been deeply rooted in people's thoughts that the Jewish people were responsible for the death of Christ. Nevertheless, on an internal power politics level, under the clergy and under the French nobility, the Ark would have been the greatest possible conceivable symbol of power. Whoever owned the Ark of the Covenant was chosen by God and was apparently invincible. This explains why Bernard of Clairvaux was urging Pope Eugenius III to call for a Second Crusade, which King Louis VII was planning together with the Preceptor of the Templar Order Everard des Barres. The Ark of the Covenant was making Bernard of Clairvaux, the King and the Templars overconfident.

As the French Capetian dynasty now had an incredible trump card – in the form of the ownership of the Ark of the Covenant and the Abbey Church of St.-Denis as its temple – together with the Templars they regarded themselves as the true Israelites. Their

Capetian insignia can be found in St.-Denis, Laon, Chartres and other cathedrals in the north of France. As Abbot Suger wrote, he now regarded King Louis VII as King David. The Capetian dynasty was a holy family because they knew they were close to the Ark of the Covenant. The Abbey Church of St.-Denis as the Gothic re-birth of the Temple of Solomon was the prototype for other, larger cathedrals as the seat of the Ark of the Covenant. The cathedrals that were first built are those whose bishops were present at the Council of Troyes: Sens, Laon, Chartres, Reims, etc. And so the Templars and King Louis VII promoted the construction of new cathedrals such as Laon, Notre Dame de Paris or Chartres. Louis's successors Louis VIII and Louis IX, the latter who was commonly known as Saint Louis, did the same thing with Chartres.

The Templars left their marks in the iconography that indicated their participation in the financing and construction of the cathedrals. Towns were chosen that fit the concept of the constellations of Virgo and Draco. This explained why massive cathedrals are standing in villages such as Sées in Normandy or Toul in Burgundy. As it was dangerous to show the Ark of the Covenant in public, the Templars left their encrypted clues in and on the cathedrals. The Order had long since begun switching from Christianity to Judaism. The Templars believed that Yahweh was the true God – the explanation why a large number of Templars interrogated stated that they had to urinate or expectorate on the Cross of Christ. Jesus Christ was passé.

When the Templars were arrested on October 13, 1307, the Ark of the Covenant was not in the Paris *Temple,* but had been hid-den in Chartres Cathedral for more than a century. So at the time of the arrest, the Ark was a vague myth within the Templar Order, the origin of which was known only to a few initiates. The uninitiated, the serving Templars, heard rumors that told of a "Baphomet."

During the trial against the Templars, innumerable Templars were asked about a bearded head, an idol. Dozens of different de-scriptions of the appearance of this supposed idol were recorded. This leads one to conclude that none of the Templars questioned had ever actually seen this idol. This supposed head didn't exist at all, but was invented before the arrests by the Inquisition to accuse the Templars of heresy. However, the word *Baphomet* was actually used within the Templar Order. As we initially had seen, the Templar trial records from the South of France mentioned the term "Baphomet" or "Bahumet."[11] The word didn't describe a corruption of the name of the Islamic prophet Muhammad because Islam forbids any kind of depictions of prophets or saints.[12]

A simple etymological study reveals something quite astonishing: the word Bahumet is made up of the Old French words "Bahut" and "Mets." "Bahut" means chest. "Mets," on the other hand, means "food" or "meal."

So the Templars were in possession of a *chest of food*: the Ark of the Covenant with the divine tablets of the covenant law, Aaron's rod and the heavenly manna, the food of God. The warrior monks stated this during the trial in just a few words. Throughout the centuries, the answer to the question about the nature of the Templar treasure was openly visible in the form of the term "Baphomet" or "Bahumet." But only now are the mosaic stones coming together to form a large overall picture.

In 1314, the last Templar Grand Master Jacques de Molay left behind graffiti in his prison in Gisors Castle depicting a dragon and a virgin – his clue to the hiding place of the Ark of the Covenant because he no longer had anything to lose.

The head of the dragon is the star Gamma Draconis: Laon Cathedral, which is dedicated to the Virgin Mary. The Virgin Mary cathedrals originate from the Mariolatry of Bernard of Clairvaux. And so we come full circle.

Arrival in *Munsalvaesche*

After about three hours, the five towers of Laon Cathedral majestically stretch into the sky – a breathtaking and awe-inspiring sight. The building was constructed on a two hundred meter high mountain of clay, sand and limestone that is perforated by caves.[13]

11   Charpentier, John, Die Templer, Frankfurt am Main: Klett-Cotta, 1981, p. 159

12   Prutz, Hans, Geheimlehre und Geheimstatuten des Tempelherrenordens: eine kritische Untersuchung, Arbeitsgemeinschaft für Religions- und Weltanschauungsfragen, Munich, 1979, p. 87f.

13   Clark, William W. and King, Richard, Laon Cathedral, London: Harvey Miller Publishers, 1983, p. 9 .

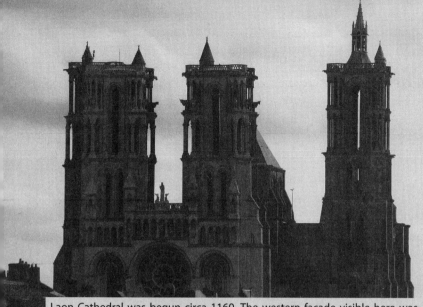

Laon Cathedral was begun circa 1160. The western façade visible here was constructed at the same time as the south and north portal of Chartres Cathedral. It is proven that the same planners and stonemasons were involved.
© Tobias D. Wabbel

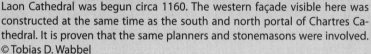

I turn on to the D967 and pass a lake near Neuville-sur-Ailette. It is remarkable that the little town of Laon, similar to the villages of Sées and Toul, should be home to such a gigantic cathedral. As far back as the 2nd century, a church is mentioned that is dedicated to Mary, Mother of God, and is located in a grotto.[14] Auguste Bouxin proved that this grotto is identical to a cavity beneath the apse of the present-day Laon Cathedral.[15]

In the 5th century, there was a church – known as *Ecclesia Laudunensis* – with an affiliated school in Laon. Saint Remigius (436-533 B.C.) was now a bishop and baptized the Merovingian King Clovis I in 499. After Noyon, Laon became the location for the coronation of the kings of France. At this time, the Romanesque Laon Cathedral was already held in high regard.[16] Crowds of pilgrims flocked to see it and this increased over the centuries. Bishop Adalbero, who was Bishop of Laon from 977 to 1032, had the right bell tower built

14   Abbé Charpentier, Saint Béat, Semaine Religieuse de Diocèse du Soisson et Laon, 1880, no. 49ff., p. 926.
15   Bouxin, Auguste, La cathédrale Notre-Dame de Laon, 2nd edition, Laon: Journal de l'Aisne, 1902, p. 8.
16   Adenauer, Hanna, Die Kathedrale von Laon, Düsseldorf: L. Schwann Druckerei und Verlag, 1934, p. 12.

and then a treasury. Laon prospered. The town that mainly lived from the manufacture and trade of wine and wheat could not afford to have a bishop who levied high tolls and taxes on their products. As a result, the population was against an expansion of the episcopal power in Laon. And of course they rejected the construction of a larger cathedral.

However, to the great dismay of the population, Bishop Waldric (Gaudry), the former Lord Chancellor of the English King, levied painfully high taxes in the town.[17] Hunting for deer and wild boar and financially blackmailing the residents of Laon was more enjoyable to him than taking care of the spiritual needs of his diocese. In 1112, the residents of Laon refused to put up with this and, without further ado, set fire to some of the Bishop's houses. The fire spread to the Romanesque basilica, which had a crypt beneath the termination to the choir.[18] The mob was raging. Gaudry lost his head. Subsequently, Bishop Barthélemy de Jur was responsible for the reconstruction that took until 1114. At this time, Laon became the preferred residence of the Carolingian kings, the Capetian dynasty.[19] Louis VI, the Fat, passed a decree that granted a pardon to those responsible for the revolt of 1112. At the same time, he abstained from being hospitably fed by the population three times a year in Laon, as well as from the reimbursement of large sums of money to fill his royal coffers. In fact, the new cathedral was built against the will of the population of Laon. However, the Regent of Laon was the King of France, who was at that time Louis VI, who had already sponsored the construction of St.-Denis by Abbot Suger. His son Louis VII was also sponsoring the construction of Laon Cathedral.

In the 12th century, circa 1160, Bishop Walter of Mortagne ordered the construction of the current cathedral. He personally donated 20 pounds a year, and one year even 100 pounds – several thirteen thousand euros, converted to today's currency. The work began on the façade of the south-east transept. The new cathedral was vastly different in its size and height from the old one. The

17   Ibid., p. 14.
18   Clark, William W. and King, Richard, Laon Cathedral, London: Harvey Miller Publishers, 1983, p. 9.
19   Ibid.

primary inspiration for the architect was the old basilica. How-ever, it is suspected that there was also a connection to Tournai Ca-thedral, which at that time belonged to the Diocese of Noyon, and which also had five towers.[20]

Documents from the time of the construction state that between 1172 and 1179 there was a cessation of the gifts from the nobility and the clergy.[21] Nevertheless, the construction of the cathedral contin-ued without any impediments. This can only be explained by the fact that the Templar Order donated considerable sums of money to the construction because the warrior monks were at this time the only institution capable of granting loans due to their immense riches. Furthermore, the gifts of the clergy and nobility, which were mostly also granted loans from the Templars, were not nearly enough to pro-vide the necessary financing for the construction.

In 1174, after the death of Walter of Mortagne, the bishop's see went to King Louis VII.[22] In other words, the King was now in charge of the construction of Laon Cathedral. In 1177, when Roger of Rozoy was elected Bishop and revolted against the King with an army, King Louis VII crushed this rebellion and forcefully took back the bishop's see.[23] So it seemed that Laon Cathedral was ex-tremely important to the King.

Meanwhile, the construction continued. The towers and the por-tals of the west façade, the nave and the crossing tower were complet-ed between 1195 and 1205.[24] It was documented that in 1205 a certain Jean of Chermizy donated the stones from a quarry.[25] From this time, the construction work progressed even faster. In addition, in 1205 the towers of the west transept, as well as the cloister and the baptistery, were begun – at a time when the north portal of Chartres was also un-der construction. In 1220, the towers of the transept aisles were built. Circa 1235, the Cathedral was dedicated to the Virgin Mary.

---

20   Adenauer, Hanna, Die Kathedrale von Laon, Düsseldorf: L. Schwann Druckerei und Verlag, 1934, p. 34f.
21   Ibid., p. 23.
22   Clark, William W. and King, Richard, Laon Cathedral, London: Harvey Miller Pub-lishers, 1983, p. 16.
23   Ibid., p. 16.
24   Ibid., p. 30.
25   Schäfke, Werner, Frankreichs gotische Kathedralen, Cologne: DuMont Verlag, 1979, p. 100.

As I drive into the city, I follow the signs for the Cathedral and creep up the narrow bends at a speed of 19 miles an hour. I pass the city walls and then drive across paving stones through the old town, past stores, busy cafés and bars from which I can hear the noise of a soccer game broadcast, music and laughter. Then I turn into Rue du Cloître. After an annoying search for a parking space, I am finally able to stop the car opposite the building of the police prefecture by the Cathedral, grab my bag and camera equipment and get out. The faraway buzz of the city traffic at the foot of the mountain hangs in the warm spring air. There are no tourists far and wide when I reach the Cathedral square.

I step back and take a look at the west portal of the Cathedral. Just like the north portal of Chartres, in Laon too the sculptures are protected by porticos. This is unique to France's Gothic architecture. However, I decide to save the portals for later and enter the Cathedral.

Inside I am received by light and a pleasant coolness. Laon is the brightest cathedral I have ever seen. The 12 bays are divided into clear lines, into pointed-arch arcades that are supported by round pillars, round-arched galleries and an accessible triforium. This is followed by the clerestories through which the light of the spring sun floods the Cathedral.

According to my observations, the Cathedral is split into an impressive tripartition: the division into narthex, nave and choir is once again emphasized by a tripartite nave and transept aisle, as well as a tripartite choir. This is the most obvious possible reference to the Temple of Solomon. The rectangular choir in the east has three main apses and two side apses. The Temple of Solomon was just as angular. There were no curves. Laon is different from all other cathedrals in the north of France that have completely semicircular choir terminations. The vault of the crossing, where the nave and transept meet, consists of eight-part ribbed vaults. The crossing is crowned by an enormous tower. With their ratio of 4:3, the dimensions of Laon Cathedral precisely match those of the Temple of Solomon.

The right, southern façade has six chapels; the left, northern façade has eight. As I enter one of the chapels of the northern transept, I catch sight of a sarcophagus made of black granite for the

Abbot of Foigny Abbey. This reminds me that Bernard of Clairvaux was in Laon twice. On January 30, 1124, he visited the third affiliate abbey of Clairvaux, Foigny, and the next day he visited Laon Cathedral.[26]

It wasn't until January 30 and 31, 1147, that Bernard came back to Laon during his trip to advocate for the Second Crusade.[27]

During this time, something remarkable happened in Laon because the preparations for the current cathedral were made during the time that Abbot Suger in St.-Denis had already consecrated the east façade and the choir of his abbey church. Documents prove that the construction of the current Laon Cathedral began in 1145, but the planning was much earlier than that and very probably at the same time as Abbot Suger's construction of St.-Denis and Sens Cathedral.[28] However, this did not seem to go unnoticed by the newly crowned King Louis VII. If the Templars were guarding the Ark of the Covenant on behalf of the Capetian dynasty, it seems probable that they had developed a plan of how to safely store the holiest artifact in the history of mankind without risking its discovery. So it's no wonder that Louis VII violently took back the bishop's see and became the patron of the cathedral. Further cathedrals also had to be built. St.-Denis wasn't enough. The consequence was unforgettable construction activity, but only the cathedrals of the royal dynasty were considered such as St.-Denis, Notre Dame de Paris, Chartres and Laon.

However, if the Ark of the Covenant was housed in Laon, where did the medieval stonemasons leave their mark on behalf of the Templars? Many sculptures were destroyed during the French Revolution, but in the 19th century they were reconstructed during various restoration projects. At least inside the Cathedral I am unable to discover any traces that might provide clues to the whereabouts of the Ark. To my astonishment, I can't see an entrance to the crypt. I jot this down in my notebook. A crypt does not officially exist in Laon. Strange.

---

26   Vacandard, Elphège, Das Leben des Heiligen Bernard von Clairvaux, Mainz: Verlag Franz von Kirchheim, 1897-1898, Volume 1, p. 263.
27   Ibid., Volume 2, p. 320.
28   Clark, William W. and King, Richard, Laon Cathedral, London: Harvey Miller Publishers, 1983, p. 25.

On the trumeau pillar of the center portico of the west portal of Laon Cathedral, we see the Virgin Mary standing on the dragon, which is writhing under her feet. Once again a reference to the constellation Draco, the head of which is formed by Laon Cathedral. © Tobias D. Wabbel

Outside I am dazzled by the sunlight. Once I have gotten used to the light, I take a look at the porticos of the portals of the west façade. At first, I notice the striking similarity to the portals of St.-Denis which also feature the Virgin Mary. As I examine the trumeau pillar of the center portal, my heart suddenly skips a beat. Here I see a sculpture of the Virgin Mary. She is holding Baby Jesus in her arms. A dragon is writhing beneath her feet. I take notes with shaking hands.

Onwards. I move on to the left portal. Dozens of small figures from the Old Testament decorate the archivolts. On the apex of the right archivolt, I spy two angels lifting up a lid. Underneath appears a kind of light. I identify it as the seven-branched Menorah from the Temple of Solomon. The Menorah is standing in a box. I examine it through my telephoto lens. On the box are inscribed the words *Arca Dei*. It is the Ark of the Covenant. But why is the Menorah stored in the Ark? It was part of the Temple treasure. The stonemasons of Laon wanted to inform the observer that they should pay attention to not only the Ark, but also the Temple treasure here. A reference to Pope Eugenius III and his confidant Nicolaus Maniacutius who described in his manuscript *Historia Imaginis Salvatoris* that not only the Ark was stored in the *Sancta Sanctorum* Chapel, but the Temple treasure was also located in the Lateran. Not far from this, I identify the crowned Virgin Mary with both Mosaic tablets of the covenant law.

In my opinion, the center Virgin portal provides no clues apart from the dragon among the saintly figures and the depiction of Moses in the left jamb of the portico who – as in Chartres – is pointing to the head of the dragon. So I turn to the right portal.

On the right jamb, Saint George is staring into the distance with a decisive expression. He has a beard, knight's armor, a chain-mail shirt with a monk's surcoat over the top of it and his helmet is adorned with a fleur-de-lis, symbol of the Capetian dynasty. George's shield is decorated with a Templar cross, similar to in Chartres, except that it has been stylized to resemble a Templar cross of the Capetian dynasty. I remind myself that the same planners of the north portal of Chartres also left behind iconographic codes on the west façade of Laon. In Chartres there wasn't a dragon

In the right archivolt of the left portico of the west portal of Laon Cathedral, two angels are lifting the lid of the Ark of the Covenant. Inside we see the seven-branched lampstand or Menorah and the jar of divine manna as part of the Templar treasure. © Tobias D. Wabbel

The striking thing here is the depiction of the Virgin Mary enthroned on a box that is flanked by two angels or cherubim. You can almost make out a dragon writhing at the feet of the Virgin Mary. The Virgin is stamping on the dragon's head. The box she is standing on is the Ark of the Covenant. © Tobias D. Wabbel

The dragon slayer George, depicted as a Templar with a Templar cross on his shield, the ends of which are stylized into the shape of fleurs-de-lis – a symbol of the closeness of the Capetian dynasty to the Templars. Here George is piercing the dragon's head – a clue to the hiding place of the Ark of the Covenant in Laon.
© Tobias D. Wabbel

Sixteen oxen decorate the bell towers of Laon Cathedral. They are a reference to the "laver," a cast bronze basin for the ritual washing of the high priests that stood in front of the Temple of Solomon and was supported by twelve bulls. Laon Cathedral is even more the depiction of the Temple of Solomon than St.-Denis or Chartres. German poet Wolfram von Eschenbach uses the term Munsalvaesche as a name for the castle where the Grail is kept by the select crowd of knights, the Templeisen. Laon Cathedral also stands on a mountain. In homage to the cattle on the towers, Laon represents a mount of holy cows: Mont des saintes vaches. © Tobias D. Wabbel

at George's feet. In Laon I finally find the dragon at the feet of Saint George – the symbol of the Templars. His lance is piercing the head of the dragon.

I shudder. Laon Cathedral corresponds to the star Gamma Draconis, in Arabic Etamin or Rastaban: both names mean "head of the dragon." My fingers are shaking so much that I am no longer capable of making any notes. "Oh my God," I whisper and step back to take a look at the entire west façade.

The first thing I notice are the unusual gargoyles. Then I blink into the sunny sky and see the towers. On the corners of the towers, four oxen are looking down on Picardy. The sight reminds me of the cast bronze basin for the high priests to wash themselves, which was situated in the courtyard of the Temple of Solomon and standing on 12 bulls.[29] So Laon Cathedral is

29   Ohly, Friedrich, Die Säulen des Salomonischen Tempels und die Doppelturm-fassade, in: Frühmittelalterliche Studien 32, 1998, p. 7ff.; cf. Sauerländer, Willibald, Funk-kolleg Kunst, Kollegstunde 4: Die Kathedralfassade, Studienbegleitbrief 1, Weinheim: Beltz Verlag, 1984, p. 134; cf. Schäfke, Werner, Frankreichs gotische Kathedralen, Cologne:

As shown in Chartres, the sculpture of Moses in Laon is also pointing at the dragon's head. © Tobias D. Wabbel

even more the Gothic depiction of the Temple of Solomon than St.-Denis. I begin to sweat. Thousands of thoughts are rushing through my head.

As I observe the oxen on the towers of Laon Cathedral, I think of Parzival, the old Grail story by Wolfram von Eschenbach.

And then I freeze. The Grail castle in Wolfram von Eschenbach's epic Parzival is called *Munsalvaesche*. Wolfram von Eschenbach wanted future generations to know that the Grail is hidden in Munsalvaesche: on the "Mount of holy cows," *Mont des saintes vaches*. Laon Cathedral with its oxen stands on a mountain – that mountain that Parzival spied during his search for the Grail after passing a lake. On the drive to Laon, I also passed a lake.

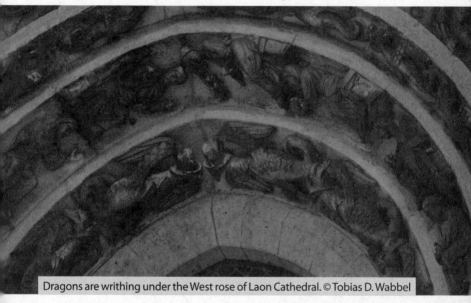

Dragons are writhing under the West rose of Laon Cathedral. © Tobias D. Wabbel

Between the towers, I catch sight of the Virgin Mary with Baby Jesus, flanked by two angels. I take another look through my camera's telephoto lens. The Virgin Mary is standing on a box. The angels correspond to cherubims – those cherubims on the Ark of the Covenant of the Israelites. And beneath the feet of the Virgin is writhing a – scarcely recognizable – dragon. Beneath the West rose I discover further dragons. There are dragons everywhere. No cathedral in France has a comparable iconography.

If Munsalvaesche corresponds to Laon Cathedral, the Grail room, where the Grail is kept by the select crowd of Templeisen, must be in the direct vicinity. Wolfram von Eschenbach describes it as a room without windows, so that could be a crypt.[30] After taking hundreds of photos, I walk along the south façade of the Cathedral across Rue du Cloître. After a few hundred meters, I discover an information sign: *Chapelle des Templiers*.

I follow the sign. Two streets on, to my surprise I catch sight of a small octagonal chapel with a bell tower. Like Laon Cathedral, the chapel also features a tripartition into portico, Holy Place and apse – once again a reference to the Temple of Solomon. The chapel was built in 1134 during the episcopate of Bishop Barthélemy de Jur, who founded Foigny Abbey together with Bernard of

The Templar chapel of Laon, not far from the Cathedral, was constructed in 1134. The Bishop, the cathedral builders and the Templars worked together in Laon. © Tobias D. Wabbel

---

30 · Kordt, Christa-Maria, Parzival in Munsalvaesche, Herne: Verlag für Wissenschaft und Kunst, 1997, p. 220.

Clairvaux, cultivated active relations with the Templars and died in 1151.[31] The reconstruction of the Romanesque basilica after the fire of 1112 and the planning and start of construction of the current Laon Cathedral all took place during his office as bishop. His closeness to the Templars proves that they made a significant contribution to the financing and construction of the Cathedral. And it is very probable that Bernard of Clairvaux did too.

As I enter, I notice the sparseness of the rooms. There are scarcely any ornaments at all. I catch sight of two sculptures in the apse that are obviously depictions of prophets. As I take a closer look at one of the figures, I recognize Moses.[32] He is holding the Torah. The two sculptures are obviously from the Cathedral's portal that depicts the Coronation of the Virgin Mary. It is still uncertain who brought the sculptures here. I am standing in a sacred place. Because the Templar chapel of Laon indicates that the Ark is in Laon. Where it is now can only be ascertained by a thorough archaeological excavation in Laon.

Now it becomes painfully clear to me that the search for the Ark of the Covenant is only just beginning. At the end of my search, the facts are as follows:

- The Templars found the Ark of the Covenant of the Israelites beneath the Temple Mount of Jerusalem and transported it to France.

- The Ark was first kept in Payns, in Clairvaux Abbey, then in Rome, St.-Denis, Chartres and finally Laon.

- The possession of the Ark of the Covenant granted the Templars the greatest possible proximity to God, as well as the greatest possible power.

- A public presentation of the Ark was thus out of the question.

- The behavior of Pope Eugenius III leads us to conclude that the Cistercians and the Templars became open to Judaism.

---

31   Frizot, Julien, Le grand sites templiers en France, Rennes: Édition Ouest-France, 2005, p. 20; cf. Frizot, Julien, Sur le pas de Templiers en Terre de France, Rennes: Édition Ouest-France, 2005, p. 32f.
32   Willibald Sauerländer, Beiträge zur Geschichte der "frühgotischen" Skulptur, in: Zeitschrift für Kunstgeschichte 19, Book 1, 1956, p. 33.

- *Baphomet* or *Bahumet* – translated as *chest of food* – is none other than the Ark of the Covenant with the jar of divine manna, the food of the Israelites.

- Chrétien de Troyes and Wolfram von Eschenbach included the Ark of the Covenant in encrypted form in the Grail stories *Perceval* and *Parzival.* The Templeisen are identical to the Templars. Parzival is Bernard of Claraval (Clairvaux). Anfortas, Parzival's uncle, corresponds to André de Montbard, Bernard's uncle.

- Marie of Champagne, the first employer of Chrétien de Troyes, was the daughter of King Louis VII, the sponsor of the cathedral construction and close friend of Abbot Suger of St.-Denis and Bernard of Clairvaux.

- The Grail castle *Munsalvaesche* is Laon Cathedral with its holy cows: *Mont des saintes vaches.*

- France's Gothic cathedrals do not represent the Heavenly Jerusalem, but instead represent the Temple of Solomon. A few of them – including St.-Denis, Chartres and Laon – were used by the warrior monks as the new Holy of Holies for storing the Ark of the Covenant.

- France's Virgin Mary's cathedrals depict the constellation Draco.

- St. Stephen's cathedrals depict the constellation Virgo.

- Laon, Gamma Draconis, is the head of the dragon.

- Judging by the iconography, even today the Ark of the Covenant is still hidden in Laon.

The National Socialists and the Ark of the Covenant

Or did the Nazis beat me to it? The question is justified because Reichsführer-SS Heinrich Himmler put great pressure on the scientists of the Forschungsgemeinschaft Deutsches Ahnenerbe (Research Community of German Ancestral Heritage) in Berlin to undertake a worldwide search for archaeological relics. The aim was to prove the supposed superiority of the Aryan race. In search of relics and proof regarding the origin of the Aryans, the prosperous pseudoscientists of the Nazis set off on expeditions to the mountains of Tibet, Palestine and the French Pyrenees. These relics included the Holy Grail which author and SS Obersturmführer Otto Rahn from the Rasse- und Siedlungshauptamt (SS Race and Settlement Main Office) was searching for under the patronage of Heinrich Himmler. Rahn searched for the Holy Grail in the Languedoc and Provence regions of the South of France. He believed that four members of the Catharism sect were able to smuggle away a treasure during the siege of Montségur Castle before the mysterious Gnostic movement was finally destroyed on March 16, 1244. This Cathar treasure is a figment of Rahn's imagination, the supposed existence of which he dreams up in his Ariosophic outburst "Crusade Against the Grail".[33]

However, Heinrich Himmler was obsessed with the Holy Grail, the occult and mysticism. He had Wewelsburg, not far from the Westphalian town of Paderborn, turned into a monstrous Grail castle. Even today, there is still a hall with a black sun wheel made up of 12 sig (victory) runes on the floor in which Himmler and 11 of his SS henchmen met to gush about their insane fantasies.

Thus, it is possible that the Germans could have found the Ark of the Covenant during the German occupation of France. We know for sure that Heinrich Himmler was interested in the Knights Templar and their esoteric doctrines.[34] Just as Himmler

studied the history of the Templars, Adolf Hitler developed an incredible interest in Laon Cathedral. Hitler visited Laon together with his two friends from the First World War, Max Amann and Ernst Schmidt. Photographs of Heinrich Hoffmann show the "Führer" on June 21 and 25, 1940, in front of and inside the Cathedral. Hitler said the following on October 18, 1941: "In the air attack on

33   Rahn, Otto, Kreuzzug gegen den Gral, Stuttgart: Verlag für ganzheitliche Forschung und Kultur, 1985, p. 183ff.

34   Wegener, Franz, Heinrich Himmler: deutscher Spiritismus, französischer Okkultismus und der Reichsführer SS, Gladbeck: Kulturförderverein Ruhrgebiet, 2004 (Politische Religion des Nationalsozialismus 4), p. 68.

Paris, we confined ourselves to the airfields – to spare a city with a glorious past ... and it would have hurt me to be obliged to attack a city like Laon, with its cathedral."[35] Laon Cathedral was miraculously saved from the destructive frenzy of the Nazis. On the pictures you can see that sand bags sacked in front of the west portal were protecting the Cathedral from being hit by grenades. So did Hitler's henchmen find the Ark of the Covenant? Or was Hitler's fascination with Laon Cathedral merely due to his enthusiasm for architecture?

We don't know. Perhaps the Nazis did find the Ark of the Covenant. Hitler was temporarily in possession of the alleged Holy Lance with which the Roman soldier Longinus pierced Christ's side to make sure the Savior was dead.

The Nazis were obsessed with Biblical relics. The possession of the Ark of the Covenant by the Nazis would have been shamefully exploited by the Reichspropagandaministerium (Reich Ministry of Public Enlightenment and Propaganda): Joseph Goebbels would have presented the Ark as divine proof of the superiority of the Aryan race over the Jewish race. But nothing of the kind occurred. Current histor-

---

35   Jochmann, Werner, Monologe im Führerhauptquartier 1941-1944, Munich: Wilhelm Heyne Verlag, p. 93.

ic research doesn't mention a single word about the Ark of the Covenant in Nazi records.

So we can safely assume that God's chest is still in Laon. The thought that the Ark, the Biblical symbol for the presence of God on earth, was hidden under Hitler's feet as he inspected one of the West's most beautiful cathedrals is both amusing and uncanny.

But now we have to ask ourselves a less amusing question: what would happen if the Ark was found by chance in the near future in Laon? Perhaps it would occur during restoration work beneath the choir because, as we have seen, there exists a cavity beneath the termination to the choir of Laon Cathedral – the old St. Mary's grotto. The mountain of Laon is also perforated by caves. Perhaps it would be discovered by geological examinations of the grottos beneath the Cathedral. Perhaps in an underground corridor or cavity beneath the Templar chapel, a stone's throw from the Cathedral.

Thus, it is not improbable that the discovery of the Ark of the Covenant could have both far-reaching political and religious consequences. Ultra-Orthodox Jews might see the Ark of the Covenant as a sign for the coming arrival of the Messiah and feel encouraged by this event to build a new Temple of Solomon – instead of the third holiest monument in Islam: the Dome of the Rock. A conflict in the Middle East would be inevitable.

People's curiosity is insatiable. Thus, it is certainly only a matter of time until the Ark of the Covenant will be found. The future will show whether humanity is ready for such a fundamental discovery. The presence of God in the form of the Ark of the Covenant and the divine tablets of the covenant law would at least warn us to peacefully inhabit this beautiful planet.

Front façade of Laon Cathedral. © Public Domain
Images pages 231-232 © Public Domain

Epilogue

Hardly anyone can resist the fascination of Gothic cathedrals. Even those who have distanced themselves from the Church or who are not particularly interested in art and cultural heritage describe a peculiar, inexplainable mood that grips them when they enter the inside of a church. Accordingly, there is extensive literature that not only attempts to capture the towering architecture and beauty of the inner lighting effects in gloriously illustrated books, but also tries to subject it to an art history analysis.

During the 14 years in which I taught Christian Art History at the Theology Faculty of the Karl Franzens University of Graz, church construction and the iconology inside the church were the focuses of my research. My access to this is primarily practical. I first studied architecture and later art history. Thanks to my involvement in maintaining the old town and in the Styrian Diocese Commission for Building New Churches, my feet are firmly planted in reality. Architecture is not an artistic genre such as painting or sculpture where I can restrict myself to the artistic premises. Construction needs a powerful client or financier. Architecture always was (and still is!) an expression of power. If there are strong clients, you will always find architects who are able to put ideas into practice. Compared to the 12th and 13th century, there was no other era in which so many magnificent cathedrals and abbey churches were built in what were often tiny villages. To describe this phenomenon with traditional clichés such as "Cathedrals – expression of belief" is just as insufficient as the reference to the pious consciousness and unpaid assistance of the population. The specialist literature mostly limits itself to the external form, the stylistic comparison and the position of the construction as part of a development history (as

if architecture were subject to a biological development process).
However, a typification that only takes into account outer forms,
datings and names of master builders doesn't do justice to church
construction in general, and certainly not to Gothic cathedrals.

The author of this book approaches this phenomenon of cathedrals with the viewpoint that the most significant epoch of
Western church construction occurs simultaneously with the era
of the Templars. France's many impressive pilgrim churches en
route to Santiago de Compostela, in some partially difficult to
access regions such as Auvergne, are today still inexplicable due
to their suddenly emerging size and artistic architecture. As these
constructions were being completed, Gothic cathedrals were just
beginning! Towards the end of the 13th century, it comes to an
end as suddenly as the beginning of monumental architecture and
monumental sculpture. The questions about clients and financiers
become decisive facts. Tobias Daniel Wabbel finds access to the
topic and further research in the architectural sculptures and the
glass windows of the cathedrals.

The classic tripartition of art books into architecture, sculpture and painting and the contribtuions by various experts is to the
detriment of the cohesiveness of the content. With reference to architectural sculpture, the sole focus on the stylistic dependence of
sculptor schools disregards one key aspect: architectural sculpture
is not about "beautification" of a building, but the key to understanding a building.

During the course of today's mostly museum-like study of cathedrals, we all too easily forget that these rooms were originally
designed for the liturgy – for a liturgy that wasn't standardized
prior to the Council of Trent. However, despite all regional differ-
ences, since the beginning of the new millennium it has become
apparent that the crossing or square choir is a defining element. In
St. Michael's Church in Hildesheim, Bishop Bernward created the
first church interior from 1001 – 1031, which was based on the dimensions of the crossing and was emphasized by its own vault with
tower. Using this crossing as a unit of measurement for the entire
church building defines the construction as a depiction of divine

order and completeness. Even if, from a purely formal perspective, there appears to be no connection between a Romanesque construction defined by wall dimensions and the construction of the Gothic cathedral based around the buttresses, the crossing remains a place for the high altar and thus the connecting element. With its quadratic dimensions, this key place was regarded as the abbreviation of the Holy of Holies of the Temple of Solomon. This is proven by Hugh of St. Victor in Paris, a contemporary of Abbot Suger and Bernard of Clairvaux. According to his manuscripts, the Christian cathedral in terms of its characteristics was a replica of the Old Testament constructions that were built according to God's will and plan – Noah's Ark, the Tabernacle and the Temple of Solomon.

The 12th century is the heyday of typology, which is the teaching of the Old Testament role models/prefigurations that are a foreshadowing of the salvation. This not only applies to architecture, but also to the entire Christian art of this era. The altarpiece at Klosterneuburg (originally an ambo), which was created in 1181 by Nicholas of Verdun, features a complete typological system in its precious gold and enamel work. The individual pictures that are arranged in three horizontal strips present a typological comparison of the era prior to the Mosaic Law, under the Law and under the mercy of Christ, where explanatory inscriptions and verses complement the salvation history presentation. The relationship between Old and New Testament is very eloquently addressed in architectural sculpture when, for example, the Apostles are shown standing on the shoulders of the Prophet in the portal jamb of Bamberg Cathedral.

The typological discourse cultivated in educated circles is reflected in all art genres. Abbot Suger himself pointed out that his typological images were openly accessible to the *literati* (the literate educated class). As a result, the depiction of the Ark of the Covenant and its typological reference in the cathedrals were something understood by every educated person of that time. Today, we can only interpret this by a painstaking search for fragmentary sources and often daring hypotheses. However, as this book shows, a far-reaching search for clues can indeed lead to an interesting and exciting result. The author Tobias Daniel Wabbel has at the very least succeeded in opening one more window in the ivory tower of relevant theories.

Dr. Wiltraud Resch, Graz, October 2009

Acknowledgments

It would be impossible to thank everyone who has contributed to this book over the last decade. Nevertheless, the following people and institutions deserve a special mention:

Dan Bahat, Malcolm Barber, Klaus Bieberstein, Adrian Boas, Christian Brachthäuser, Martin Büchsel, Gilbert Dahan, Israel Finkelstein, Gisors town council, Julian P. Haseldine, Rainer Hilbig, Marie-Françoise Leccia, E. Ann Matter, Musée Hugue de Payns, National Trust for Scotland, Frank Paulikat, Emeline Priadka from the Rashi Institute, Douglas J. Preston, Leen Ritmeyer, Wilhelm Schlink, Günter Sponheuer and the Wabbel family. I owe a big thank you to Sarah Downing for her translation.

I am particularly grateful to my wife Anja Gerritzen and my friend Emile Chmiel for the encouragement, patience and the inspiring, but sobering comments during the production of this manuscript and my many research trips. Last but not least, I would like to thank Dr. Wiltraud Resch for the excellent epilogue.

One last word: I am not a scientist. I am only a very curious and sceptical journalist and writer. Sceptical about the gaps in historical research. The missing Templar treasure is a huge historical gap. Therefore, this book is not a scientific paper, but also not a Douglas Preston novel – it is a chronicle of a quest that, like Indiana Jones' quests, will probably last my whole lifetime. If archaeologists and historians ever scrutinize my research results and start seriously investigating at Laon Cathedral or elsewhere for the whereabouts of the Ark of the Covenant, this would be the greatest honor I could ever experience. If nothing is found, however, it is not the end of the search. So when you happen to travel to France, I ask you the readers: "Keep your eyes open!" – you might discover the greatest archaeological treasure of all time. If you do so, drop me a line. I will be happy to hear from you.

— Tobias Daniel Wabbel, September 2013

Index

241

H

I

J

K

Torah 11, 79, 104, 229
Toul 182, 213, 215
Tournai 182, 217
Tracery 189, 192
Transept 161, 193, 218
Triforium 160, 218
Troyes 7, 11, 15, 21-22, 39, 63, 70-71, 77, 85, 87, 103, 174
Troyes commandery 39
Tunic 177, 190
Tutankhamen 102, 106, 172
Tympanum 157-158, 187, 195
Typology 158, 187

U

Uzzah 111

V

Vacandard, Elphège 10
Valley of Wormwood 29
Valois dynasty. 170
Vézelay 145, 155, 176
Villard de Honnecourt 188
Virgin Mary 28, 29, 31, 157-160, 175, 177-178, 182, 195, 214, 217, 221, 227
Virgo 213
Von Simson, Otto 151, 154
Vulgate 9, 88, 202

W

Walter of Mortagne 216-217
Waqf, Antiquities Authorities 130
Warren, Charles 19, 120, 133-34
Welf VI 148
Wewelsburg 231
Wife of Hugues de Payns 8
William, Castellan of St. Omer 17
William III of Nevers 147
William II of Nevers 146
William of Champeaux 30, 31
William of Tyre 13, 16
William St. Clair 53-54, 59, 61, 63
Wilson, Charles 133

Wolfram von Eschenbach 32, 78, 81-83, 85-89, 174, 211, 227-228, 230

Z

Zadok 111, 122
Zedekiah 117
Zengi, Imad ad-Din 145
Zerubbabel 129
Ziegert, Helmut 128
Zion 110, 112, 117